WHAT MAKES AN ALCOHOLIC
DIFFERENT FROM A NONALCOHOLIC?

The physiology of the alcoholic—not psychological makeup or cultural background—is the chief determining factor, a conclusion that has had major impact on the way we perceive and understand alcoholics today.

Under the Influence removes the stigma of guilt from alcoholism. It explains how enzymes, hormones, genes, and brain chemistry work together to create this abnormal, addictive reaction. Moreover, it suggests changes that can be made in our social programs, our research, and our medical profession so that alcoholism can finally be recognized for what it really is—a disease.

"I give *Under the Influence* to my patients when I first make the diagnosis of alcoholism. It's been very effective. A tremendous teaching tool, and one of the best books on the subject I know."
—Dr. Nicholas A. Pace, M.D., specialist, Internal Medicine

"I find Dr. Milam's concept absolutely extraordinary and very exciting."
—Mrs. Marty Mann, founder-consultant, National Council on Alcoholism

"This is the one book to be left somewhere for the alcoholic to find and read."
—Toby Rice Drews, author, *Getting Them Sober*

UNDER THE
INFLUENCE

UNDER THE INFLUENCE

A LIFE-SAVING GUIDE TO THE MYTHS
AND REALITIES OF ALCOHOLISM

JAMES R. MILAM, PH.D.,
AND KATHERINE KETCHAM

BANTAM BOOKS
New York

2021 Bantam Books Trade Paperback Edition

Copyright © 1981 by James R. Milam and Katherine Ketcham

All rights reserved.

Published in the United States by Bantam Books, an imprint of Random House, a division of Penguin Random House LLC, New York.

Bantam Books and the House colophon are registered trademarks of Penguin Random House LLC.

Originally published in hardcover in the United States by Madrona Publishers in 1981.

Appendix B and Appendix C: Copyright © 2021 by University of Wisconsin Hospitals and Clinics Authority. All rights reserved. Printed with permission. Produced by the Department of Nursing.

Library of Congress Cataloging-in-Publication Data
Names: Milam, James Robert, 1922– author. | Ketcham, Katherine, 1949– author.
Title: Under the influence: a life-saving guide to the myths and realities of alcoholism / James R. Milam, Ph.D., and Katherine Ketcham.
Description: New York: Bantam Dell, 2021. | "2021 Bantam Books Trade Paperback edition"—Title page verso.
Identifiers: LCCN 2021005972 (print) | LCCN 2021005973 (ebook) | ISBN 9780593358221 (trade paperback) | ISBN 9780307801739 (ebook)
Subjects: LCSH: Alcoholism. | Alcoholism—Psychological aspects.
Classification: LCC RC565 .M442 2021 (print) | LCC RC565 (ebook) | DDC 362.292—dc23
LC record available at https://lccn.loc.gov/2021005972
LC ebook record available at https://lccn.loc.gov/2021005973

Printed in the United States of America on acid-free paper

randomhousebooks.com

2 4 6 8 9 7 5 3 1

PERSPECTIVES FROM THE FIRST EDITION

I am thrilled with this book. It meets a great need. I know that it will be understood and utilized so that millions of lives can be saved.

Under the Influence clearly points out that the accumulated evidence from all the life sciences positively indicates that physiology, not psychology, determines whether a drinker will become addicted to alcohol or not. The alcoholic's genes, enzymes, hormones, brain chemistry, and other body chemistries work together to create their abnormal and unfortunate reaction to alcohol. This concept has not been and is not now understood or accepted even by the majority of alcoholism professionals, who seem committed to the misconception that alcoholism is, at least in part, caused by social, cultural, and psychological factors and is therefore treatable through mental health methods such as various psychotherapies and behavior modification techniques.

In 1970 James R. Milam wrote and self-published *The Emergent Comprehensive Concept of Alcoholism*. The book was enthusiastically welcomed by thousands of readers, both professionals and laypersons. Many of us said, "Here for the first time is someone who really knows what alcoholism is all about and who has finally put it down on paper." Fifty thousand copies of Milam's *Concept*, which was written in a relatively technical and clinical language, have been sold to date. This was accomplished without benefit of marketing, advertising, or the sponsorship of a publishing house. The demand for and acceptance of this new idea has indeed been phenomenal.

In *Under the Influence,* this original concept has been expanded, restated, and presented in a thoroughly understandable and fascinating explanation of alcoholism. It has been written with such clarity that many of the highly complex issues related to alcoholism become clear for the first time. Indeed, I feel this book is not only intended to be a textbook for professionals, clinicians, and academicians, but will also be welcomed and easily understood by the lay public. The authors have articulated ideas and truths that many of us have "known" or felt intuitively were underlying the disease of alcoholism. For the first time, these ideas, concepts, and truths have been expressed with a validity based on research, documentation, and fifteen years of extensive clinical experience at Alcenas Hospital and elsewhere.

Thousands of alcoholics are seen every year by professionals—psychiatrists, psychologists, social workers, clergy, counselors, nurses, and doctors—yet, tragically, they are almost always misdiagnosed and often harmfully treated. It is my belief that alcoholism has suffered more malpractice out of ignorance than any other disease in recent times. Yet it is a disease that strikes our society so severely that, if unchecked, it could bring our nation to its knees.

It is my prayer and fervent hope that the concepts so clearly and boldly stated in *Under the Influence* have emerged at a time when they can be broadly recognized and accepted. They are truly ideas whose time has come. It is my further hope and prayer that the treatment approach described herein will be widely adopted as a basis for treatment of alcoholism in the future.

Under the Influence will aid and advance by light-years the understanding of alcoholism and the recovery process. The labors of Milam and Ketcham in researching, documenting, and writing *Under the Influence* have placed us all in their debt. Let us hope that this book will spread light into darkness and bring us closer to a complete understanding of the disease of alcoholism, and through this new understanding reach millions of our fellow men and women who today are suffering—and dying—because of society's ignorance.

MEL SCHULSTAD

Cofounder and past president
of the National Association of Alcoholism Counselors
(now known as the National Association of Alcoholism
and Drug Abuse Counselors or NAADAC)

FOR A NEW GENERATION

Alcohol has been described as an ambiguous molecule—often referred to as humankind's oldest friend and oldest enemy. Its global influence and historical impact across the ages and among different cultures cannot be overstated. It has taken on mythical, supernatural, even deistic dimensions. Embedded deeply into the psyche and traditions of many societies around the world, it is viewed and experienced by many as balm and elixir, social lubricant and somatic sedative, reliable dissolver of psychic pain.

Economically, it is a profitable industry, large employer, and reliable producer of national tax revenues. At the same time, alcohol can cause acute and chronic physical disease; produce psychological angst, panic, and depression; create violence and social unrest; and dissolve our closest human relationships. It is an intoxicant, it creates toxicity, it is a known carcinogen, and it is an addictive drug. Economically, it is also a major drain on economies, causing increased healthcare and criminal justice costs and large financial losses due to illness-related lost work productivity. As a diagnosable disorder—alcohol use disorder—it is highly prevalent. Approximately 75 percent of all diagnosable cases of addiction to any psychoactive drug in the United States are cases of alcohol addiction. Alcohol kills roughly 3.3 million people around the globe each year—ten times more than all illicit psychoactive drugs combined. Despite this shockingly high casualty rate, alcohol is not headline news. We seem to be largely inured to its effects, seemingly willing to absorb these casualties quietly into the social fabric. As a molecule, CH_3CH_2OH, it is astonishingly simple compared to the molecular structure of other addictive drugs—a simplicity that clearly belies the complexity of its physical, psychological, and social impact.

It is with this complexity and its cultural, medical, psychological, and social impact that this book concerns itself. This updated volume brings in many new findings since its first edition. It provides helpful information related to the nature of alcohol and its effects on the human body. It details new knowledge on the psychological and physical processes involved as a result of exposure to it. It describes the human vulnerabilities to its influence and the course of progression that, for too many, results in full-fledged manifestation of addiction. It provides useful information on treatment and recovery from it.

In many ways, *Under the Influence* takes the ambiguous molecule that is alcohol and unambiguously clarifies and unravels much of its complex impact. The book is likely to educate as well as offer help and hope to the many suffering from its seductive but ultimately punishing allure.

JOHN F. KELLY, PH.D., ABPP

Elizabeth R. Spallin Professor of Psychiatry in Addiction Medicine,
Harvard Medical School
Director, MGH Recovery Research Institute
Program Director, MGH Addiction Recovery Management Service (ARMS)
Associate Director, MGH Center for Addiction Medicine

CONTENTS

UNDER THE
INFLUENCE

1

Every Human Soul

Every human soul is worth saving; but . . . if a choice is to be made, drunkards are about the last class to be taken hold of.

—From "Drunkenness a Vice, Not a Disease," by J. E. Todd, 1882

Bob is twenty-six years old and a talented songwriter. He says he drinks heavily for any number of reasons—when he is depressed because his work is not progressing well, when he is elated because he finished a song, when he is frightened about his future, or when he is concerned about his financial problems.

When he drinks, he has problems. His car is scarred with dents and scratches from his erratic driving. He sometimes "forgets" what he did while he was drinking, and the next day he tries to piece together the night before. On one drunk, he broke his leg jumping over a fence. His wife takes a lot of verbal and emotional abuse when Bob drinks. After a New Year's Eve party, Bob was driving, drunk, and his wife asked him to let her drive. Furious, he stopped the car, leaned across her, opened the door, and pushed her out. Then he sped away, leaving her stranded on the highway.

After these episodes, Bob feels guilty and ashamed and vows to cut back on his drinking. He begs his wife's forgiveness, and together they try to understand what bothers him when he is drinking and why he cannot just stop after a few drinks. Bob thinks the problem is psychological. He tells his wife that his career is difficult and demanding; the ups are euphoric, he explains, but the downs are devastating. Anyone would drink in this work, he tells her; it just comes with the territory. His wife blames the heavy drinking and violent behavior on his upbringing. His mother was a big drinker and set a bad example; furthermore, she never gave her kids any love or affection. Bob is just insecure, his wife insists. He needs understanding and tender loving care. She knows that he is a sensitive, loving man, and she believes she can be most helpful by supporting and helping him through the rough times.

Both Bob and his wife believe the drinking is just a symptom of some deep insecurity or emotional hang-up. Once Bob becomes successful and their financial situation is secure, they believe, he will have the confidence to work his problems out more rationally. "It is just a temporary problem," they agree.

Bob is an alcoholic.* His wife, doctor, friends, and relatives do not know that he is addicted to alcohol. He does not know it either, although he is often afraid that something terrible is happening to him. He worries that he may have some kind of mental health problem, although he struggles with these fears by himself, convinced that once he admits them they will be confirmed. He is deeply ashamed of himself and full of guilt about his inability to control his drinking and keep his promises to his wife.

What will happen to Bob? If he is like most of the 26 million

---

* We use the words *alcoholism* and *addiction* throughout this book because this is the everyday language most people use and because these words call attention to the progressive nature of the disease as it moves from its early to its middle and late stages. Early-stage symptoms (see pages 49–62), which are often overlooked or dismissed, can and should be recognized as potential warning signs of addiction. The American Psychiatric Association, in its *Diagnostic and Statistical Manual of Mental Disorders, 5th Edition (DSM-5)*, uses the term *alcohol use disorder*, with three sub-classifications: mild, moderate, and severe. See Appendix E.

alcoholics in the United States,* his children will be ashamed of him, his friends will shun him, his doctors will despair of helping him, and his wife will finally leave him. His personality will be gradually distorted, his talents and intelligence wasted, and his integrity and self-respect eroded. He will take tranquilizers and sedatives in an effort to combat his depression and anxiety. He will switch doctors, hoping to find one who can tell him what is wrong. He will see a psychiatrist and spend countless hours and thousands of dollars trying to dig up the roots of his unhappiness. He will be reprimanded by his boss, and eventually he will be fired.

Throughout it all, he will drink. He will try to stop drinking, and sometimes he will succeed. But he will shake, sweat, and feel sick to his stomach when he stops drinking. After a week or a month, he will start drinking again. As he continues to drink, these withdrawal symptoms will get worse, and he will drink more, and more often, to relieve his pain.

As his disease progresses, his blood pressure will escalate and his depression will increase. The drinking will not stop but instead will become more and more of a problem, causing difficulties at home, on the job, with the children. His heart, liver, and nervous system will begin to function less effectively. He will be hospitalized from time to time for various complications caused by his excessive drinking.

He will have numerous accidents—falling down the stairs or off a ladder, driving his car into a tree, overdosing on sleeping pills or tranquilizers—and one of these accidents may kill him. He may commit suicide. Or he may eventually die from acute alcohol poisoning, cirrhosis of the liver, pancreatitis, heart or respiratory failure, pneumonia, infections, or cancer.

* Experts estimate that there are over 26.5 million alcoholics (one in eight adults) in the United States. Bridget F. Grant, S. Patricia Chou, Tulshi D. Saha, et al. (2017). "Prevalence of 12-Month Alcohol Use, High-Risk Drinking, and *DSM-IV* Alcohol Use Disorder in the United States, 2001–2002 to 2012–2013." *JAMA Psychiatry* 74(9): 911–923.

Most alcoholics will die an average of twenty-nine years earlier than their nonalcoholic friends.[1] Most will never receive treatment for their primary disease, alcoholism. Their death certificates will typically state heart failure, accident, suicide, or respiratory failure as the cause of death. The chances are that no one—physician, social worker, family member, or alcoholic—will diagnose the cause of the problem as addiction to alcohol.

WHILE TENS OF thousands of alcoholics like Bob die every year, scientists, physicians, and professional alcoholism specialists disagree, often heatedly, about the nature of the disease that destroys them. Those involved in trying to understand alcoholism—and that includes psychologists, psychiatrists, physicians, nutritionists, biologists, neurophysiologists, biochemists, anthropologists, and sociologists—operate in a confused and chaotic system where prejudiced opinion, fierce competition for resources, and deep distrust abound. Professionals argue about the causes of the disease, how it should be treated, and how it can be prevented.

The problem is deeper than a superficial disagreement among scholars. Violent feeling lurks here. Hatred, distrust, and prejudices abound. Profound insecurities and long-standing feuds smolder. Each scientist or research team appears to be working in a narrow compartment, oblivious of work conducted by others outside their special field. Scientists in the laboratory accuse the clinicians, who work directly with alcoholics, of ignoring scientific data and conforming to old-fashioned and outdated treatment methods. Clinicians accuse the scientists of dismissing all firsthand experiences with alcoholics as "nonscientific" and therefore invalid. Neuroscientists argue with social scientists about the causes of alcoholism while researchers from all disciplines accuse government bureaucrats of pandering to fads and special interests.

These deep and often painful schisms were once again thrust into the spotlight at the 2015 Nobel Conference titled "Addiction: Exploring the Science and Experience of an Equal Opportunity

Condition."[2] Panelists from various academic disciplines including psychology, philosophy, sociology, epidemiology, and neurobiology struggled for days to find common areas of agreement. In one telling exchange, neuroscientist Eric Kandel stated his conviction that addiction is a genetically transmitted brain disease characterized by progressive loss of control, and developmental psychologist Marc Lewis vehemently disagreed.

"I would not agree that addiction is a disease," Lewis said. "There's lots of stuff that's genetic, like having an impulsive personality or a low frustration tolerance, that I would not call a disease."

"It's a disease of the brain," Kandel repeated with some irritation.

"How can you show genetically that it's a disease?" Lewis responded.

"If your father has it and you get it, that's a gene," Kandel said.

"My father has a big nose and I've got a big nose. That doesn't make it a disease," Lewis said with a chuckle.

"I think we need a course in biology before we go further, to be honest with you," Kandel responded, clearly exasperated.

"That's below the belt," Lewis muttered.

"I think this is a long discussion which we're not going to solve," Kandel said, summarizing the proceedings. "It really requires a common culture. It was as if we came into this room a Tower of Babel. We are each speaking different languages, and we're not quite communicating with each other because we don't share a common culture."

AS LONG AS the experts continue to speak different languages and find themselves incapable of discovering a "common culture," the layperson will be confused and misinformed about alcoholism. The scope of this confusion and misunderstanding is truly astonishing, given the abundance of factual information already known about the disease. For example, alcoholism is known to be a true physiological disease that transforms its victims, leaving them in its later stages with little or no control over their behavior. Yet the majority of people in this country—professionals and nonprofessionals alike—stubbornly cling to the belief that alcoholism is an emotional "weakness" and a moral evil capable of destroying society. Note such influential views as the following:

- Morris Chafetz, director of the National Institute on Alcohol Abuse and Alcoholism (NIAAA), in addressing a special prevention task force on alcoholism, December 17, 1973: "I do not happen to believe that alcoholism is a disease." Instead, it is "a symptom of a myriad of psychological and social problems."
- Representative Samuel Devine (R-Ohio) in 1974 in explaining to Congress why he did not believe alcoholism is a disease: "My opinion is that it is a weakness, because otherwise we could attribute all our weaknesses to disease."
- Representative Robert K. Dornan (R-Calif.), as reported in the *Congressional Record*, October 25, 1979: "There is one major cause underlying alcohol abuse, drug abuse, and many other of the ills that afflict our society; it is an absence of self-discipline. This has broader implications than the statistics of premature death and disability would indicate. The social and economic disruption caused by such widespread self-abuse can undermine the strength of an entire society. A democratic society cannot survive and prosper without a virtuous people. And virtue is impossible without self-discipline."
- Thomas Szasz, M.D., psychiatrist, in a 1996 public TV show: "Addiction is a form of behavior. Behavior is not caused; it has reasons. Drugs can no more cause addiction than sex hormones or genitals can cause perversions or sexual acts."
- Lawrence Dodes, M.D., in a 2011 post on *Psychology Today:* "The only 'disease-like' aspect of addiction is that if people do not deal with it, their lives tend to get worse . . . addiction is essentially the same as other compulsive behaviors like shopping, exercising, or even cleaning your house. Of course, addiction usually causes much more serious problems. But inside, it is basically the same as these other common behaviors."

- Psychologist Stanton Peele, in a 2015 interview with historian William White: "Addiction is not a primary disease, [but] a way of coping for people who feel inadequate to the task, or who have insufficient life satisfaction otherwise."

- Development psychologist Marc Lewis, Ph.D., in the introduction to his 2015 book *The Biology of Desire:* "Addiction is a habit, which, like many other habits, becomes entrenched through a decrease in self-control. Addiction is definitely bad news for the addict and all those within range. But the severe consequences of addiction don't make it a disease, any more than the consequences of violence make violence a disease, or the consequences of racism make racism a disease, or the folly of loving thy neighbor's wife makes infidelity a disease. What they make is a very bad habit."

- Physician and author Gabor Maté, M.D., in a 2017 blog post: "Addiction is neither a choice nor a disease, but originates in a human being's desperate attempt to solve a problem: the problem of emotional pain, of overwhelming stress, of lost connection, of loss of control, of a deep discomfort with the self."

- Journalist and author Maia Szalavitz in a 2017 interview: "Most people who compulsively seek to escape through drugs do so because they find their consciousness unbearable. That's the real source of addiction. It's not a property of the drug. You can get rid of the substance but as long as people are feeling miserable, something will come along to replace it."

Pronouncements such as these by compassionate, highly educated individuals undoubtedly color public opinion, buttress innate prejudices, and shape public policies. In a 2003 study, "Alcoholism: Low Standing with the Public," published in the international journal *Alcohol and Alcoholism,* researchers interviewed 5,025 residents of Germany to assess attitudes about allocating financial resources to various diseases.[3] Asked to choose from a list of nine conditions or disorders—cancer, AIDS, heart disease, diabetes, rheumatism, Alzheimer's disease, alcoholism, schizophrenia, and depression—and select the condition least deserving of resources, most respondents selected alcoholism. Most participants agreed that research funds should be allocated last—or not at all—to studying alcoholism.

A 2014 survey conducted by researchers at the Johns Hopkins Bloomberg School of Public Health focused on public attitudes about alcoholism and mental illness, specifically stigma, discrimination, treatment, and public policy, and reported these findings:[4]

- Ninety percent of respondents said they would be unwilling to have a person with alcoholism or other drug addiction marry into their family (compared to 59 percent for people with mental illness).
- Seventy-eight percent said they would be unwilling to work closely with someone who has a drug addiction (versus 38 percent for mental illness).
- Sixty-four percent believe employers should be able to deny employment to people with a drug addiction (compared to 25 percent for mental illness).
- Fifty-four percent believe landlords have the right to deny housing to drug-addicted individuals (compared to 15 percent for mental illness).
- Forty-three percent oppose giving drug-addicted individuals health insurance benefits equivalent to those of the public at large (versus 21 percent for mental illness).
- Roughly 30 percent believe that even with treatment, people with drug addiction and mental illness *cannot* get well and return to productive lives.

"The American public is more likely to think of addiction as a moral failing than a medical condition," the study's lead author, Colleen Barry, concludes. "In recent years, it has become more socially acceptable to talk publicly about one's struggles with mental illness.

But with addiction, the feeling is that the addict is a bad or weak person."

The stigma of this disease is tragic given the horrific toll it exacts on every man, woman, and child in this country. There are over 26.5 million alcoholics in the United States. Every year an estimated 95,000 people die from alcohol-related causes—more than twice the annual death toll of opioid overdoses. Alcohol is the third-leading preventable cause of death; the first is tobacco and the second is poor diet and physical inactivity, both of which are related directly or indirectly to alcohol use.

Every fifty minutes someone is killed in a drunk driving crash. Twenty-nine percent of all traffic deaths are alcohol-related. In 2019, 6,590 pedestrians were killed by drivers who had been drinking; 50 percent of all pedestrian fatalities involved alcohol.

More than any other drug, alcohol is linked to crime. Alcohol is a factor in 57.7 percent of incarcerations for violent crimes, including murder, rape, robbery, and aggravated assault. More than 2.2 million minors have alcohol- or drug-addicted parents currently in prison.

Every year nearly five thousand teenagers die from alcohol-related causes (more than all illegal drugs combined).

When asked, one in nine pregnant women report drinking in the prior thirty days; one-third of these women report binge drinking (four or more drinks), with an average of 4.5 binge episodes reported in this thirty-day period. Although researchers don't know exactly how many children are born each year with fetal alcohol spectrum disorders (FASDs) as the result of alcohol exposure in utero, the number may be as high as 5 percent, with five of every one hundred babies demonstrating one or more signs of FASDs such as low birth weight, slow rate of growth, and irreversible brain damage.

In a 2019 study reported in the *Journal of the American Medical Association,* the rate of alcoholism in the general population rose by 49.4 percent from 2000 through 2010, with the greatest increases in women (83.7 percent increase), African Americans (92.8 percent increase), individuals with only a high school education (57.8 percent increase), individuals with income less than $20,000 (65.9 percent increase), and the elderly (106 percent increase).

The visible cost to the economy approaches a staggering $249 billion each year. Alcoholics fill up our prisons, mental institutions, hospitals, and welfare rolls. In terms of lost workplace productivity, alcohol costs over $179 billion each year; health and medical costs run over $28 billion, motor vehicle losses over $13 billion, and criminal justice costs over $25 billion. The hidden costs of undiagnosed and unrecognized alcoholism and the pain and suffering caused by alcohol-related injuries and diseases raise the toll even higher, leading researchers to conclude that the study "underestimates the cost of excessive drinking."[5]

ALCOHOLISM IS TRAGICALLY and fundamentally misunderstood. Every aspect of the disease is confused, distorted by myth and misconception, and colored by opinions that have no firm basis in fact. The roots of these myths are deeply buried in an ethical code of behavior that stretches back in time thousands of years. The Roman philosopher and lawyer Seneca (4 BCE–65 CE) pronounced an opinion about drinkers and drunkenness that continues to mold public opinion: "Drunkenness is nothing but a condition of insanity purposely assumed."

Even today, despite the abundance of scientific research to the contrary, alcoholics are generally considered to be moral degenerates who choose a life of abasement and, through lack of willpower and maturity, allow themselves to lose their job, their family, and their self-respect. The typical alcoholic, the myth informs us, is a person who would rather be drunk than sober, who lacks confidence and maturity, who is riddled with guilt and shame over past sins and misdeeds, yet lacks the strength of character to change their ways, and who has no guiding purpose or motivation in life. This myth is only one of many that rule the way we think about the disease and its victims.

The myths and misconceptions surrounding the disease of

alcoholism and its victims must be rooted out and replaced by already established facts. Only then will professionals come to an agreement about the causes of the disease; only then will an understanding be reached about why alcoholics drink excessively and what must be done to help them overcome their disease. Only when the myths no longer cloud perception and shape opinion can alcoholics and their disease finally be understood.

A substantial body of scientific facts and information about alcoholism already exists—more than enough to guide prevention, education, research, intervention, and effective treatment. The problem is not a lack of knowledge but the fact that this knowledge is scattered all over the landscape of the various life sciences. What is needed is not more isolated facts and information but a truly unifying scientific view of alcoholism. To be successful, such a concept must meet two primary criteria: (1) all hard data and facts must be respected and accommodated, and (2) only those theories and beliefs that are compatible with the established hard data and facts should be accommodated.

It is the primary purpose of this book to present just such a view of alcoholism. *Under the Influence* is a guide to the myths and realities of alcoholism. It offers—for the alcoholic and those who hope to understand and treat them—a clear explanation of a disease that continues to be misunderstood, misdiagnosed, and mistreated. This book looks at alcohol, the substance that causes the disease, and explains why this combination chemical, drug, and food is relatively harmless for some but addictive for others. It examines the causes of alcoholism and its gradual but inevitable progression from an early, hidden stage through the first noticeable signs of trouble and on to the catastrophic later stages. The alcoholic's symptoms are described, and the question "Why do they drink when drinking is destroying them?" is clearly answered. The reader learns how to help the alcoholic into treatment and what kind of treatment alcoholics must receive if they are to break their addiction and achieve a permanent, lasting sobriety.

Finally, the fundamental changes that must occur in social programs, government agencies, research, education and prevention efforts, and the medical and legal professions are carefully outlined and explained. The very workings of our society in all these areas must shift and change focus if alcoholics are ever to receive the kind of help they deserve.

Separating myth from reality is not an easy task. Myth is reality for many people; to suggest that another reality exists is to turn their world upside down. But if the truth about alcoholism is ever to be understood, the myths must be attacked and destroyed. Only facts can destroy myths. And facts are the backbone of this book.

The Myth and the Reality

MYTH: *Alcohol is predominantly a sedative or depressant drug.*

REALITY: Alcohol's pharmacological effects change with the amount drunk. In small quantities, alcohol is a stimulant. In larger quantities, alcohol acts as a central nervous system depressant or sedative. In all amounts, however, alcohol provides a rich and potent source of calories and energy (Chapter 2).

MYTH: *Alcohol has the same chemical and physiological effect on everyone who drinks.*

REALITY: Alcohol, like every other food we take into our bodies, affects different people in different ways (Chapters 2, 3).

MYTH: *Alcohol is an addictive drug, and anyone who drinks long and hard enough will become addicted.*

REALITY: Alcohol is a selectively addictive drug; it is addictive for only a minority of its users, namely, alcoholics. Most people can drink occasionally, daily, or even heavily without becoming addicted to alcohol. Others (alcoholics) are genetically and physiologically susceptible to the drug's addictive effects (Chapters 2, 3).

MYTH: *Alcohol is harmful and poisonous to the alcoholic.**

REALITY: Alcohol is a normalizing agent for alcoholics and the best medicine for the pain it creates, giving the alcoholic energy, stimulation, and relief from the pain of withdrawal. Its harmful and poisonous aftereffects are most evident when the alcoholic stops drinking (Chapters 3–7).

MYTH: *Addiction to alcohol is often psychological.*

REALITY: Addiction to alcohol is primarily physiological. Alcoholics become addicted because their bodies are physiologically incapable of processing alcohol normally (Chapters 3–5).

MYTH: *People become alcoholics because they have psychological or emotional problems that they try to relieve by drinking.*

REALITY: In general, alcoholics have the same range of psychological and emotional problems as everyone else before they start drinking. Some alcoholics may have significant emotional problems that may make addressing their alcoholism more challenging; some may have fewer such problems, and some have the same level of emotional problems as the general population. Whatever emotional problems the alcoholic may have, however, are aggravated by their addiction to alcohol. Alcoholism undermines and weakens the alcoholic's ability to cope with the normal problems of living. Furthermore, the alcoholic's emotions become inflamed both when they drink excessively and when they stop drinking. Thus, when they are drinking and when they are abstinent, they will feel angry, fearful, and depressed in exaggerated degrees (Chapters 3–5).

MYTH: *All sorts of social problems—marriage problems, a death in the family, job stress—may cause alcoholism.*

---

*Heavy use of alcohol can cause toxicity-related problems such as cancer and liver disease independent of addiction to it. Alcohol can also cause acute psychological impairment independent of addiction to it.

REALITY: As with psychological and emotional problems, alcoholics experience all the social pressures everyone else does—trauma and chronic stress, for example, are well-known stress factors that may underlie the decision to drink alcohol in the first place—but their ability to cope is undermined by the disease and the problems get worse (Chapters 3–5).

MYTH: *When alcoholics are drinking, they reveal their true personality.*

REALITY: Alcohol's effect on the brain causes severe psychological and emotional distortions of the normal personality. Sobriety and long-term recovery reveal the alcoholic's true personality (Chapters 3–10).

MYTH: *The fact that alcoholics often continue to be depressed, anxious, irritable, and unhappy after they stop drinking is evidence that their disease is caused by psychological problems.*

REALITY: Alcoholics who continue to be depressed, anxious, irritable, and unhappy after they stop drinking are often suffering from a phenomenon called protracted or post-acute withdrawal syndrome.* The physical damage and underlying nutritional deficiencies caused by years of excessive drinking have not been completely reversed; such people are, in fact, still sick and in need of more effective treatment (Chapters 5, 9).

MYTH: *If people would only drink responsibly, they would not become alcoholics.*

REALITY: Many responsible drinkers become alcoholics. Then, because it is the nature of the disease (*not* the person), they begin to drink irresponsibly (Chapters 3, 4, 11).

MYTH: *An alcoholic has to want help to be helped.*

REALITY: Many drinking alcoholics resist help because they are sick, unable to think rationally, and incapable of giving up alcohol by themselves. Many recovering alcoholics were forced into

---

* Some alcoholics have independent affective/anxiety disorders that persist independent of the protracted withdrawal syndrome; these disorders can predate or coincide with the onset of alcoholism or emerge in early recovery.

treatment against their will. Self-motivation usually occurs during treatment, not before (Chapters 8, 9).

MYTH: *Some alcoholics can learn to drink normally and can continue to drink with no ill effects as long as they limit the amount.*

REALITY: Alcoholics can never safely return to drinking because drinking in any amount will sooner or later reactivate their addiction. Once the alcoholic stops drinking alcohol, the body begins to heal from the tissue and organ damage caused by the alcohol. However, the underlying susceptibility to addiction does not change; thus, any return to drinking is extremely risky and potentially life-threatening (Chapters 9, 11).

MYTH: *Psychotherapy can help many alcoholics achieve sobriety through self-understanding.*

REALITY: Psychotherapy as a primary treatment method risks diverting attention from the physical causes of the disease, compounds the alcoholic's guilt and shame, and aggravates rather than alleviates the alcoholic's problems. Individual and group counseling may be helpful adjunctive therapies, especially in the long-term recovery process, but abstinence from alcohol must come first (Chapters 9, 11).

MYTH: *Craving for alcohol can be offset by eating high-sugar foods.*

REALITY: Foods with a high sugar content cause erratic fluctuations in blood sugar levels that will only increase the alcoholic's depression, irritability, and tension and intensify the desire for a drink to relieve these symptoms (Chapter 9, Appendices B, C).

MYTH: *If alcoholics eat three balanced meals a day, their nutritional problems will eventually correct themselves.*

REALITY: Alcoholics' nutritional needs are only partially met by a balanced diet. They also may need vitamin and mineral supplements to correct any deficiencies and to maintain nutritional balance, especially in the short term (Chapter 9, Appendices B, C).

MYTH: *Tranquilizers and sedatives are sometimes useful in treating alcoholics.*

REALITY: Tranquilizers and sedatives are useful only during the
acute withdrawal period. Beyond that, these substitute drugs are
destructive and, in many cases, deadly for alcoholics (Chapters 9,
10, Appendices A, D).

MYTH: *Alcoholics should avoid all drugs after treatment and in long-
term recovery.*

REALITY: Medication-assisted treatment to reduce craving and
treat co-occurring disorders, under the careful supervision of a
medical specialist, may be one of the many pathways to recovery
(Chapter 10).

2

Alcohol

> As better knowledge and understanding of the actions of alcohol become available, more sensible attitudes regarding it are arising, [but] it is also interesting to observe how little the people wanted to learn about alcohol in a scientific way. They seem much to prefer their violently differing emotional fantasies about it.
>
> —Chauncey D. Leake, Ph.D., in a symposium called "Alcoholism," 1957[1]

Alcohol is an infinitely confusing substance. In small amounts it is an exhilarating stimulant. In larger amounts it acts as a sedative and as a toxic, or poisonous, agent. When taken in very large amounts over long periods of time, this combination chemical and drug can be damaging to cells, tissues, and organs. Yet alcohol is addictive for only a minority of its users—in the United States, an estimated 10 percent. Most people can drink lightly or occasionally without experiencing serious physical or psychological harm.*[2]

To further the confusion, alcohol is the only drug that can also be classified as a food. Rich in calories and a potent source of energy for the body, alcohol is used by the cells to perform their complicated

---

*The benefits of occasional drinking are still debated, but recent studies show that even moderate drinking (less than two drinks a day) is associated with higher rates of stroke, fatal aneurysms, heart failure, and death, and raises the risk of cancers of the mouth, throat, larynx, esophagus, colon, rectum, liver, and, particularly in women, breast cancer. Furthermore, from a public health and public safety perspective, alcohol actually causes more harm in a population not through addicted users but instead from the larger number of moderate and heavy drinking but nonaddicted users—simply because there are more of them.

functions. Unlike most foods, however, alcohol contains negligible amounts of vitamins and minerals and contributes little or nothing to the cells' nutritional requirements. As a result, continual heavy drinking inevitably leads to malnutrition.

Perhaps alcohol's most surprising property is its ability to relieve the distress it creates in the first place. An alcoholic suffering from withdrawal has only one priority: alcohol. A malnourished alcoholic does not want food; the malnourished alcoholic wants alcohol. Alcoholics drink because drinking makes them feel good and, later in the disease, because it immediately relieves the craving for alcohol experienced by the alcoholic, whose body has adapted over time to the presence of high levels of alcohol. Only when the alcoholic stops drinking do they experience the full effect of alcohol's disruptions in the body.

Understanding the disease of alcoholism must begin with an understanding of the substance alcohol—a combination chemical, drug, and food capable of creating both extraordinary pleasure and extraordinary pain.

Alcohol the Chemical
What It Is

Ethyl alcohol or ethanol (hereafter called simply alcohol) is actually the excrement of yeast, a fungus with a ravenous appetite for sweets. When yeast encounters honey, fruits, berries, cereals, or potatoes, for example, it releases an enzyme that converts the sugar in these materials into carbon dioxide (CO_2) and alcohol (CH_3CH_2OH). This process is known as fermentation. The yeast then continues to feed on the sugar until it literally dies of acute alcohol intoxication—the very first victim of "drunkenness."

Because yeast expires when the alcohol by volume (ABV) measures 13 to 15 percent, natural fermentation stops at this point. Beer generally ranges from 3.0 to 13.0 percent ABV but can be weaker or stronger depending on the quantity of fermentable sugars and variety of yeasts used. Table wine contains between 10 and 14 percent alcohol, the limit of yeast's alcohol tolerance.

Distillation, which was discovered about 800 CE in Arabia, is the human-initiated process designed to take over where the vulnerable yeast fungus leaves off. Distilled or hard liquors, including brandy, gin, whiskey, Scotch, rye, bourbon, rum, and vodka, contain between 40 and 75 percent pure alcohol. Pure alcohol is also added to fortify wines such as port and sherry, boosting their alcohol content to 18 or 20 percent.

The percentage of alcohol in distilled liquors is commonly expressed in degrees of "proof" rather than as a percentage of pure alcohol. This measure developed from the seventeenth-century English custom of "proving" that an alcoholic drink was of sufficient strength by mixing it with gunpowder and attempting to ignite it. If the drink contained 49 percent alcohol by weight or 57 percent by volume, it could be ignited. Proof is approximately double the percentage of pure alcohol. A 100 proof whiskey is therefore 50 percent pure alcohol; an 86 proof whiskey is 43 percent alcohol.

Pure alcohol is a colorless, somewhat volatile liquid with a harsh, burning taste, which is widely used as a fuel and as a solvent for various fats, oils, and resins. This simple and unpalatable chemical is made to look, taste, and smell appetizing by combining it with water and various substances called congeners. Congeners make bourbon whiskey taste different from Scotch whiskey, distinguish one brand of beer from another, and give wine its "nose" and sherry its golden glow.

Congeners include a wide variety of substances, many of which appear to have no business in a beverage designed for human consumption. Inorganic substances such as aluminum, cadmium, cobalt, chromium, copper, lead, manganese, nickel, silicon, and zinc are frequently found in alcoholic beverages, as are glucose, fructose, acetic and lactic acids, carbon dioxide, small amounts of vitamins and minerals, salts, acids, ketones, esters, carbohydrates, and various other alcohols (including propyl, butyl, amyl, hexyl, hyptyl, octyl, nonyl, decyl, methyl, and fusel). In minute or trace amounts, most congeners are harmless, but they have also proven toxic and even fatal for unsuspecting drinkers. Cobalt, for example, was once used to increase the foamy "head" in certain beers. Years went by before researchers finally linked the mineral with a rising cancer rate in beer drinkers.

How It Works

When human beings drink alcohol, it travels rapidly to the stomach, where approximately 20 percent immediately passes through the stomach walls into the bloodstream. The remaining 80 percent is transferred from the stomach to the small intestine, where it is then absorbed into the bloodstream.

The concentration of alcohol in the body is described by researchers in terms of the blood alcohol content (BAC), which is simply a measure of alcohol in the bloodstream or on one's breath. A .05 BAC, for example, indicates approximately 5 parts alcohol to 10,000 parts other blood components. When a person drinks more alcohol than his or her body can immediately eliminate—the average rate of elimination is approximately one-half ounce per hour, which is the equivalent of 1 ounce of 100 proof whiskey or about 3 ounces of wine—alcohol accumulates in the bloodstream, and the BAC rises. As the BAC rises, the drinker's behavior, thoughts, and emotions are increasingly affected, with severe disruptions in behavior occurring at high BACs. A person with a .08 BAC, for example, is considered legally "under the influence" in most states.

A number of factors can affect the rate at which the BAC rises and thus the rate at which behaviors are altered. Weight is one factor. The more the drinker weighs, the more water there is in the body to dilute the alcohol and therefore the lower the BAC. A 200-pound male might have an approximate 0.15 BAC after drinking eight cans of beer, whereas a 150-pound male drinking at the same rate might have an 0.20 BAC with the same intake. The higher BAC would, of course, make the 150-pound male act drunker. It is therefore the BAC and not the amount consumed that determines the effect on behavior.

Sex is another factor that affects the BAC. Females reach higher BACs faster because they have less water in their bodies and more adipose tissue (fat), which is not easily penetrated by alcohol. Hormones also affect the BAC. With the same intake of alcohol, women experience the highest BACs premenstrually and the lowest BACs on the first day of their menstrual cycle, fluctuations that are almost certainly caused by changing hormone levels.

Food or lack of it can alter the BAC. An empty stomach has no food with which to dilute alcohol and slow down its absorption into the bloodstream. As a result, the BAC rises more rapidly in those who drink on an empty stomach. When there is food in the stomach, particularly high-protein foods such as cheese, meat, and eggs, the absorption rate is slowed down.

The type of mixer also affects absorption. Water and fruit juices slow the process, while carbon dioxide speeds it up. The carbon dioxide in champagne and carbonated mixers such as Coca-Cola, ginger ale, and tonic water rushes through the stomach and intestinal walls and into the bloodstream, carrying alcohol along with it and creating a rapid rise in BAC.

The strength of the drink will have a significant effect on absorption rates, with higher concentrations of alcohol resulting in more rapid absorption. Pure alcohol is generally absorbed faster than diluted alcohols such as 86 proof gins, which are, in turn, absorbed faster than wine or beer. An unusual effect may occur, however, in certain drinkers. Alcohol taken in concentrated amounts can irritate the stomach lining to the extent that it produces a sticky mucus that delays absorption. Furthermore, the pylorus valve, which connects the stomach and small intestine, may go into spasm in the presence of concentrated alcohol, trapping the alcohol in the stomach instead of passing it on to the small intestine, where it would be more rapidly absorbed into the bloodstream. As a result, the drinker who downs several straight shots of alcohol in an effort to get a quick high may actually experience a delayed effect.

Finally, the temperature of the beverage affects its absorption, with warm alcohol being absorbed more rapidly than cold alcohol.

ONCE IN THE bloodstream, alcohol is distributed throughout the body in simple diffusion. Its small and relatively simple molecular structure allows it to pass right through cell membranes and mix in the entire water content of the body. The brain, liver, heart, pancreas, lungs, kidneys, and every other organ and tissue system are infiltrated by alcohol within minutes after it passes into the bloodstream.

Alcohol's immediate effect on the brain is most unusual. The brain is usually protected from chemicals and drugs by an electrical-chemical filter system known as the blood/brain barrier, which makes sure that only very simple molecules such as those of oxygen and water can pass through. The simple molecular structure of alcohol allows it to penetrate this selective screen and gain easy access to the brain and its extension, the spinal cord.

Consequently, alcohol has immediate and profound effects on behavior. At low doses, alcohol stimulates the brain cells, and the drinker feels happy, talkative, energetic, and euphoric. After one or two drinks, most drinkers will experience some improvement in thought and performance. As the BAC rises, however, the amount of alcohol in the brain also rises, and alcohol begins to disrupt the brain's electrical and chemical circuitry, causing complicated behavior changes.

With large amounts of alcohol surging through the brain's labyrinthine passageways, the central nervous system cells can no longer function normally. The brain malfunctions, and the major visible effect is a change in the drinker's psychological and emotional state. After several drinks, most drinkers will begin to show signs of intoxication. They may become emotionally demonstrative, expressing great joy, sadness, or anger. They may also begin to show signs of motor incoordination and slowed reflexes, staggering slightly when they walk, knocking their drink over as they leave the table, or slurring their words. If they continue to drink, their vision may blur and their emotions, thoughts, and judgment may become noticeably disordered.

When blood alcohol concentrations reach very high levels, the brain's control over the respiratory system may actually be paralyzed. A 0.30 BAC is the minimum level at which death can occur; at 0.40 the drinker may lapse into a coma. At a 0.50 BAC, respiratory functions and heartbeat slow drastically, and at 0.60 most drinkers are dead.

The body, in the meantime, is doing its best to eliminate alcohol. Small amounts are eliminated in the urine, sweat, and breath, but the primary site of alcohol elimination is the liver, which is located behind the ribs on the right side of the body. This vital organ is responsible for numerous life-sustaining processes, including the control and elimination of drugs and chemicals that are toxic to the body's cells and the conversion of various nutritional substances into materials that can be used in the life processes of cells (such as eliminating wastes, making repairs, and creating new cells).

The process of elimination begins as soon as alcohol enters the liver. An enzyme called alcohol dehydrogenase (ADH) attacks the alcohol molecule, quickly removing two hydrogen atoms to create a new substance called acetaldehyde. Since acetaldehyde is a highly toxic agent that can produce nausea, rapid heartbeat, dizziness, headache, and mental confusion when present in the body in large quantities, the liver quickly initiates the second step in the elimination process.* It employs another enzyme with a similar name, aldehyde dehydrogenase (ALDH), to transform acetaldehyde into acetate ($C_2H_3O_2$). Acetate is then converted to carbon dioxide and

---

* Antabuse, a medication that has been used for many years with recovering alcoholics as a deterrent to drinking, blocks the liver's ability to eliminate acetaldehyde and causes an immediate and severe reaction. See Chapter 10, page 181.

water and eventually eliminated from the body. During these two steps in alcohol oxidation, a great deal of energy is released. In fact, with ordinary rates of alcohol metabolism, almost the entire energy needs of the liver can be satisfied. Most of the acetate is passed into the bloodstream and oxidized to carbon dioxide and water in other organs. The energy produced in these reactions contributes to the energy needs of the entire body. In the alcoholic, up to two-thirds of the body's total energy needs may be satisfied by substituting alcohol for other foods. This helps to explain why alcoholics often neglect eating for several weeks at a time.

The conversion of alcohol into acetaldehyde and acetate is an efficient process in most drinkers. The liver works at maximum efficiency, converting alcohol at the rate of approximately one-half ounce per hour, until all the alcohol in the body is broken down and its energy released to the cells. The liver is then able to return to its other duties.

If alcohol is present in the body in large amounts for long periods of time, however, the liver must work constantly to break it down and flush it out. The liver's preoccupation with alcohol results in the neglect of its other duties, and as a result, toxins accumulate and nutritional functions are disrupted. The health and vitality of the body's cells, tissues, and organs begin to suffer.

Alcohol the Drug

Alcohol is the most commonly used drug in the world, and yet even habitual users do not understand exactly how it affects them. When asked to describe alcohol's pharmacological properties, most people, including alcohol specialists, would reply that it is a central nervous system depressant or sedative. When asked if alcohol is an addictive drug, the majority of drinkers and nondrinkers would answer yes.

Both answers are only partially true. Alcohol in larger amounts is a sedative but initially, in small amounts, it is a true stimulant directly to nerve tissues. Furthermore, alcohol is an addictive drug only for the minority of its users who are genetically and physiologically susceptible.

Stimulant and Sedative

A shot of whiskey, a glass of wine, or a bottle of beer will trigger a variety of stimulating responses throughout the body. Numerous studies report that low doses of alcohol increase blood flow, accelerate heart rate, step up the conduction and transmission of nerve impulses, and excite simple spinal and brain stem reflexes. Performance on highly complex problem-solving tasks is improved with low doses of alcohol, memory and concentration are sharpened, and creative thinking is enhanced.[3]

Anyone who drinks can attest to these stimulating effects of low doses of alcohol. After a drink, or even a few sips, the average drinker feels warm and suffused with a sense of well-being. Ideas multiply, confidence increases, frustrations ease, and feelings of camaraderie, amusement, and contentment grow. For most people, the world definitely seems a better place after a drink or two. Through simple conditioning or learning, even the anticipation of a drink can trigger some of these pleasant effects.

If it were not for these stimulating effects of alcohol, most people would soon lose interest in drinking. In fact, when alcohol's sedative effects begin to take over after several drinks, the pleasure and excitement of drinking are gradually cancelled out, and the average drinker simply stops drinking. A built-in deterrent to overdrinking seems to be working in most drinkers, somewhat like the natural deterrent to overeating that most people have, although the mechanism is different. The average person enjoys sweets, for example, and will eat a piece of candy if it is offered. Some people will eat two or three, and a few will gobble down the whole box. Most people, however, will feel sick if they eat more than a small amount of concentrated sweets.

Likewise, the average drinker is unable to comfortably drink more than a few beers, a glass or two of wine, or several mixed drinks. The benefits of drinking are usually available only with low doses of alcohol, and when sedation begins to override the stimulation, most drinkers stop drinking. Another deterrent is the toxic effect of several drinks in the average drinker—nausea, dizziness, sweating, and other unpleasant sensations.

The point at which alcohol's stimulating effects are overshadowed by the sedative and toxic effects varies from drinker to drinker. For some people, one drink is the limit. Others can consume four, five, or more drinks and still experience alcohol's stimulating and euphoric effects. Alcoholics develop an increased physical resistance to alcohol's effects (called tolerance), and some can drink many times more than nonalcoholics while continuing to behave as if they were on their first few drinks.* Thus alcohol remains stimulating and pleasurable for alcoholics even after they have drunk amounts that would cause nonalcoholics acute discomfort.

For alcoholics as well as nonalcoholic drinkers, however, alcohol's stimulating effects will eventually be erased with continued drinking. After several drinks—again, depending on the initial tolerance of the drinker—the average person will begin to experience a slowing down in their mental and physical reactions. They may not be able to grasp the thread of a conversation; reflexes will be somewhat delayed, speech slurred, and gait unsteady. As they continue to drink, the alcohol increasingly depresses the central nervous system, and sleepiness, mental sluggishness, and physical incoordination intensify.

Only rarely, however, will a normal, nonalcoholic drinker take in enough alcohol to lose consciousness. This is fortunate, for alcohol taken in large enough quantities to cause unconsciousness is dangerously near the amount needed to paralyze the respiratory center, shut off the breathing apparatus, and kill the drinker. As an anesthetic or painkiller, therefore, alcohol is inferior because it numbs

* See Chapter 4 for a discussion of tolerance.

the senses only at extremely high, nearly lethal doses. Stories from the Old West about soldiers or cowboys who are facing amputation gulping a lot of whiskey and then screaming horribly when the doctor starts sawing demonstrate the point. The unfortunate patient may have succeeded in becoming drunk, but the alcohol did not obliterate the pain. Even a drunken Clint Eastwood winces when, in the movies, arrows and bullets are being removed from his body.

A Selectively Addicting Drug

In the 1970s, the World Health Organization (WHO) defined addiction-producing drugs as those drugs that produce in the great majority of users an irresistible need for the drug, an increased tolerance to the effects of the drug, and physical dependence on the drug, manifested in severe and painful symptoms when the drug is withdrawn.[4] Examples cited were heroin, morphine, and codeine. With these drugs, dependence occurs after approximately four weeks of use, and the drug-dependent individual typically graduates to quantities well above the normally lethal dose, usually from twenty to one hundred times the initially effective dose.

Alcohol did not qualify as an addictive drug under the WHO guidelines simply because it causes addiction in only a minority—approximately 10 percent—of its users. Furthermore, addiction to alcohol for some requires a period of years, not weeks, to become established, and tolerance may be only three to four times greater in some alcoholics than in nonalcoholics.

It was also difficult to place alcohol in the category "habit-forming drug," which was defined by the WHO as a drug capable of causing an emotional or psychological (rather than physical) dependence in the user and which can be withdrawn without causing physical harm or pain. Of course, alcohol does qualify in the limited sense that millions of people—alcoholics and nonalcoholics alike—become psychologically and emotionally dependent on it. However, alcohol does not fit snugly in this category because it does cause physical dependence in a minority of its users and those users definitely suffer both physical and mental anguish when the drug is withdrawn.

The WHO concluded that alcohol belongs in a category somewhere between the habit-forming and addiction-producing drugs and described it as "intermediate in kind and degree" between the two categories of drugs. But even this label was inaccurate. *The fact is that the effects of alcohol simply cannot be generalized for both alcoholics and nonalcoholics.* For most drinkers, alcohol is not addictive. Yet for the minority who are alcoholics, the criteria of true drug addiction are fulfilled: an increased tissue tolerance to the drug, a physical dependence on the drug with physical withdrawal symptoms, and an irresistible need for the drug when it is withdrawn.

Even after all these years confusion still lingers about what kind of drug alcohol is and how to categorize it. The only way to clear up the confusion is to label alcohol a *selectively addicting drug*. It is addictive only for those individuals who are physically susceptible.

Alcohol the Food

Because alcohol contains calories, it is considered a food. And in terms of calories, it is a very rich food indeed. One ounce of pure alcohol delivers about 170 calories when broken down in the body. Medical writer Berton Roueché notes in the classic *The Neutral Spirit*:

> That approximates the caloric vigor of a dozen Blue Point oysters, one broiled lamp chop, a hard roll, an average baked potato, a glass of milk, or a large orange. As a concentrated source of energy, alcohol thus ranks among the very richest of foods. Only the fats, which assay around two hundred and seventy calories per ounce, are richer.[5]

Alcohol's calories are quickly available to the body and require the cells to do relatively little work to release them. Unlike most fats, proteins, and carbohydrates, which require one to four hours of soaking in the digestive acids secreted by the mouth, stomach, and small intestine, alcohol requires virtually no preparation before being absorbed into the bloodstream and distributed throughout the body. The breakdown process in the liver is relatively simple, and within minutes after ingestion alcohol's calories are supplying the body with a boost of energy. Unfortunately, these calories are empty, containing only tiny amounts of vitamins, minerals, and amino acids. Without sufficient amounts of these essential nutrients, the cells cannot replace damaged cell parts, create new cell materials, or carry on the normal everyday functions of a living, healthy cell.

Alcohol's energy "kick" is therefore its most beneficial and potentially its most deadly characteristic. As normally consumed, alcohol is usually in the body in small amounts and for relatively short periods of time, and its effects are therefore temporary. Furthermore, in small amounts, alcohol's benefits are noticeable and the penalties nonexistent: the cells receive a quick jolt of energy, the heartbeat accelerates, the brain cells speed up their communications, and the drinker feels euphoric and stimulated. The chemical causing these pleasurable effects is easily eliminated in an orderly and efficient manner, and the body then returns to normal activities. The brain cells quickly recover from their alcohol bath, the liver cells return to their everyday functions, nutritional materials once again flow in adequate proportions and amounts to the cells, and waste materials are efficiently eliminated.

In large and continuous amounts, however, the penalties of drinking far outweigh the initial benefits. The drinker is taking in so many calories from alcohol that they will automatically require fewer calories from other, more nutritious foods. Alcohol also disrupts the cells' ability to take in and use nutrients from other food. It interferes with the absorption of various vitamins from the gastrointestinal tract, inhibits the absorption of numerous amino acids, and increases the loss of certain vitamins in the urine, including thiamine (B_1), riboflavin (B_2), pantothenic acid (B_5), pyridoxine (B_6), folate (B_9), vitamin A, and vitamin C. As a result, even if an alcoholic is eating well, alcohol denies them the full nutritional benefit of what they eat. Put another way, alcohol literally robs the body of substances that are essential for life. Thus all alcoholics develop malnutrition regardless of what or how much they eat.

ANYONE WHO HAS experienced the pleasant stimulating and euphoric effects of alcohol will find it easy to understand why nearly 140 million people in the United States age twelve or over drink beverage alcohol.[6] And there is certainly nothing complicated or mysterious about why alcoholics take up drinking, or why they continue to drink. The short answer is that they drink for all the reasons other people do—stimulation, euphoria, relaxation, and, perhaps, mild intoxication. The significant question, then, is not why alcoholics drink, which is obvious, but why their motivation to drink becomes progressively stronger as they drink more, and more often. Once again, a look at the relevant facts will dispel any mysteries and provide a clear answer to this question.

3

What Makes an Alcoholic

PREDISPOSING FACTORS

In my judgment such of us who have never fallen victims [to alcoholism] have been spared more by the absence of appetite than from any mental or moral superiority over those who have. Indeed, I believe if we take habitual drunkards as a class, their heads and their hearts will bear an advantageous comparison with those of any other class.

—Abraham Lincoln, address to the Washington Temperance Society, 1842

Over 140 million people in the United States drink alcohol in any given year. Nearly 30 million of those drinkers are diagnosed with alcohol use disorder, defined by the National Institute on Alcohol Abuse and Alcoholism as "a chronic relapsing brain disorder characterized by an impaired ability to stop or control alcohol use despite adverse social, occupational, or health hazards"—in other words, they are an alcoholic. What makes an alcoholic different from a nonalcoholic? Does the alcoholic drink too much because their body is somehow abnormal, or does their body become abnormal because they drink too much? To answer these questions, both the alcoholic's and the nonalcoholic's reasons for drinking alcohol must be examined.

Why People Drink Alcohol

The alcoholic starts drinking the same ways and for the same reasons the nonalcoholic starts drinking. They drink to gain the effects of alcohol—to feel euphoric, stimulated, relaxed, or intoxicated.

Sometimes they drink to ease their frustrations; other times they drink to put themselves in a good mood. If they are tense, they may drink more than usual in an effort to unwind and get their mind off their troubles; if shy, they may drink to gain confidence; if extroverted, they may drink because they like the company of other drinkers.

Alcoholics, like nonalcoholics, are influenced in the way they drink, where they drink, how much they drink, and how often they drink by numerous psychological, social, or cultural factors. They may start drinking to impress their friends, to prove they are not afraid of their parents' disapproval, or because they are taunted into it by their friends. They may drink regularly because alcohol makes them laugh and forget their troubles or because they feel self-assured after a few drinks. If their partner has a cocktail every night, they may drink to keep them company. If their coworkers are heavy drinkers, they may learn to drink heavily.

Again like the nonalcoholic, the alcoholic learns to drink a variety of alcoholic beverages and develops preferences among beers, wines, and liquors. They learn how much and how fast people ordinarily drink on various occasions, and they learn how well they can "hold their liquor"—how much it takes for them to feel good, to get high, or to get drunk.

Alcoholics as well as nonalcoholics may change their drinking habits because of life changes: death of a loved one, divorce, loss of a job. Loneliness, depression, fears, and insecurities may also affect the way a person drinks. *The point is that none of these psychological or social factors are unique to either the alcoholic or nonalcoholic. Members of both groups drink for the same reasons and with the same reinforcement by alcohol's stimulating and energizing effects.* The same variety of personality traits is found in both groups. Earlier advocates of an "alcoholic personality" have long since abandoned this hypothesis, and the theory of an "addictive personality" has also been discredited by lack of supportive evidence.

At some point, however, the drinking patterns of the two groups begin to diverge. The alcoholic starts to drink more, and more often. They do not want to stop drinking once they have started. In the later stages of their drinking, they may keep a six-pack of beer in their desk drawer or a pint of whiskey in the glove compartment. They may stop regularly at the corner tavern for a few quick ones after work. They may gulp their first drink or switch to martinis or straight whiskey.

Particular personality traits may become intensified or may undergo bizarre transformations. The sensitive may become insensitive, the extrovert introverted, the gentle violent, the tactful belligerent, and the compassionate uncaring. Early-stage alcoholics are often irritable, moody, and depressed when they are not drinking. They angrily deny that they are drinking too much, blame their drinking on a nagging spouse or a demanding boss, and stubbornly refuse to stop drinking. Their promises to cut down are broken within days or weeks. Their marriage slowly and painfully deteriorates, friendships dissolve, and interest in their work wanes.

The alcoholic appears to be using alcohol to solve their problems. Their drinking seems to be an effort to drown their depression, forget work or relationship difficulties, obliterate loneliness and insecurities, and ease mounting tensions. *The reality, however, is very different from the appearance. In reality, an abnormal physiological reaction is causing the alcoholic's increasing psychological and emotional problems. Something has gone wrong inside.*

Why Some People Are Alcoholics

Researchers have worked relentlessly, like detectives on a tough case, to discover exactly what goes wrong. Their accumulated evidence shows that no one mysterious X factor or isolated gene causes alcoholism; no silver bullet exists that can make the alcoholic well again. Instead, their studies have uncovered a number of physiological differences between alcoholics and nonalcoholics. When taken together, these predisposing factors explain the alcoholic's vulnerability to alcohol and the onset of alcoholism.

The susceptible person must drink, of course, if he or she is to become addicted to alcohol. If the alcoholic stops drinking for any reason—religious, cultural, social, or psychological—the disease is arrested. Furthermore, although psychological factors do not cause alcoholism, they can influence the alcoholic's attempts to control their drinking and their reaction to the addiction. Professional athletes trained to believe in the importance of health and fitness may go on the wagon repeatedly in an effort to halt a growing addiction to alcohol. When they start drinking again, they may suffer crippling feelings of guilt and shame. A lonely or bored widow or widower, on the other hand, may slide helplessly and resignedly into the disease, having few psychological or social incentives to fight the addiction.

In other words, while psychological, cultural, and social factors definitely influence the alcoholic's drinking patterns and behavior, they have no effect on whether or not he or she becomes an alcoholic in the first place. *Physiology, not psychology, determines whether one drinker will become addicted to alcohol and another will not.* The alcoholic's enzymes, isoenzymes, hormones, genes, and brain chemistry work together to create their abnormal and unfortunate reaction to alcohol.[1] Discussions of the basic predisposing factors to alcoholism—abnormal metabolism, preference, heredity, prenatal influences, and ethnic susceptibilities—follow.

Abnormal Metabolism

Pioneering research in the 1970s revealed that acetaldehyde, the intermediate byproduct of alcohol metabolism, is a major villain in the onset of alcoholic drinking. The trouble begins in the liver. Dr. Charles Lieber, then chief of the research program on liver disease and nutrition at the Bronx Veterans Administration Hospital, found that the same amount of alcohol produced very different blood acetaldehyde levels in alcoholics and nonalcoholics, with much higher levels reached in alcoholics. Lieber theorized that this unusual buildup of acetaldehyde was caused in part by a malfunctioning of the liver's enzymes.[2]

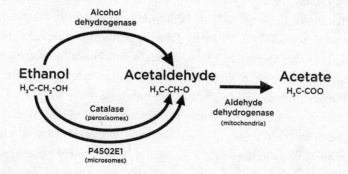

Marc Schuckit, a psychiatrist and researcher at the University of California in San Diego, took the acetaldehyde difference in alcoholics one step further than Lieber. His studies confirmed that in alcoholics, the breakdown of acetaldehyde into acetate—the second step in alcohol metabolism—is performed at about half the rate of "normal" (i.e., nonalcoholic) metabolism. It is this slowdown in metabolism that apparently causes acetaldehyde to accumulate.[3]

Both Lieber and Schuckit wanted to find out whether this enzyme malfunctioning was caused by heavy drinking or preceded heavy drinking. In other words, they hoped to answer this question: Do alcoholics drink too much because their bodies are somehow abnormal, or do their bodies become abnormal because they drink too much? Lieber discovered that the liver mitochondria in alcoholics are abnormal and unable to change acetaldehyde into acetate as rapidly as in nonalcoholics. Significantly, this low capacity was evident even in the early stages of heavy alcohol consumption, indicating that the alcoholic's cells are altered before they start drinking heavily and continually.[4] Schuckit's studies with the offspring of alcoholics also indicate that the metabolic abnormality exists prior to heavy drinking. Like their alcoholic parents, the children of alcoholics (who before this experiment had never drunk alcohol) were unable to convert acetaldehyde to acetate at normal speed.[5] Heredity is clearly implicated in these studies.

Essentially, then, alcoholics appear to have a liver cell malfunction that causes acetaldehyde to accumulate when they drink. Unfortunately for the alcoholic, acetaldehyde is a dangerous substance to have around in any quantity. Directly irritating to the cells and capable of hampering cellular activities, acetaldehyde can also react explosively when combined with other chemical substances. Lieber theorized that the rising levels of acetaldehyde in the liver disturb many of the intricate activities of the cells, making it even more difficult for them to get rid of acetaldehyde, which in turn results in further damage to the cells. The cells may be permanently damaged if acetaldehyde is present in large quantities for long periods of time.

Moreover, acetaldehyde's harmful effects are not confined to the liver. High acetaldehyde levels can inhibit the synthesis of proteins in heart muscle, leading to impaired cardiac function. In the brain, a piling up of acetaldehyde can lead to bizarre and complicated chemical reactions. When acetaldehyde flows through the brain, it competes with other chemical substances known as brain amines (or neurotransmitters) for the attention of certain enzymes. Acetaldehyde wins this competition and, as a result, blocks the enzymes from accomplishing their primary duty of inhibiting the amines' activity.

If alcohol metabolism and acetaldehyde were confined to the liver, addiction to alcohol might never occur. Acetaldehyde, however, is a volatile substance that reacts with just about any other chemical that happens to be in the vicinity. The brain amines, which have been piling up while the acetaldehyde preoccupies their enzymes, interact with acetaldehyde to form compounds called isoquinolines. These chemical agents are responsible for a number of fascinating and far-reaching events.

Like acetaldehyde, the isoquinolines suppress enzymes that are responsible for deactivating many of the brain amines. The isoquinolines also release stored brain amines. In mice, this can aggravate alcohol withdrawal symptoms. For alcoholics, the isoquinolines have one characteristic that makes their other properties pale in significance: they are astonishingly like opiates, and researchers suggest that they may act on the opiate receptors in the brain, thus contributing to addiction to alcohol.[6]

More recent research on the role of alcohol metabolism underlying the alcoholic's need to drink supports and elaborates upon this earlier research. One focus is the metabolism of ethanol and its metabolites in the brain. Of particular interest is the growing body of evidence elucidating the role of ethanol metabolites in mediating the dopaminergic system of the mesolimbic areas of the brain, which are thought to be involved in the effects of addictive opioid drugs. Of specific interest is the role of salsolinol (a tetrahydroisoquinoline that results from the condensation of acetaldehyde with the neurotransmitter dopamine) in the brain and in the neurobiological basis of alcohol addiction.

Preference for Alcohol

Everyone has a different reaction to the taste and effect of alcohol. Some people appear driven by the desire to drink; some enjoy the taste and effect and so drink whenever they have the chance; others like a drink every once in a while but prefer nonalcoholic beverages most of the time; still others feel sick to their stomachs, dizzy, flushed, or drunk after just one or two drinks. The last group will generally avoid drinking alcohol.

The concept of "initial sensitivity" describes the response of a person to alcohol consumption experienced during the earliest episodes of drinking.[7] A person's initial sensitivity to alcohol can be assessed in several ways, including subjective self-reporting, objective third-party observations, and monitoring of biochemical parameters such as changes in blood alcohol concentration. Individuals who, based on their initial sensitivity assessment, experience "innate tolerance" or "low response" to alcohol typically must consume higher levels of alcohol to pass from the stimulating, euphoric effects of alcohol (which result from the rising concentration of alcohol in the blood) to its sedative, negative effects (which result from relatively higher blood alcohol concentration). Thus, the person with a low response to alcohol may appear to have a greater preference for it because they must consume more alcohol to experience the sedative, negative effects of the alcohol than a person having a high response to alcohol. This innate tolerance or low response to the effects of consuming alcohol may also be correlated to a higher risk of heavy drinking later in life.[8]

The same range of likes and dislikes for alcohol is found in rats and mice bred to be genetically alike. The DBA strain of mice, for example, are teetotalers. These animals probably find alcohol's taste or effect unpleasant. The C57BL strain, on the other hand, are heavy drinkers and will consistently choose an alcohol solution over water or a sugar-water solution. Other animals are more mixed in their likes and dislikes and can be compared to the typical social drinker who will slowly sip one or two drinks over the course of an evening.

Preference for alcohol is undoubtedly regulated by complicated chemical activities in the brain. In a 1968 experiment, rats dramatically reduced or completely stopped drinking alcohol when given a chemical substance that depleted the brain's supply of serotonin.[9] Serotonin, a brain amine responsible for relaying messages from one brain cell to another, appears to increase the animal's preference for alcohol. The brains of alcohol-seeking mice and rats, for example, contain higher levels of serotonin than the brains of alcohol-avoiding animals. Further, drinking alcohol increases serotonin concentrations in the brains of the animals that show a preference for alcohol but not in those that avoid it.[10]

Serotonin is only one of many chemical substances that regulate how much an animal will drink. Tetrahydropapaveroline (THP), the product of the interaction of acetaldehyde and dopamine, a brain amine similar to serotonin, is another. When THP was injected into rats' brains, it caused rats that normally rejected alcohol to drink excessive amounts.[11] In what the experimenters called an "addictive-like intake," rats injected with THP drank to the point of intoxication and suffered withdrawal symptoms when they stopped drinking. They continued to drink as though to avoid the disagreeable and painful withdrawal symptoms. The animals' behavior, in short, mimicked the alcoholic's drinking behavior.

An animal's initial liking or dislike for alcohol is clearly only one factor involved in a biological predisposition to alcoholism. The THP study shows that preference is not even a necessary factor, since rats that at first refused to drink could be made to drink addictively when THP was injected into their brains. A number of chemical activities in the brain, therefore, appear to be at the root of addictive drinking.

Heredity

Accumulated evidence clearly indicates that alcoholism is hereditary. Professionals and researchers, however, were reluctant for a long time to accept heredity as a major cause of alcoholism, in part because they were committed to the common misconception that alcoholism is caused by social, cultural, and psychological factors.* Genes may influence the alcoholic's reaction to alcohol, these professionals admitted, but can genes explain every nuance of the alcoholic's behavior? What about their personal problems, including their troubled marriage, financial difficulties, emotional insecurities, and belligerent refusal to stop drinking? People do not inherit functional, or nonorganic, psychological problems; therefore, if these problems are the causes of alcoholism, as many insisted, then obviously alcoholism cannot be hereditary.

Once again, the consequences of alcoholism are confused with the causes. The weight of evidence clearly links alcoholism

---

* Multiple interacting/moderating factors—developmental, environmental, social, cultural—affect the risk of onset of alcoholism. Heredity is not destiny.

to heredity. In the late 1970s, psychiatrist and researcher Donald Goodwin provided, for the first time, clear and strong corroboration that alcoholism is indeed passed from parent to child through genes.[12] Goodwin was able to separate hereditary influences from environmental influences by studying the children of alcoholics who were taken from their parents at birth and adopted by nonrelatives. He postulated that if alcoholism was indeed inherited, these children would have a high rate of alcoholism even though they were not living with their biological alcoholic parent. If environmental influences were more important, the adopted child would be no more likely to become alcoholic than the children of nonalcoholic parents.

Goodwin found that the children of alcoholics do have a much higher risk of becoming alcoholics themselves—four times that of nonalcoholics—despite having no exposure to their alcoholic parent after the first weeks of life.* They were also likely to develop the disease earlier in life, usually in their twenties. The children of nonalcoholic parents, on the other hand, showed relatively low rates of alcoholism even if reared by alcoholic foster parents.

In an effort to discover the relationship, if any, between alcoholic drinking and psychiatric problems, Goodwin compared the children of alcoholics with the children of nonalcoholics. The two groups were "virtually indistinguishable" with regard to depression, anxiety neurosis, personality disturbance, psychopathology, criminality, and drug abuse. As already indicated, psychiatric problems are clearly not relevant to the onset of alcoholism.

In a second adoption study, Goodwin compared the sons of alcoholics who were adopted and raised by an unrelated family with their brothers who had been raised by the alcoholic parent. He found that the children raised by the biological alcoholic parent were no

* Recent twin studies support a heritability range from 40 to 70 percent, which is as high or higher than the risk of inheriting type 2 diabetes or cardiovascular disease. Elisabeth A. Tawa, Samuel D. Hall, and Falk W. Lohoff (2016). "Overview of the Genetics of Alcohol Use Disorder." *Alcohol and Alcoholism* 5(5): 507–514.

more likely to become alcoholic than their brothers who were raised by nonrelatives.

These astonishing findings shattered theories that insisted that the children of alcoholics become alcoholics themselves because they learn bad habits from their parents or model their behavior on that of their alcoholic parent. The findings also destroyed one other misconception—the belief that problem drinking and alcoholism are directly related. The terms *alcohol abuse* and *alcoholism* are commonly used to imply that the former causes the latter. Most people believe problem drinkers, or those people who use alcohol to solve personal problems, become alcoholics. Problem drinkers, the theory goes, abuse alcohol because they are unhappy, lonely, depressed, angry, hostile, unemployed, divorced, poor, or generally dissatisfied with life. As they drink more and more often for relief, they become addicted to alcohol.

Not only did Goodwin fail to find this connection between alcoholism and problem drinking, but he found an inverse relationship: the children of nonalcoholic parents had a much lower rate of alcoholism but were more likely to be heavy or problem drinkers. As Goodwin summarized the results: "Our findings tend to contradict the oft-repeated assertion that alcoholism results from the interaction of multiple causes—social, psychological, biological . . . The 'father's sins' may be visited on the sons even in the father's absence."[13] Problem drinking, then, appears to be caused by psychological, emotional, or social problems, while alcoholic drinking is caused by hereditary factors.*

Goodwin's studies provided compelling evidence that alcoholics do not drink addictively because they are depressed, lonely, immature, or dissatisfied. They drink addictively because they have inherited a physical susceptibility to alcohol that results in addiction if

---

* The important distinction between "problem drinking" and "alcoholic drinking" is discussed in more detail in Chapter 11. It's important to remember that people without family histories of alcoholism can still meet clinical criteria for addiction and die from alcohol-related causes.

they drink. Furthermore, this evidence has profound implications for treatment. While it may be possible to teach the problem drinker how to drink in a more responsible way, the alcoholic's drinking is controlled by physiological factors that cannot be altered through psychological methods such as counseling, threats, punishment, or reward. In other words, the alcoholic is powerless to control their reaction to alcohol.

Prenatal Influences

When a pregnant woman drinks, the fetus drinks with her. If the mother drinks too much, so does the fetus. The fetus, of course, has no defenses against these large doses of alcohol. Alcohol is a teratogen, meaning it has the potential to cause birth defects and health problems if a developing fetus is exposed to it in utero.

Fetal alcohol spectrum disorders (FASDs) are a group of conditions that can occur in a child exposed to the teratogen alcohol as a result of maternal alcohol consumption during pregnancy. FASDs range from severe, as in full-blown fetal alcohol syndrome (FAS), to milder conditions depending on the amount of alcohol to which the child is exposed in utero. Symptoms of FASDs can include low body weight, hyperactive behavior, short attention span, learning disabilities, abnormal facial features, and even birth defects affecting the heart, kidneys, or bones.

Since alcoholism is hereditary, a fetus that is subjected to large amounts of alcohol may also become addicted while still in the womb. When the baby is born and the umbilical cord supplying alcohol is severed, the newborn child may experience withdrawal symptoms. As one researcher describes it:

> The alcoholic mother who has been drinking heavily through pregnancy and particularly that mother who has actually had acute alcoholic withdrawal during pregnancy may have ingested sufficient alcohol to have developed incipient signs

WHAT MAKES AN ALCOHOLIC 45

and symptoms of tolerance and physical dependence in the newborn child. . . . Such a child, in addition to having the hypothesized genetic propensity toward alcoholism, has probably been exposed to high levels of alcohol during his intrauterine development. Such a child may actually have developed some level of tolerance and physical dependence during pregnancy and may be born—in a manner similar to that of children of heroin addicts—in an acute alcoholic withdrawal state.[14]

The newborn is, in fact, an alcoholic. Years later, when they take their first voluntary drink, they may experience an instant reactivation of this addiction. Many alcoholics do appear to be instantly addicted to alcohol from their very first drink, experiencing immediate tolerance changes, craving for alcohol, and withdrawal symptoms when they stop drinking. This "instant alcoholic" may actually have triggered an addiction that began before they were born.[15]

Ethnic Susceptibilities to Alcohol

Extreme differences in alcoholism rates have been found among various ethnic groups. For example, in the past, Jews and Italians had been found to have low alcoholism rates, about 1 percent, while at the other extreme, Native Americans exhibited extraordinarily high rates, somewhere around 80–90 percent. Once again, physiological factors—not psychological, social, or cultural issues—prove to be the key determinants of an ethnic group's susceptibility to alcoholism.

Dr. Bert Vallee and his colleagues at Harvard Medical School studied biochemical and genetic aspects of alcoholism in the 1980s. They isolated fifteen different forms of the ADH liver enzyme and discovered that the number and variety of these enzymes vary widely from person to person. The complex patterns appeared to be genetically controlled, and different ethnic groups presented a typical variation of the number and type of these isoenzymes.

Vallee suspected that each combination of isoenzymes reacts with alcohol differently and determines the person's specific physiological response. Flushing, nausea, violent behavior, sleepiness, and hyperactivity, for example, are probably brought about by the drinker's specific grouping of isoenzymes.[16]

Vallee's findings helped to explain the abundance of research showing different physiological reactions to alcohol among various ethnic groups. In 1971, for example, D. Fenna and colleagues discovered that a group of Native Americans were unable to oxidize and eliminate alcohol as quickly as whites; and in 1972 Peter H. Wolff found that Japanese, Koreans, and Taiwanese had aversive reactions, including flushing and mild to moderate intoxication, to alcohol doses causing no obvious reaction in the majority of whites. He ruled out the possibility that this reaction was acquired or learned by testing Asian and white newborn infants and finding similar responses.[17] Researchers have also found higher levels of acetaldehyde, alcohol's highly toxic breakdown product, in Asians than in whites after drinking alcohol.[18] These high acetaldehyde levels are probably the result of differences in the enzymes that break down ethanol in different racial groups; the flushing and nausea that result could explain why Asians tend to drink sparingly or not at all.

Subsequent research has, in fact, substantiated differences in the forms and efficiencies of the enzymes that break down ethanol in various ethnic groups. For instance, the rates of occurrence of five different forms of the enzyme ADH (the enzyme that breaks the alcohol molecule down to its metabolite acetaldehyde) in different racial populations are shown in the following table. The form of ADH found in 85 percent of people of Japanese ancestry, ADH1B*2, has been shown to be especially efficient at breaking alcohol down to acetaldehyde. As the acetaldehyde accumulates in the body as a result of the enhanced efficiency of the ADH1B*2 form of ADH, the adverse effects of higher acetaldehyde levels, such as flushing, nausea, headaches, and faster heart rate, occur quickly, which may deter further consumption of alcohol. Racial groups characterized by lower rates of the ADH1B*2 form of the ADH enzyme, such as whites in the United States (less than 5 percent of whom have the ADH1B*2 form of ADH), do not experience this accelerated buildup of acetaldehyde or its adverse effects, and thus may not be deterred from further alcohol consumption. Given this, the ADH1B*2 form of ADH that occurs so prevalently in those of Japanese ancestry is considered to have a protective effect against the occurrence of alcoholism.

FREQUENCY OF ADH ALLELES IN RACIAL POPULATIONS

	ADH1B*1	ADH1B*2	ADH1B*3	ADH1C*1	ADH1C*2
White-American	>95%	<5%	<5%	50%	50%
White-European	85%	15%	<5%	60%	40%
Japanese	15%	85%	<5%	95%	5%
Black-American	85%	<5%	15%	85%	15%

Another interesting finding is the discovery that a direct relationship exists between the length of time an ethnic group has been exposed to alcohol and the rate of alcoholism within that group. Jews and Italians, for example, have had access to large amounts of alcohol for more than seven thousand years, and their alcoholism rate is very low. Alcohol was first introduced in quantity to the northern European countries, including France, Ireland, and the Scandinavian countries, some fifteen hundred years ago, and the rates of alcoholism are relatively higher there. Native Americans, who suffer from extremely high alcoholism rates, did not have easy access to large supplies of alcohol until approximately three hundred years ago.[19]

These differences in susceptibility are exactly what we should expect given the fact that alcoholism is a hereditary disease. The implication is that the longer an ethnic group is exposed to alcohol, the lower its members' susceptibility to alcoholism. This relationship is consistent with the principle of natural selection, whereby those people with a high genetic susceptibility are eliminated over many generations, resulting in a lower susceptibility rate for the entire group. People with low susceptibility to alcoholism survive and pass on their low susceptibility. Thus, the rate of alcoholism among high-susceptibility groups should lower significantly over time if they continue to drink.

WHAT MAKES AN ALCOHOLIC: PREDISPOSING FACTORS

ETHNIC GROUP	TIME EXPOSURE	SUSCEPTIBILITY TO ALCOHOLISM	ALCOHOLISM RATE
Jews, Italians	7,000 + years	Low	Low
Scandinavians, Irish, French	1,500 years	Medium	Medium
North American Indians, Eskimos	300 years	High	High

From James R. Milam, *The Emergent Comprehensive Concept of Alcoholism*, 1974. (Out of print)

THE SCIENTIFIC EVIDENCE clearly indicates an interplay of various hereditary, physiological factors—metabolic, hormonal, and neurological—that work together to determine an individual's susceptibility to alcoholism. It is a mistake to oversimplify the interactions in the body and claim that one specific gene, one enzyme, or one hormone is solely responsible for a chain of events leading in a straight line to physical dependence and addiction. Even a slight difference in the number or type of liver enzymes, for example, could alter a person's drinking patterns, preference, and problems. Yet while additional predisposing factors to alcoholism will undoubtedly be discovered, abundant knowledge already exists to confirm that alcoholism is a hereditary, physiological disease and to account fully for its onset and progression.

4

The Early, Adaptive
Stage of Alcoholism

It [alcoholic beverages] sloweth age, it strengtheneth youth, it helpeth
digestion, it abandoneth melancholie, it relisheth the heart, it lighteneth
the mind, it quickeneth the spirits, it keepeth and preserveth the head
from whirling, the eyes from dazzling, the tongue from lisping, the
mouth from snaffling, the teeth from chattering, and the throat from
rattling; it keepeth the stomach from wambling, the heart from swelling, the hands from shivering, the sinews from shrinking, the veins
from crumbling, the bones from aching, and the marrow from soaking.

—Anonymous, thirteenth century

One of the first symptoms of alcoholism is, ironically and tragically,
an ability to increase alcohol intake and still function "normally." It is
ironic because most diseases incur immediate and obvious penalties,
not benefits, and result in reduced functioning rather than improvement in functioning. But in the early stages of alcoholism, the alcoholic is not sick, in pain, or visibly abnormal. In fact, the early, adaptive
stage of alcoholism appears to be marked by the opposite of disease,
for the alcoholic is "blessed" with a supernormal ability to tolerate
alcohol and enjoy its euphoric and stimulating effects.

This improvement of functioning is tragic because the alcoholic
has little or no warning of the deterioration inevitably to follow.
Neither early-stage alcoholics nor their friends have reason to suspect that they are suffering from a progressive and often fatal disease. The disease is difficult to recognize or diagnose in its early
stages because the symptoms are so subtle and so easily confused

with normal reactions to alcohol. No pain or visible malfunction is involved. Early-stage alcoholics do not complain, have no reason to visit a doctor because of their drinking, and do not suffer when they drink. Indeed, they appear to be just like all other drinkers. They have hangovers when they overdrink, but so do their friends. They enjoy drinking, but so do their friends. They look forward to their evening cocktails, but so do their friends.

In this early stage, it would be difficult if not impossible to convince the alcoholic to stop drinking. Why should they stop if they don't feel sick but in fact feel better when they drink? An early-stage alcoholic confronted with a diagnosis of alcoholism and the advice to stop drinking would probably respond, "Who do you think you're kidding? Me, an alcoholic? I can drink more than my friends, I rarely get a hangover, I'm never belligerent or violent, I never miss work, I don't drink in the morning, I can stop whenever I want, and I feel terrific when I drink. Go pick on someone who really has a problem!"

Because the early alcoholic shows no sign of disease, the logical but wholly mistaken idea persists that alcoholism begins only when the drinker does suffer from drinking and does show some deterioration in physiological functioning, such as severe withdrawal symptoms, personality disintegration, or inability to control their intake. Before these visible symptoms appear, most people assume that alcoholics and nonalcoholics experience precisely the same physical reaction to alcohol.

In fact, they do not. The alcoholic reacts physically in an abnormal way to alcohol, and the disease begins long before they behave or think like an alcoholic. The reactions or adaptations of the body's cells to alcohol remain hidden in the early stages of the disease, but they are nevertheless happening. In months or years, the cells will have been so altered by alcohol that the alcoholic's behavior and thought processes will be affected. Then the disease will no longer be hidden, and the alcoholic will clearly be in trouble with alcohol.

In the early stage, however, the disease is subtle and difficult to recognize. It is characterized by adaptations in the liver and central nervous system, increased tolerance to alcohol, and improved performance when drinking.

Adaptation

Homeostasis is the process of dynamic equilibrium, or adjustment, by which biological systems self-regulate to maintain the stability required for survival. It follows that when any bodily system is under stress, it either adapts or suffers damage. Adaptation is actually a tool of survival, helping the body endure stressful changes in internal or external environments. Adaptational responses occur rapidly, spontaneously, and in most cases without the person's conscious knowledge. To cite the obvious example, muscles that are stressed grow and get stronger—a fundamental principle of exercise. Excessive stress, of course, will damage the muscles.

In the onset of alcoholism, adaptation is central. Alcoholics initially experience physical stress whenever they drink. Numerous enzymes, hormones, and biochemical processes are thrown out of balance by alcohol, and the normal ebb and flow of materials into and out of the cells is upset. To counteract this confusion, the cells make certain changes in their structures. These adaptations gradually allow the cells to work smoothly and efficiently even when alcohol is present in the body in large quantities. In fact, the alcoholic's cells become so competent at using alcohol for energy that they prefer alcohol over other food sources of energy.

For the alcoholic, however, alcohol is a distinctly unlovable and ungrateful guest. Although it gives the cells a rich supply of energy and provides stimulation and sedation in different amounts, these benefits are inevitably turned into stiff penalties. Gradually alcohol attacks the cells, destroying their delicate chemical balances, eating away at the membranes, and deforming the cell innards. If the alcoholic continues to drink, sooner or later the penalties of drinking outweigh the benefits as the alcoholic gradually progresses into the later, deteriorative stages of the disease. The length of time between adaptation and deterioration varies from one alcoholic to the next. For some alcoholics, adaptation occurs rapidly, and within weeks or months after first taking a drink the alcoholic is clearly addicted to alcohol. In other cases, many years go by before the earliest symptoms of adaptation and addiction develop.

The critical point, however, is this: the preliminary adaptation begins before the alcoholic starts drinking heavily, and in fact this adaptation causes the heavier drinking. Adaptation does not occur because a person drinks too much. On the contrary, when a person starts drinking more, and more often, and the pattern persists, they are displaying one of the first symptoms of alcoholism.

The adaptations that occur in the early stage of alcoholism are of two kinds: those affecting the metabolism of alcohol, and those taking place in the central nervous system and contributing to addiction. Both types of adaptation have direct effects on the alcoholic's ability to drink large amounts of alcohol without becoming intoxicated (tolerance) and actually to function better when they are drinking than when they are not drinking (improved performance).

The degree of adaptation that occurs in the body of an alcoholic moving from the early stage of alcoholism to the later stages may change. In the early stages, the alcoholic may experience small adaptive metabolic changes to reestablish a relatively normal homeostatic baseline within the body. As the alcoholic moves into the later stages, the body makes more significant metabolic adaptive changes in response to the chronic exposure to high levels of alcohol; some researchers hypothesize that these additional changes may even reset the body to a new, pathologic homeostatic baseline, which in turn may trigger further high consumption of alcohol in an attempt to maintain this pathologic homeostasis.[1]

Metabolic Adaptations

Metabolic adaptations take place primarily in the liver, where most alcohol metabolism takes place. But the brain is also capable of metabolizing small amounts of alcohol, and evidence shows that the brain's metabolic activity, like the liver's, increases through various adaptive changes.

The Microsomal Ethanol Oxidizing System (MEOS).   In most alcoholic and nonalcoholic drinkers, the ADH pathway (operating primarily in the liver) eliminates approximately two-thirds of the alcohol present in the body. Because of genetically controlled liver enzyme abnormalities, however, alcoholics are unable to eliminate the alcohol breakdown product acetaldehyde as quickly as nonalcoholics (see the discussion in Chapter 3). As a result, acetaldehyde builds up and threatens the cells with its toxic effects.

The liver has an amazing capacity to adjust and adapt, and when necessary it gears up an additional system for processing alcohol. This system was identified by Charles Lieber as the microsomal ethanol oxidizing system, or MEOS.[2] In alcoholics, MEOS adapts by revving up its activity—the enzymes responsible for oxidizing alcohol are increased, and new cells are created. As a result, the alcoholic's ability to convert alcohol into acetaldehyde also increases.

Unfortunately, the ability to get rid of the resulting acetaldehyde does not keep pace. MEOS actually compounds the alcoholic's problems rather than solving them, because it increases the ability to tolerate and process very large doses of alcohol and yet does not sufficiently improve the ability to eliminate acetaldehyde.[*] Most of the incoming alcohol is still directed to the overwhelmed ADH pathway. Thus, both MEOS and the ADH pathway contribute to ever-increasing levels of acetaldehyde. A vicious cycle begins when the alcoholic must drink more to maintain a level of alcohol sufficient to override and block the devastating effects of the rising level of acetaldehyde. This is, in part, the basis of the alcoholic's physiological

---

[*] People who have a high level of acetaldehyde without the ability to tolerate and process very large doses of alcohol may develop an aversion to alcohol and drink sparingly or not at all. This may explain why some people of Asian ancestry avoid alcohol as a result of the buildup of high acetaldehyde levels after consuming alcohol, as noted in Chapter 3.

imperative to keep drinking once they start—something that is regu-larly mistaken for a psychological compulsion to drink.

The Mitochondria.   The mitochondria are tiny structures within each cell that are responsible for releasing energy from food. Since alcohol contains a richer supply of energy than most foods and since this energy is easily released, alcohol is a ready source of fuel.

In alcoholics, the mitochondria adapt their structure to accom-modate large amounts of alcohol in order to capitalize on this rich energy source. Normal mitochondria are round with clearly defined outer walls and inner structures; in alcoholics, the mitochondria become enlarged and misshapen, and their inner architecture is redesigned.

Unfortunately, for all that alcohol gives the cells, it eventually takes away much more. Electron micrographs of chronic alcohol-ics' liver cells depict an eerie battleground: the mitochondria are scattered haphazardly, some grotesquely misshapen, others with gaping holes in their membranes, and still others white and vacant, bled dry of everything inside. Once again, the cells' early adaptations support the heavier drinking that eventually leads to widespread cell injury and death.

Adaptations in the Cells and Cell Membranes

The cell membranes are more than simple walls keeping the vital parts of the cell from leaking out. They are actually complex chemi-cal and electrical doorways that let various substances into the cells while denying access to other substances, and that allow wastes to be eliminated from the cell. In a sense, they are the guardians of the cell, protecting the vulnerable cell materials that are vital to life. The membranes' activities ultimately affect everything that goes on inside and outside the cell.

Not surprisingly, the balance of incoming and outgoing elements is critically important to the health and vitality of the cell. Nutrients must get into the cell in adequate amounts and proportions to allow the cell to make repairs, feed itself, and stay healthy and strong. Waste materials must be eliminated quickly and properly, or the cell will become poisoned with its own wastes. Enzymes, hormones, fats, and proteins must all be let into the cells at the right time and in the correct amounts or the cells' orderly functioning will be threatened. Since cells are the building blocks of tissues, and tissues are the building blocks of the major organs, any injury to the cells will eventually be felt throughout the body.

Alcohol consumption interferes drastically with the normal events going on within and across the cell membranes. It changes the chemical structure of the cell membranes, forcing certain materials to be imprisoned within the cell while letting other vital materials escape. For nonalcoholics, alcohol causes only minor inconveniences for the cells.

When alcohol is taken in large amounts over long periods of time, however, the cell membranes adapt by developing methods of coping with these large doses of alcohol. In experiments with rats made tolerant to and physically dependent on alcohol, the cell membranes showed an increased resistance to alcohol's toxic effects. The membranes actually toughened up in an apparent effort to remain stable when alcohol was present in large quantities. Researchers conclude that large and continuous doses of alcohol stimulate the cells to adjust the structure and thus the functioning of their membranes.[3] As a result, the cells are able to cope with increasingly large doses of alcohol; they become, in other words, tolerant to alcohol.

If the alcoholic continues to drink in large quantities, however, the toughened membranes are continually battered and gradually damaged by alcohol's toxic aftereffects. They weaken and in some cases dissolve. No longer able to function as selective doorways, the membranes now let poisonous substances into the cells while vital fluids and enzymes leak out. The results are catastrophic. Vital chemical processes are interrupted or altered, and throughout the body, cells sicken and die. The destruction of cell membranes is linked with many of the conditions that afflict alcoholics in the late stage of their disease, including severe withdrawal symptoms (such as convulsions, hallucinations, and delirium tremens) and damage to the heart muscle (alcoholic cardiomyopathy).

Deterioration is a slow and gradual process, however, and despite the destruction that inevitably comes later, adaptation in the early stage of alcoholism is initially responsible for an acceleration, not a slowdown, of functioning. The alcoholic's cells are better able to cope with alcohol and withstand its toxic effects. The first visible indication that adaptation has occurred is the phenomenon called tolerance.

Tolerance

The word *tolerance* has many meanings. To most people, tolerance denotes a capacity to consume large amounts of alcohol without passing out or feeling nauseated. "He has an amazing tolerance for the stuff," an admirer might comment about someone who consistently drinks everyone else under the table and then proceeds to drive home without incident.

This interpretation is not quite accurate, for *tolerance* is actually a term that applies to all drinkers. Every drinker has a specific tolerance to alcohol. Below this tolerance level, the drinker can function more or less normally; at levels above this tolerance threshold, they will act intoxicated. Tolerance is therefore a condition that can only be measured accurately in a laboratory, where the drinker's blood level and behavior can be carefully monitored.

Nonalcoholics fairly quickly establish a stable tolerance level, which may be high or low. Alcoholics, however, typically experience a dramatic climb in tolerance in the first stage of alcoholism and can often drink huge amounts of alcohol without showing obvious impairment of their ability to walk, talk, think, and react. Anyone who observes the early- and middle-stage alcoholic's drinking behavior is familiar with the fact that the typical alcoholic can drink as much as a liter of wine, a dozen beers, or even a bottle of whiskey without acting drunk.

This ability to tolerate large amounts of alcohol can develop over a period of weeks or years, depending on the individual. Some alcoholics experience a subtle, gradual shift from normal drinking to a drinking pattern of increased frequency and stepped-up amounts over a period of many years. Most alcoholics, however, experience a more immediate change in their tolerance level and are able to drink more than their friends and show less impairment soon after they first start drinking.

Regardless of how long it takes to develop increased tolerance, the same adaptational processes underlie its development. Adaptations in the MEOS and the mitochondria are basically responsible for increased metabolic tolerance, which is evident in the alcoholic's ability to metabolize alcohol more quickly and efficiently. Cellular or tissue tolerance is the result of central nervous system adaptations to alcohol's toxic effects and is evident in the alcoholic's ability to drink large amounts of alcohol without becoming intoxicated. As one research team described it in 1970, tissue tolerance indicates "a change in the nervous system leading to improvement of physiological functioning in the presence of a given concentration of alcohol."[4]

TWO MAJOR MISCONCEPTIONS about the phenomenon of tolerance should be straightened out. The first is the belief that tolerance is a learned response. Many people think that the more the alcoholic drinks, the more they learn how to compensate for the effects of drinking. But tolerance is not learned, nor is it subject to the alcoholic's conscious control or willpower. Tolerance is caused by physiological changes that occur primarily in the liver and central nervous system. These changes cause alterations in the brain's electrical impulses, its hormone and enzyme levels, and the chemical structure of cell membranes, all of which contribute to tolerance. Learned behavior cannot possibly account for these physiological and biochemical shifts.[5]

The second and very misleading misconception is that tolerance initially develops because the person drinks too much. Many alcoholism theorists and professionals insist that psychological or emotional problems are the primary cause of increased drinking; as the person drinks more frequently, the theorists contend, they run the risk of becoming tolerant to alcohol. Again, the implication is that alcoholics are responsible for contracting their disease—by drinking too much, they make themselves tolerant to alcohol. Yet the opposite is true. Tolerance is actually responsible for the alcoholic's continued and increasingly large intake of alcohol. In fact, an increase in the amount and frequency of drinking is the typical symptom of a developing tolerance to alcohol and one of the first warning signs of alcoholism.

When alcoholics become tolerant to alcohol's effects, they are responding to changes that are occurring inside them. They are not responsible for initiating these changes. They are not even conscious that these changes are taking place.

Improved Performance

In this early, hidden stage of alcoholism, the only visible difference between the alcoholic and the nonalcoholic is improved performance in the alcoholic when they drink and a deterioration in performance when they stop drinking. Their improved performance is the result of metabolic and tissue tolerance to alcohol's effects, as mentioned in the previous section. The following chart illustrates the dramatic differences in physiological functioning between alcoholics and nonalcoholics when they drink and then stop drinking.

When the typical nonalcoholic drinks, physical and psychological functioning improve with approximately one-half ounce to one ounce of alcohol. Nonalcoholic drinkers experience feelings of euphoria, relaxation, and well-being. Their performance is slightly better than normal. Concentration, memory, attention span, and creative thinking are all improved with an ounce or less of alcohol.

The stimulating and energizing effects of a small amount of alcohol are offset, however, by the sedative effects brought on by additional drinking, and the nonalcoholic's performance soon falls below the normal level. If the nonalcoholic continues to drink, the blood alcohol concentration rises even higher, and behavior rapidly deteriorates. They slur their words, they have difficulty walking, and their memory and thinking abilities gradually worsen. When the nonalcoholic stops drinking, the BAC slowly descends toward normal, and behavior also gradually returns to normal.

Psychological and Physiological Functioning

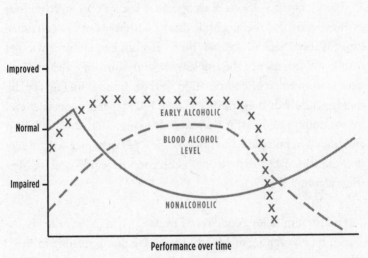

Performance over time

Something completely different happens when the early-stage alcoholic drinks. Alcoholics in the early, adaptive stage of their disease also show improvement of functioning as the blood alcohol concentration begins to rise. But unlike the nonalcoholic, this improvement continues with additional drinking. Even when blood alcohol remains at fairly high levels—levels that would overwhelm nonalcoholics, causing them to stumble, slur, and sway—the early alcoholic is often able to talk coherently, walk a straight line, and skillfully maneuver a car.[6] Only when the alcoholic stops drinking and the BAC descends does performance deteriorate—and it does so very rapidly.

Understanding the relationship between alcohol and improved performance is crucial to an understanding of alcoholic behavior. The alcoholic's increasing motivation to drink, for example, can be partially explained by alcohol's "normalizing" effect on their behavior and emotions, confirmed by researchers more than sixty years ago.[7] Because alcohol immediately makes the alcoholic feel better, think clearly, and act normally, another drink is the specific preventive for a drop in blood alcohol concentration and a corresponding drop in performance.

The therapeutic effects of alcohol may last for prolonged periods of time, provided the alcoholic drinks within his or her tolerance limit. If they drink more than their cells can handle, they will get drunk and experience the unpleasant symptoms of nausea, dizziness, tremors, loss of coordination, and confused thinking. For the therapeutic effect, they must keep their BAC at a fairly constant level by continuing to drink; if they stop drinking, their BAC will drop and both psychological and physiological performance will rapidly deteriorate. Mike's experience is common for early- and middle-stage alcoholics:

> Friday night Mike went directly from work to his favorite tavern for an evening of beer and pool. He drank steadily from 6 p.m. to 1 a.m., but he never felt or acted drunk. In fact, he dominated the pool table, winning every game.
>
> When he left the tavern and started home, Mike felt fine. He was clearheaded, mentally alert, and physically in control. Friends who saw him leave later told him they had no idea he was drunk.
>
> After fifteen or twenty minutes on the road, however, he began to feel slightly weak and nauseated. He was driving erratically when the police stopped him. When he tried to walk a straight line, he was dizzy and confused. The tests were repeated at the police station an hour later, and Mike could barely stand on two feet, let alone balance on one. He

seemed to be getting drunker and drunker, and the arresting officer decided to lock him up for the night, blaming his deteriorating condition on the delayed effects of alcohol. "He drank too much, and it finally caught up with him," the officer concluded.

Mike was later charged with drunk driving. Because it was his first offense, the judge dismissed the charges on the condition that he enter alcoholism treatment. At his first session, Mike was both embarrassed and bewildered. "I don't understand it," he told the counselor. "I felt just fine at the tavern. I was thinking straight and playing terrific pool. When I stopped drinking and headed for home, I was suddenly drunk and out of control. What happened?"

When Mike was drinking at the tavern, he was able to talk coherently, play a competitive game of pool, and continue to drink steadily without feeling or acting intoxicated—even though his BAC was as high as 0.20, which would cause severe motor disturbances in most nonalcoholics. It was when Mike left the bar and stopped drinking that his BAC began to descend and his physiological and psychological functioning rapidly deteriorated. In other words, not until he stopped drinking did he feel drunk, sick, shaky, and out of control. The same cells that were able to function well as long as the BAC was ascending or staying level were unable to function normally as soon as the BAC started to drop. Not only could these cells handle large amounts of alcohol, but they actually needed it to function normally. They were, in fact, addicted to alcohol.

Most alcoholics discover "maintenance drinking" early on in their drinking careers, and they learn ways to protect themselves against the disastrous drop in blood alcohol level. One alcoholic in long-term recovery, when told of Mike's experience, said, "If Mike continues to drink, he will learn fast enough. Either he'll keep a bottle in the car to maintain him until he gets home, or he'll pick a tavern closer to home and gulp a last drink just before leaving."

Maintenance drinking is not gluttony or irresponsible drinking, but a protective device whereby the alcoholic delays the drop in BAC until safely off the road and back in bed. By drinking continuously but never overdrinking, the alcoholic attempts to hold on to the benefits of drinking while forestalling the penalties.

Tragically, the alcoholic can only temporarily control their drinking behavior. Over a period of years, the cells' dependence on alcohol becomes more firmly entrenched until at some point the alcoholic no longer has a choice. They need alcohol to function, and they suffer terribly when they stop drinking. The early benefits of adaptation are gradually overshadowed by the penalties of deterioration.

5

The Middle Stage of Alcoholism

One thing about alcohol, it works. It may destroy a man's career, ruin his marriage, turn him into a zombie unconscious in a hallway—but it works. On short term, it works much faster than a psychiatrist or a priest or the love of a husband or a wife. Those things, they all take time. They must be developed. But alcohol is always ready to go to work at once. Then minutes, half an hour, the little formless fears are gone or turned into harmless amusement. But they come back. Oh yes, and they bring reinforcements.

—From *Carlotta McBride,* a fictional study of an alcoholic
by Charles Orson Gorham

There is no actual demarcation line between the early and middle stages of alcoholism, but there are several characteristic features that signal a new stage in the progression of the disease. As physiological changes gradually occur, the penalties of drinking begin to outweigh the benefits. Pleasurable drinking for a "high," a lift in feeling and performance from a relatively normal base, gives way to a more urgent "drinking for medicine" to "cure" the pain and misery caused by previous drinking. The basic cause of the increase in penalties is deterioration. Organs and systems that once welcomed the large doses of alcohol and were able to tolerate its toxic aftereffects are being damaged. Now when the alcoholic drinks, the pleasant effects (stimulation, euphoria, relaxation) become less pronounced and the unpleasant effects (tremors, insomnia, nausea, depression) are increasingly obvious. And when the alcoholic stops drinking, the suffering is more severe and prolonged.

As the withdrawal symptoms intensify, the alcoholic relieves the physical and psychological pain with more alcohol, which inevitably makes the withdrawal symptoms worse. The alcoholic's every action, mood, and emotion are increasingly governed by the need to drink. This physiological need for alcohol is often referred to as "craving." A spiral of drinking, suffering, and drinking again gradually progresses to the point where the alcoholic is no longer able to control his or her drinking consistently. Noticeable loss of control helps define the end of the middle stage and the beginning of the later, deteriorative stage of alcoholism.

This transition from the middle stage to the later deteriorative stage of alcoholism may, ironically, be accelerated the more times the alcoholic tries to stop drinking. It has been observed clinically that in an alcoholic who is struggling to stop drinking, and who cycles through periods of alcohol consumption followed by withdrawal symptoms during periods of abstinence, the withdrawal symptoms, including tremors and even seizures, may actually get worse with increasing periods of abstinence from alcohol. This phenomenon has been called "kindling." The kindling hypothesis proposes the adaptive changes to alcohol in the alcoholic's brain over time may account for the increased severity of withdrawal symptoms.[1]

The middle stage of alcoholism, then, can be characterized by three basic features: *physical dependence,* as experienced in acute and protracted withdrawal syndromes; *craving;* and *loss of control.* These features deserve careful examination.

Physical Dependence

In the adaptive stage, when the cells of the central nervous system change their functioning to accommodate alcohol, the alcoholic's tolerance increases, and they are able to drink greater quantities of alcohol without becoming drunk. As they drink more, and more often, to get the desired effect, the cells of their body are soaked in alcohol for long periods of time. The cell membranes become increasingly resistant to alcohol's effects, and the mitochondria within the cells increase in size and shift functions in order to accommodate the alcohol. With these changes, the adapted cells are able to live and thrive in an environment where alcohol is continually present in large amounts.

This situation continues as long as the alcoholic does not drink more than his or her cells can process—in other words, as long as they drink within their tolerance—and as long as they continue drinking. If the alcoholic drinks beyond their tolerance, the cells will be overwhelmed, and the person will get drunk. If the alcoholic stops drinking, the addicted cells will suddenly be thrown into a state of acute distress, unable to function normally without alcohol. The cells' distress when alcohol is no longer present in the body, or when the BAC is falling, is evident in various symptoms known collectively as the withdrawal syndrome. Withdrawal symptoms demonstrate that physical dependence exists; they are the visible signs of addiction.

The withdrawal syndrome occurs in two phases: the *acute withdrawal syndrome,* which is experienced immediately after the alcoholic stops drinking and lasts up to a few days, and the *post-acute withdrawal syndrome,* which lasts for months and even years of abstinence if the alcoholic's nutritional balance is not restored. Most people are familiar with the acute withdrawal syndrome, but the post-acute withdrawal syndrome is not so well known or appreciated. Yet a complete understanding of alcoholism is impossible without an understanding of the nature and progression of these related syndromes. The acute withdrawal syndrome helps to explain why alcoholics are in such mental and physical distress immediately after they stop drinking and why the urge for a drink is overpowering; the post-acute withdrawal syndrome explains why alcoholics continue to be depressed, shaky, and irritable many days, months, or even years after their last drink, and why so many alcoholics return to drinking after a period of sobriety.

The Acute Withdrawal Syndrome

One of the most confusing aspects of alcoholism is that *alcoholics feel most sick not when they drink but when they stop drinking.* Their bodies have adapted to the constant presence of alcohol—their cells are accustomed to functioning with alcohol as their major source of energy and stimulation and as an antidote for the ever-present toxicity.

Thus when the alcoholic stops drinking, all hell breaks loose. Blood vessels constrict, cutting down on the flow of blood and oxygen to the cells. The blood glucose level drops sharply and remains unstable. The brain amines serotonin and dopamine decrease dramatically. Hormones, enzymes, and body fluid levels fluctuate erratically. The body's cells are malnourished and toxic from long exposure to large doses of alcohol and acetaldehyde.

These chaotic events cause fundamental disruptions in the brain's chemical and electrical activity. As soon as the blood alcohol level begins to descend, the brain cells, or neurons, become excited and agitated. The entire brain is affected, as the sensitive neurons send out highly disorganized and chaotic distress signals. The brain is, in a sense, short-circuiting, and the resulting pandemonium creates numerous psychological and physiological problems for the alcoholic, including profound mental confusion, anxiety, depression, memory defects, lack of muscular coordination, convulsions, hallucinations, paranoia, violent or fearful behavior—all the symptoms associated with the acute withdrawal syndrome.

More recent research substantiates the essential role of brain chemistry—specifically a class of chemicals called neurotransmitters that interact with brain cell receptors, exciting or inhibiting brain function—in the development of alcoholism from short-term alcohol exposure through the alcohol-seeking behavior underlying the disease of alcoholism. Specifically, the normal delicate balance between neurotransmitters, such as dopamine, serotonin, GABA, and glutamate, changes with longer-term alcohol exposure. As the period of exposure to higher levels of alcohol lengthens, the brain attempts to compensate for this imbalance in the levels of inhibitory and excitatory neurotransmitters and bring the balance back to normal. These neurological adaptions of the brain to long-term alcohol exposure correspond to the development of tolerance to alcohol. And when alcohol is discontinued or reduced, these neurological adaptations—that is, the brain's dependence on high levels of alcohol—result in withdrawal symptoms.[2]

In early-stage alcoholics, the major withdrawal symptoms are anxiety, irritability, and agitation—symptoms that many nonalcoholics also experience after a night of heavy drinking. As the disease progresses, however, the alcoholic's withdrawal symptoms become more and more severe, and they may suffer from tremors ("the shakes"), increased heart rate (tachycardia), increased blood pressure, body temperature dysregulation, heavy sweating, gastrointestinal disturbances (nausea, vomiting), and, in the later stages of the disease; severe hangovers, convulsions, hallucinations, and delirium tremens (DTs). The withdrawal symptoms vary according to how much the alcoholic drinks and how long they continue to drink without stopping. In general, the more the alcoholic drinks, the more they will suffer when they stop drinking; if they drink for a week, they will suffer more than if they drink for one or two days. Furthermore, the frequency, duration, and intensity of the symptoms vary from one alcoholic to the next, depending on gender, constitutional differences, malnutrition, and other diseases or medical complications. The simultaneous or alternating use of other drugs can also increase the severity of the acute withdrawal syndrome.

Early Symptoms of Withdrawal.   Often the first evidence of the alcoholic withdrawal syndrome is a shaky and agitated feeling the morning after drinking and the growing desire for a remedy for these symptoms. In the early-stage alcoholic, the cells are mildly agitated when alcohol is withdrawn. While the symptoms are uncomfortable and unpleasant, they last for a relatively short time and are not incapacitating. The alcoholic in mild withdrawal can get out of bed, give a speech, and play a game of racquetball at the end of the day with no major difficulties.

Other mild withdrawal symptoms experienced by almost all early-stage alcoholics include nervousness, weakness, insomnia, vivid dreaming, nausea, excessive perspiration, loss of appetite, and impairment of memory. These symptoms are often dismissed by the alcoholic as "normal" reactions to excessive alcohol intake, particularly in the very beginning of the disease. "I overdid it last night," the alcoholic confesses to a nonalcoholic friend, who nods in sympathy, having experienced some dreadful hangovers themselves.

Most drinkers, of course, are familiar with the hangover. It usually begins when the drinker gets out of bed in the morning. A pounding headache signals the start of a rough day, and the unhappy victim walks into the bathroom, searching for aspirin, Alka-Seltzer, or some other remedy to relieve the pain. The creak of the door hurts their head, and the light blinds their eyes. They are thirsty, and no matter how much they drink, the thirst lingers on. Their mouth is cottony dry. The mere thought of alcohol turns their stomach upside down. When they finally make it through the day, they may swear to themselves that they will never drink that much again.

The hangover can be excruciating for the nonalcoholic, but it becomes much worse for the alcoholic in the later stages of their disease. As one expert put it, "[Hangovers] are so extreme for the alcoholic that they really should have a different name. No normal drinker would recognize them as what he has."[3] The source of the physical and mental pain of the alcoholic hangover is, to repeat, the state of hyperactivity in the central nervous system caused by the withdrawal of alcohol that may reflect adaptation of the neurochemical state of the central nervous system. The cells, which are accustomed to the presence of alcohol and dependent on it for energy, stimulation, and sedation, become agitated when it is suddenly not available. The cells' distress is experienced by the alcoholic

as the headache, eye ache, dizziness, nausea, and anguish characteristic of the hangover.*

Alcoholics feel physically wretched during a hangover, but they
also feel deeply and profoundly ashamed. From past experience,
they know better, but they got drunk anyway, and wonder why.
Ignorant of the powerful workings of the addiction, they can only
blame themselves. Remorse, self-loathing, and guilt therefore go
hand in hand with the throbbing headache and queasy stomach. At
one point, some students of alcoholism believed—wrongly—that
these emotions were actually responsible for causing the pain of the
hangover. "The increasing misery of the hangover is not due to the
headache, the nausea, the cold sweats, the chills and fever, or even
the shakes," wrote psychiatrist Benjamin Karpman in 1957, "but to
the emotional pain which accompanies them—the guilt, anxiety,
self-accusation, the sense of hopelessness and despair."[4] But Karpman placed the cart before the horse. The alcoholic hangover is not
an emotional illness, as he implied, but a very real and very painful
physiological disorder.

The increasing misery of the alcoholic's hangover is directly
caused by the drinker's physical dependence on alcohol. As the disease progresses and the alcoholic drinks more, and more often, the
withdrawal symptoms—experienced in those minutes, hours, or
days without a drink—become more severe. The alcoholic begins
to feel shame and remorse when they repeatedly fail in their efforts
to stop drinking or control their intake. They cannot make good
on their intentions to drink as everyone else does, and this personal
failure causes great guilt and despair. The alcoholic believes that they
should be able to control themselves by a sheer force of will. They
do not know that the physical addiction is in command of their every
thought and action and subverts their persistent efforts to control it.

---

*Anguish is an older term than anxiety and refers to both mental and physical
pain or suffering. Anxiety is most often used to refer to psychological conflict
or tension.

Alcoholics may swear to themselves, their spouse, their children, their clergymember, or anyone else concerned with their drinking that they will control their intake. But their addiction makes certain that they will drink in spite of their best intentions and heartfelt promises. The alcoholic's most cherished values—their honesty, their integrity, their self-discipline, even their love for their family— are repeatedly overthrown because they cannot reliably predict or control their own drinking behavior. Any normal human being would feel disgust and self-loathing at this repeated inability to exert control and exercise willpower; and so does the alcoholic, who may be normal in every respect except their reaction to alcohol.

The alcoholic's guilt, depression, self-loathing, and despair are therefore understandable reactions to a bewildering and mysterious inability to stop the ravages of drinking. Neither the alcoholic nor those around them know that the alcoholic's cells have become abnormal, for the physical dependence and cellular addiction have worked inside them for months or perhaps years, invisible and unnoticed. No wonder alcoholics believe they are weak-willed and pathetic. No wonder many of the people who observe their behavior believe that the alcoholic is psychologically unstable, self-destructive, and perhaps suicidal. Without an understanding or knowledge of the addiction, they have no way of knowing that the alcoholic's irrational behavior is beyond their control.

Later Symptoms of Withdrawal.   Convulsions, hallucinations, and DTs are rare in the early stages of the disease but are occasionally seen in the middle stages and are more frequently found in the later stages. Late-stage alcoholics who drink heavily for long periods of time are prime candidates for these severe withdrawal symptoms.

Alcohol-related seizures appear six to forty-eight hours after the last drink and usually occur singly or in brief clusters. These seizures are typically classified as tonic-clonic seizures and are similar to grand mal epileptic convulsions. Such seizures may involve loss of consciousness and bodily control, extreme body rigidity or tenseness, and jerking movements in various areas of the body. These seizures may be triggered by a number of physical disorders brought about by the withdrawal of alcohol, including extremely low blood sugar, low levels of certain hormones in the blood, changes in the neurochemical state of the central nervous system, malnutrition, and the accumulation of waste products and toxins in the bloodstream.

Hallucinations, like other symptoms of withdrawal, indicate a profound disorder in the central nervous system. They are usually terrifying for the alcoholic, as they involve such horror-film ingredients as butcher knives, ghosts, excrement, bloody body parts, ants, bees, lions, and rodents. However, not all hallucinations are frightening and horrible, and sometimes alcoholics are even aware that they are hallucinating.

An elderly man, hospitalized for chronic alcoholism and suffering from frightening hallucinations involving brown furry animals with teeth like nails, was placed in restraints overnight. The next day the nurse found him staring peacefully at the ceiling, clearly enchanted with some happy daydream.

"Mr. Smith," she asked, "are you all right?" He nodded dreamily. "What has happened?" she asked curiously.

"I learned to switch channels," he replied.

Delirium tremens, sometimes referred to as "the horrors," are the most dramatic and dangerous expression of withdrawal. Translated directly from Latin, the term *delirium tremens* means "trembling delirium" or "shaking insanity." The DTs typically begin a few days after the alcoholic's last drink, when alcohol is completely eliminated from the bloodstream, and they usually last two to three agonizing days but may continue for a week or longer.[5] Alcoholics who are severely malnourished and have been drinking heavily for prolonged periods are the most common victims, but brain injuries and other traumas or medical complications can aggravate withdrawal and trigger DTs in early- and middle-stage alcoholics.

An alcoholic experiencing DTs is mentally disoriented, hallucinating, and unable to control the movements of his or her body. Like all the symptoms of acute withdrawal, however, the DTs have any number of outward expressions. Some alcoholics experience violent and terrifying hallucinations, others become aggressive and dangerous, and still others may sweat and shake while concentrating intently on playing a game of cards with a nonexistent deck. As Mark Twain's description in *Huckleberry Finn* so masterfully illustrates, the disorder is completely in control of the victim's body and mind:

> I don't know how long I was asleep [Huck Finn confides] but all of a sudden there was an awful scream and I was up. There was pap looking wild, and skipping around every which way and yelling about snakes. He said they was crawling up his legs; and then he would give a jump and scream, and say one had bit him on the cheek—but I couldn't see no snakes. He started to run round and round the cabin, hollering "Take him off! take him off; he's biting me in the neck!" I never see a man look so wild in the eyes. Pretty soon he was all fagged out, and fell down panting; then he rolled over and over wonderful fast, kicking things every which way, and striking and grabbing at the air with his hands, and screaming and saying there was devils a-hold of him. He wore out by and by, and laid still awhile, moaning. Then he laid stiller, and didn't make a sound. I could hear the owls and wolves away off in the woods, and it seemed terrible still. He was laying over by the corner. By and by he raised up part way and listened, with his head to one side. He says, very low: "Tramp—tramp—tramp; that's the dead; tramp—tramp—tramp; they're coming after me, but I won't go. Oh, they're here! don't touch me—don't! hands off—they're cold; let go. Oh, let a poor devil alone!" Then he went down on all fours and crawled off, begging them to let him alone, and he rolled himself up in his blanket and wallowed in under the old pine table, still a-begging; and then he went to crying.

No matter how violent, distracted, or peaceful the alcoholic might seem, the DTs are clearly a sign of deep disturbances in the brain and throughout the body. The condition is so stressful that any other medical complication occurring simultaneously, such as gastrointestinal problems, pancreatitis, heart disease, or liver disease, can cause a fatal breakdown in the alcoholic's already seriously over-stressed body. In some instances, the trauma of DTs alone may be severe enough to precipitate a massive coronary, brain hemorrhage, or respiratory shutdown, any of which can be fatal.

The mortality rate of untreated patients suffering from DTs is as high as 37 percent; with early intervention and appropriate ther-apy, the mortality rate can be less than 5 percent.[6] The DTs would undoubtedly kill even more alcoholics if accidents, suicides, or other diseases did not kill them first. Most alcoholics, however, either recover or die from their disease before reaching this most severe and life-threatening stage of alcoholism.

The Protracted Withdrawal Syndrome

Even if the alcoholic is able to endure the acute withdrawal syn-drome without taking a drink to relieve their anguish, their troubles are not over. The majority of alcoholics continue to be anxious, depressed, nervous, and fearful long after they stop drinking. Alco-holics abstinent for months and even years may complain of insom-nia, depression, agitation, moodiness, and an overwhelming desire for alcohol. Because so many alcoholics experience these symptoms to some degree, many people conclude that the alcoholic is and always has been psychologically troubled. Some experts even label those alcoholics who suffer recurring psychological or emotional problems "neurotic," "anxiety prone," or simply "immature." These alcoholics are sometimes given tranquilizers or sedatives in hope of alleviating their mental suffering. Those who finally break down and drink, no longer able to endure life without alcohol, may be considered hopelessly depressed or morbidly suicidal.

The sober "recovering" alcoholic is baffled by their continuing depression and anxiety, and they, too, may conclude that their problems are primarily psychological. Their hopelessness and despair are overwhelming, and they are haunted by questions that already appear to be answered in the affirmative: "Am I simply an emotionally unstable person who drinks to ease my problems? Will I always return to drinking because I am so weak and psychologically sick?" When their problems persist, the sober alcoholic is frustrated and afraid. They may very well believe that they were better off when they were drinking, for alcohol always seemed to ease their problems. Their options appear to be few, and their future precarious.

Yet the alcoholic's persistent problems are not caused by any inherent psychological flaws or emotional weaknesses but by the physical disease itself. The depression and anxiety are actually long-term (or protracted) withdrawal symptoms, and they indicate that the cells are still suffering from the damage caused by alcohol. They are clear signs of adaptive, cumulative, persistent, and pathological changes in the structure and functioning of the brain. The healing process is not automatically completed when the alcoholic stops drinking. Alcohol has created widespread destruction throughout the body, and the cells need time to heal. They also need help if the healing process is to be rapid and complete.[7]

The major causes of the protracted withdrawal syndrome—also sometimes referred to as "protracted abstinence"—are malnutrition, hypoglycemia, autonomic nervous system dysfunctions, cognitive impairment, and brain amine depletion. Each of these physiological abnormalities needs to be understood in the context of alcoholism.

Malnutrition.   All alcoholics are malnourished to some extent because excessive alcohol intake interferes with the body's ability to absorb and use various nutrients regardless of what the alcoholic may be eating. The cells, of course, are dependent on an adequate supply of nutrients to perform their everyday functions, heal themselves, and create new cells.

Alcohol's massive assault on the structure and functioning of the alcoholic's cells cannot be reversed just by removing alcohol from the body—abstinence alone does not make malnourished cells healthy again. The cells need vitamins, minerals, amino acids, proteins, fats, and carbohydrates, and they need them in therapeutic amounts and proportions. Without an adequate supply of these nutrients, the cells cannot get on with the long process of repairing the damage done by excessive drinking. Dr. Charles Lieber explained the relationship between alcoholism and nutrition and the importance of nutritional therapy in recovery:

> Many alcoholics are malnourished, either because they ingest too little of essential nutrients (e.g., carbohydrates, proteins, and vitamins) or because alcohol and its metabolism prevent the body from properly absorbing, digesting, and using those nutrients. As a result, alcoholics frequently experience deficiencies in proteins and vitamins, particularly vitamin A, which may contribute to liver disease and other serious alcohol-related disorders. Furthermore, alcohol breakdown in the liver, both by the enzyme alcohol dehydrogenase and by an enzyme system called the microsomal ethanol-oxidizing system (MEOS), generates toxic products such as acetaldehyde and highly reactive, and potentially damaging, oxygen-containing molecules. These products can interfere with the normal metabolism of other nutrients, particularly lipids, and contribute to liver cell damage. Nutritional approaches can help prevent or ameliorate alcoholic liver disease.[8]

The liver is not the only organ profoundly affected by nutritional deficiencies, as noted by Korean neuropsychiatrists Byung Joo Ham and Ihn-Geun Choi:

> Chronic alcoholics exhibit a number of neurological disorders which are related to nutritional deficiencies, in particular vitamin deficiencies that are essential for normal cerebral

functioning. Specific vitamin and nutrient deficiencies arising in chronic alcoholics may result in severe functional impairment and tissue damage, mainly neuronal and vascular, in the brain. Nutritional deficiency in alcoholics also causes neurotransmitter dysfunction, ion channel dysfunction, oxidative stress and metabolic dysfunction in the brain. Nutritional deficiency in chronic alcoholics frequently leads to a mild to moderate cognitive impairment, including impairment in perceptual-motor skills, visual-spatial functions, learning/memory, and abstraction and problem solving.[9]

Most recovering alcoholics do not even know that they are suffering from nutritional damage, and even if informed about their condition, they probably do not realize that a balanced diet and nutritional supplements will help them make a rapid and complete recovery. As discussed previously, they are more likely to suppose that their psychological distress is caused by psychological problems—a misconception widely shared by society and even many therapists.

Hypoglycemia.   Another aspect of malnutrition that is widely misunderstood and overlooked is hypoglycemia, or chronic low blood sugar. This condition, which is prevalent in early-, middle-, and late-stage alcoholics, is usually caused by diseases or disorders in the liver, endocrine glands (including the pancreas), and possibly the brain that affect the body's ability to store and release blood sugar or glucose. Alcoholics may also have various malfunctions in liver enzyme activities that may result in a decreased ability to convert glycogen into glucose.[*]

When the blood sugar drops to abnormally low levels, the alcoholic experiences symptoms of fatigue, headache, sleepiness, forgetfulness, inability to concentrate, moodiness, anxiety, depression, hunger, and shakiness. Alcohol immediately brings the blood sugar level up and makes the symptoms disappear. After one or two

---

* See Chapter 3 for additional discussion of liver enzyme malfunctions.

drinks, the hypoglycemic feels remarkably better. Their headaches and sleepiness are gone, tremors settle down, and the mental confusion, depression, and anxiety miraculously fade away.

Alcohol is thus an attractive first aid for hypoglycemia, but it is poor therapy because it triggers a series of chemical changes that soon make the blood sugar level drop like a rock once again. As the blood sugar level crashes down, the symptoms of hypoglycemia return with a vengeance—and a reinforcement: the desire for alcohol to relieve the symptoms.

Hypoglycemia is a chronic condition. The symptoms do not simply disappear when alcoholics stop drinking, and they must therefore carefully regulate their nutrient and sugar intake to control the level of glucose in their blood. This can be accomplished through simple dietary measures and nutritional supplementation.*

Tragically, most alcoholics are not aware of this condition or its significance. Many treatment programs ignore or compromise the hypoglycemic diet and thus do little or nothing to enlighten their patients. Without an adjustment in sugar intake, the alcoholic's feelings of depression, anxiety, and irritability may continue indefinitely, and they may never escape the desire for a drink to relieve their "psychological" symptoms.

THERE ARE OTHER areas in which the healing process will be blocked or slowed down if malnutrition and hypoglycemia are not recognized and treated. In particular, certain dysfunctions related to central nervous system damage, including autonomic nervous system dysfunction, cognitive impairment, neurotransmitter imbalances, and sleep disturbances, may continue.

Autonomic Nervous System (ANS) Dysfunction. Large amounts of alcohol taken over a prolonged period of time can upset the orderly workings of the autonomic nervous system, which

---

* See Appendices B (Guidelines for a Hypoglycemic Diet) and C (Sample One-Day Menu for a Hypoglycemic Diet).

is responsible for overseeing the work of the involuntary glands, the cardiac muscle, and the smooth muscles such as those of the digestive system, the respiratory system, and the skin.[10] As many as 73 percent of alcoholics suffer from ANS dysfunction, with the greatest impact on the parasympathetic nervous system; the most common symptom is erectile dysfunction. Particularly during the first months of sobriety, the alcoholic may show signs of tremor, excess perspiration, and rapid pulse and heart rates—all indications of malfunctioning in the ANS. These disturbances are found in lesser degrees in alcoholics abstinent for up to two years, and they lessen further as sobriety lengthens. As in the treatment of hypoglycemia, comprehensive nutritional therapy will promote more rapid healing of the ANS and an end to the alcoholic's continued suffering.

Cognitive Impairments.   Approximately half of late-stage alcoholics experience measurable deterioration of function in the cortex, the layer of gray matter blanketing the two hemispheres of the brain.[11] The cortex is involved in a number of functions, including the major senses of sight, hearing, touch, taste, and smell, the direction of conscious movements of the body, reasoning, and memory. Damage to one or more of these functions may be permanent, but most alcoholics with cortical damage will gradually recover normal functioning as the period of sobriety lengthens and the body is allowed to heal itself. Nutritional therapy is once again a crucial element in ensuring improvement and promoting rapid recovery. That said, however, while about half of the alcoholics in the United States may appear to experience little or no cognitive impairments, the other half (roughly 10 million alcoholics) may experience neuropsychological difficulties, with as many as 2 million alcoholics developing permanent and incapacitating conditions that may require custodial care for the rest of their lives.[12]

Brain Amine Depletion.   In alcoholics, the levels of at least two brain amines—the substances responsible for transmitting chemical messages from one brain cell to another and regulating various emotional states—are significantly lower in the protracted withdrawal period. Specifically, lowered serotonin and dopamine levels may contribute to the alcoholic's continuing depression, anxiety, tension, irritability, and even insomnia and nightmares during this period of withdrawal.[13] The amines usually return to normal activity after several weeks or months of sobriety, although insomnia and nightmares may persist for years. A decrease in serotonin, in particular, seems to be at least partially responsible for persistent sleep disturbances. Studies have shown a connection between decreases in serotonin, insomnia, and disruptions of deep (stage IV) sleep.[14] With comprehensive nutritional therapy, sleep disturbances eventually abate, but they may linger for a significant period of time after cessation of alcohol consumption.[15]

Craving

Craving is the overwhelming need for a drink. Like everything else in alcoholism, craving is progressive. During the early stages of the disease, craving is related to the benefits the alcoholic experiences from drinking—alcoholics want to drink because drinking makes them feel so good. In the middle stages of the disease, craving becomes a need—alcoholics need to drink because their cells are physically dependent on alcohol. In the deteriorative stages of the disease, the alcoholic drinks more directly for the purpose of relieving the psychological and physiological distress of withdrawal. Craving has gradually evolved into an overpowering obsession—the alcoholic craves alcohol because it is the most effective remedy for the pain they feel when they stop drinking.

Early in the disease alcoholics can usually control their craving for alcohol, but since there are so few penalties associated with drinking and so many benefits, they feel no need for control. As tolerance increases and physical dependence sets in, they gradually lose psychological control over their physiological need for alcohol. Finally, willpower, self-restraint, and the ability to say "no" have no power over alcoholic craving. The physical need for alcohol overshadows everything else in the alcoholic's life.

A great controversy surrounds this experience of craving. Most experts agree that alcoholics experience a physical need for alcohol whenever their alcohol intake is delayed during a drinking bout. This physical need is caused by the acute withdrawal symptoms—the alcoholic's great physical distress when the blood alcohol concentration starts to drop. In an effort to forestall these painful symptoms, the alcoholic keeps on drinking.

Disagreement prevails, however, over whether the sober alcoholic actually needs a drink in between drinking bouts or just thinks they do. Withdrawal symptoms are no longer present, some experts insist, and the alcoholic therefore is motivated only by a psychological need or desire to drink again. Such theories are long-lasting; in 1960, E. M. Jellinek, a renowned authority on alcoholism and author of *The Disease Concept of Alcoholism*, wrote, "[The alcoholic's continuing complaints] . . . seem to be . . . indications of insufficient adaptation on the symbolic level to an alcohol-free life."[16]

Jellinek appears to be saying that the alcoholic's adjustment to a sober lifestyle is dependent on inner strength and resilience and if problems persist, they are basically psychological. But, as has been stressed, most of the alcoholic's problems are caused by physiological factors. Months or years after their last drink, the alcoholic may experience physical withdrawal symptoms, and craving for alcohol is a true physiological need to relieve these symptoms. The abstinent alcoholic will continue to suffer from protracted withdrawal symptoms until the healing process is complete. Again, without nutritional therapy they may never fully recover.

Loss of Control

As the alcoholic progressively loses control over their drinking, they are no longer able to restrict it to socially and culturally accepted times and places. They often drink more than they intended, and the drinking continues despite extremely punishing consequences. They may drink in the morning, at lunch, in the middle of the night; they may drink in the car, the bathroom, the garage, or the closet as well as the tavern. Their drinking behavior can no longer be disguised as normal or even heavy drinking. Their inability to stop drinking—despite their firm resolution that they will stop after one or two—is striking confirmation that they are physically addicted to alcohol.

Alcoholics begin to lose control over their drinking because their tolerance decreases and the withdrawal symptoms increase. The alcoholic's tolerance, which was so high in the early stages of the disease, begins to decrease because the cells have been damaged and can no longer tolerate large amounts of alcohol. While tolerance is lessening, the withdrawal symptoms are increasing in severity. Alcoholics are now in the dangerous position of needing to drink (because they suffer terribly when they stop drinking) but being unable to handle the high levels of alcohol needed to relieve the symptoms. They have also lost the ability to judge accurately how much alcohol their body can handle. As a result, they often overmedicate themselves with alcohol, drinking to the point where they either lose consciousness or become so violently ill that they are forced to stop drinking.

Severe impairment in the ability to control the use of alcohol does not happen all of a sudden, nor is it always characterized by the alcoholic's drinking everything in sight. Loss of control occurs gradually and is sometimes evident in the early stages of the disease when the alcoholic occasionally drinks past their tolerance. The effects of overdrinking are extremely unpleasant, however, and early-stage alcoholics will make every attempt to drink within their tolerance level. At this point in the disease, they are usually able to exert considerable control over their drinking and thus can usually avoid the penalties.

As alcoholism progresses, the episodes of uncontrolled drinking become more frequent and severe. Middle- or late-stage alcoholics may start drinking in the morning in an attempt to alleviate the tremors in their hands, the queasiness in their belly, and the ache in their head. The first drink works quickly, and the second drink makes them feel almost normal. Soon, however, their blood alcohol content begins to descend as the alcohol is gradually broken down and eliminated; the acetaldehyde level builds up, and the alcoholic starts feeling jittery again. They throw back another drink and then another in an attempt to forestall their agitation and anxiety. Some alcoholics may never drink in the early morning or never after dinner, but the progression will still be there. A drink or two may be "necessary" at lunch. Lunch may stretch out until midafternoon. For the rest of the workday, the alcoholic may sip from a bottle hidden in their desk. They may have a drink as soon as they get home, and the pre-dinner drinks may step up in number.

This cycle of drinking is, in fact, an effort to relieve the impending withdrawal symptoms, and it may go on for some time. Healthier alcoholics can drink for days or even weeks, precariously balancing the benefits of drinking with the increasing penalties of withdrawal. Severely malnourished alcoholics whose tolerance for alcohol has decreased significantly or alcoholics with liver disease or gastritis may only be able to put off the penalties for a few hours or perhaps a day or two of drinking.

Soon enough, more alcohol must be drunk to compete with the rate at which alcohol is being eliminated. It is a race against time—a losing race. At some point, alcohol is no longer capable of neutralizing the increasing anguish, tremors, and nausea, and the alcoholic is forced to stop drinking because they pass out or become acutely ill. The alcoholic who drinks to this extreme has clearly lost control.

6

The Late, Deteriorative
Stage of Alcoholism

Among all sources of disease, alcohol stands preeminent as a destroyer. . . . This pestilent principle generally seeks for asylum where it may practice its deadliest deeds in some important and vital organ of the body. It sometimes makes the brain more particularly the seat of its venom, and victim of its cruelties. At another time, it hides itself in the inmost recess of the heart, or coils around it like a serpent; now it fixes upon the lungs; now upon the kidneys, upon the liver, the bladder, the pancreas, the intestines or the skin. It can agitate the heart until it throbs and bursts, or it can reduce pulsation until it becomes impalpable. It can distract the head until the brain sweats blood, and horrified reason flies away and leaves the man a maniac or a madman. I never knew a person become insane who was not in the habit of taking a portion of alcohol daily.

—Benjamin Parsons, an English clergyman, in *Anti-Bacchus:
An Essay on the Crimes, Diseases, and Other Evils Connected with the Use
of Intoxicating Drinks,* 1840

Once again, although the distinction between the middle and late stages of alcoholism is somewhat arbitrary, it can be identified as that point at which symptoms associated with adaptation to alcohol are gradually overcome by symptoms that reflect increasing toxicity and damage to body organs and systems. The alcoholic's tolerance to alcohol is progressively lessening because of cell damage in the liver and central nervous system, and their withdrawal symptoms are increasing in severity. The late-stage alcoholic spends most of his or her time drinking, since otherwise the agony is excruciating.

When most people think of an alcoholic, they think of them in this final stage of the disease: destitute, deathly ill, mentally confused, and living only for alcohol. Yet the alcoholic's deterioration began long before this last stage, in most cases years before any physical damage became apparent. Deterioration, in fact, began in the early and middle stages of the disease, as described in Chapters 4 and 5, when the alcoholic's cells adapted to alcohol, allowing it into the body in ever larger doses. It progressed gradually as the cells became physically dependent on alcohol, until finally there were so many alterations in normal functioning that the disease could no longer remain hidden and emerged full-blown.

During the late stages of alcoholism, the alcoholic's mental and physical health are seriously deteriorated. Damage to vital organs saps the alcoholic's physical strength; resistance to disease and infection is lowered; mental stability is shaken and precarious. Late-stage alcoholics are so ravaged by their disease that they cannot even understand that alcohol is destroying them. They are only aware that alcohol offers quick and miraculous relief from the constant agony, mental confusion, and emotional turmoil. Alcohol, their deadly poison, is also their necessary medicine.

If alcoholics continue to drink, alcohol will kill them in one way or another. Over 95,000 people die every year (260 per day) in the United States due to excessive alcohol use. * "Given previous reports that death certificates often fail to indicate the contribution of alcohol," NIAAA researchers conclude, "the scope of alcohol-related mortality in the United States is likely higher than suggested from death certificates alone."[1]

As the disease progresses into the final stages, alcohol destroys in a scattergun approach, hitting the heart, liver, brain, stomach, lungs, kidneys, and pancreas. The alcoholic dies when one specific organ stops functioning, but every vital organ suffers massive damage. The major medical consequences of alcoholic drinking include

---

* This number includes large numbers of individuals who never suffered alcohol addiction but died from alcohol toxicity and intoxication-related effects.

heart failure, liver disease, gastrointestinal disorders, respiratory tract disease, cancer, pancreatitis, malnutrition, and immune system disruption.

Heart Failure

Heart failure is a major cause of death in alcoholism. High levels of alcohol and acetaldehyde act directly on the cell membranes in the heart muscle (myocardium), altering their shape and functioning with such effects as cell enlargement and death, tissue scarring, and stretching and thinning of the left ventricle, the heart's main pumping chamber. Various enzymes then leak from the cells, cell mitochondria are damaged, and the cells are slowly infiltrated with fat. The symptoms of alcoholic cardiomyopathy (disease of the heart muscle) are fatigue; swelling in the legs, ankles, and feet; heart palpitations; and labored or difficult breathing. Neural and chemical mechanisms that regulate the heart may be overcome, and death is commonly caused by cardiac arrhythmia (abnormal variations of the heartbeat). High blood pressure (hypertension) is another common condition among untreated alcoholics and a contributor to heart failure.

Most alcoholic heart problems are reversible, particularly if treated in the early stages. Continued abstinence and necessary interventions to protect the alcoholic through the acute withdrawal stage are the first priorities. If the heart muscle is extensively damaged, bed rest and dietary control may be necessary.

Fatty Liver, Hepatitis, and Cirrhosis (Alcohol-Related Liver Disease, or ARLD)

The body needs fuel to continue functioning, and its primary fuel sources are carbohydrates and fat. The liver is the major organ for converting these substances into energy. When alcohol is in the body, however, the liver has a choice. It can use either alcohol or the fat and carbohydrates for fuel. Because alcohol requires less time and effort to be oxidized than these other sources of fuel, and the calories available from its breakdown provide a rich and potent energy kick, the choice is quickly made. The liver uses the alcohol as a fuel, the carbohydrates are stored as glycogen or converted to fat, and the fat is kept in storage.

Thus, whenever alcohol is in the body, the liver uses it for fuel rather than the more difficult and time-consuming fat. This substitution of alcohol for fat as a fuel is not restricted to the alcoholic but, in fact, occurs in everyone who drinks a significant amount of alcohol. The nonalcoholic drinker, however, usually drinks only for short periods, with relatively long periods of abstention in between. When there is no alcohol in the body, the fat is pulled out of storage and converted by the liver into energy to fulfill the body's needs. Alcoholics, on the other hand, keep a fairly constant supply of alcohol in the liver, and as a result, fat accumulates.

Alcohol contributes to the buildup of fat in the liver in another major and potentially disastrous way. Large amounts of alcohol trigger various hormonal discharges that mobilize the fat stored and deposited in other body tissues and move it toward the liver, which must then make room to store it. Surplus fat also circulates in the bloodstream as triglycerides.

As the fat accumulates, it begins to crowd the highly specialized liver cells, many of which suffocate and die. This condition is termed *fatty infiltration of the liver*. As more and more liver cells are injured, the fatty deposits enlarge, causing the liver to swell. A healthy liver is normally neatly tucked away behind the rib cage on the right side. But as the fat and swelling increase, the inflamed liver can be felt by pressing up under the bottom rib. In advanced cases, the swelling can extend down to the pelvis on the right side. The typical person with a severe case of alcoholic fatty liver has been drinking heavily for weeks or months and may feel tired or have discomfort on the upper right side of the abdomen. Most people with fatty liver disease, however, experience few or only mild symptoms. While approximately

40 percent of moderate drinkers experience fatty liver changes, such changes in the liver are virtually universal in heavy drinkers.[2]

In some alcoholics, estimated to be about one in five late-stage alcoholics, large numbers of cells in the liver get sick and begin to die, and the liver becomes inflamed, swollen, and extremely tender. This condition is known as *alcoholic hepatitis*. The alcoholic with hepatitis may become nauseated, feverish, and jaundiced, and may lose weight, suffer ascites, experience spider angioma, or complain of abdominal pain. A buildup of toxins in the blood, as the result of deterioration of the liver, can lead to confusion and other mental and behavioral changes. Both fatty liver and hepatitis are reversible with abstinence from alcohol and good nutrition to promote healing. But if the alcoholic continues to drink, so many liver cells may be destroyed that scar tissue begins to form, signifying the condition known as *cirrhosis* of the liver.[3] Overall, approximately 10–15 percent of alcoholics develop liver cirrhosis, while up to 40 percent of alcoholics with hepatitis will develop cirrhosis. Many alcoholics are unaware they have cirrhosis of the liver, with 30 to 40 percent of cirrhosis diagnoses in alcoholics first made after death during autopsy.[4]

A cirrhotic liver is a plugged-up liver, something like a drain that is clogged. Blood cannot flow smoothly through the congested organ; it backs up and is gradually saturated with toxic materials. As the poisoned blood flow reaches the brain, the cells become poisoned and sick, profoundly affecting the alcoholic's behavior and emotions. The toxic alcoholic is confused, thought processes are jumbled and rambling, and memory and judgment are muddled. Even balance and equilibrium may be affected.

As the scar tissue in the liver accumulates and ages, it also constricts, choking the blood vessels and cutting off the blood supply to the remaining liver cells, which causes further cell death. If the alcoholic continues to drink, the combined effects of fatty liver, hepatitis, and cirrhosis have additional serious consequences. When the blood can no longer circulate freely through the congested liver, the pressure created causes the small blood vessels in the head, face, and chest to rupture, resulting in tiny, spiderlike patterns of broken blood vessels called *spider angioma*.

As the body's blood vessels become constricted, alternative routes to the heart must be found. One route is through the thin-walled and delicate veins of the esophagus. The increased blood flow through these veins can cause them to dilate and, like a bicycle tire blown up with too much air, rupture and hemorrhage. Bleeding from the esophageal vessels (or varices) is evident when the alcoholic vomits up fresh blood. These hemorrhages are obviously dangerous and one of the major causes of death of cirrhosis victims.

Ascites is another complication of the pressure created by a cirrhotic liver. Specifically, ascites is a symptom of pressure in the lymphatic system, part of the circulatory and immune systems. When the pressure grows too great, lymph leaks out of the vessels, accumulating in the abdomen, which then swells. Infection is a serious concern, for the fluids can become infected with bacteria (a condition called spontaneous bacterial peritonitis), which causes fever and pain. Ascites is sometimes mistaken for the common and relatively harmless beer belly, but a swollen stomach in a heavy drinker should be a clear warning of serious trouble in the liver.

Many other serious and sometimes fatal complications occur as a result of cirrhosis. Because so many of its cells are dead or injured, the liver's ability to detoxify poisons is greatly reduced, and potentially dangerous chemicals build up in the bloodstream. One of these is ammonia, which can cause personality changes, lethargy, coma, and death. Bilirubin is another chemical that builds up in the blood when the liver is plugged up with scar tissue. This orange bile pigment is a breakdown product of hemoglobin, and its accumulation causes yellowing of the skin, or jaundice.

As liver damage progresses, other essential chemical and hormonal substances are produced at a slower rate because the liver is simply not functioning normally. Among these is prothrombin, an ingredient necessary for clotting blood. As the prothrombin level decreases, the alcoholic may bruise easily and bleed excessively from a small cut or scratch. They may have bleeding gums, frequent and severe nosebleeds, or bleeding under the skin. If the prothrombin level gets too low, the alcoholic is in danger of dying from internal hemorrhage.

Up to the point of scar tissue development, the liver has extraordinary regenerative powers, and amazing transformations take place when the liver is given proper nutrition, rest, and no alcohol. The body slowly eliminates the accumulated fatty tissue, the liver rebuilds itself, the blood is cleansed of its impurities, and the chemical balance in the brain is gradually restored.

If the alcoholic continues to drink and if scar tissue accumulates, however, the blood vessels gradually will be choked off and the liver cells will sicken and die until the formerly mighty and complex factory of the liver is reduced to a decrepit, fragile structure clogged with poisons, wastes, and dead cells and incapable of sustaining life.

Gastrointestinal Disorders

The stomach is the site of astonishingly powerful chemical reactions that can reduce substances as difficult to digest as fish bones, toothpicks, and gristle to a soft mush, which is then easily transported through the small intestine and eliminated from the body. Something has to protect the stomach from digesting itself in this process, however, and this role belongs to the mucous membrane that lines the stomach and to a layer of specialized cells directly beneath the mucous membrane. One of the most important parts of this protective barrier is the cell membrane, which contains a layer of fats and proteins tightly cemented together to prevent leakage of digestive juices. This multilayered barrier allows the digestive enzymes and gastric acid to do their violent work while protecting the soft stomach walls from being dissolved in the process.

In the early- and middle-stage alcoholic, alcohol sabotages this intricate protective system by assaulting the fat and protein layer of the membranes and weakening the tight links between the cells.

Digestive juices, including gastric acid, may now leak through the cells and onto the membranes. The lining of the stomach may then become seriously inflamed, a condition known as *gastritis*. Gastritis can be severe enough to cause bleeding, and its symptoms include indigestion, bloating, nausea, headache, and abnormal increase or decrease in appetite. Ironically, the best temporary first aid for gastritis may sometimes be alcohol. In a 1974 study published in the *Journal of the American Medical Association,* researchers reported:

> Studies of two subjects whose stomachs previously had been photographed with a gastrocamera are presented with pictures made after heavy alcoholic ingestion. Both subjects had severe hangovers. Observations made before and after drinking of an alcoholic beverage on the "morning after" showed a remarkable calming of the stomach after ingestion, demonstrated by the gastrocamera.[5]

Taken in large enough amounts, however, alcohol will once again aggravate the inflammation.

More recent research supports the complex effect of alcohol on the stomach. It is reported that alcoholic beverages having a lower alcohol content, such as wine and beer, increase the secretion of the gastric acid that causes gastritis more than alcoholic beverages having a higher alcohol content, such as whiskey, gin, and cognac. In fact, it has been shown that pure alcohol in low concentrations (less than 5 percent by volume) is only a mild stimulant of gastric acid secretion, whereas at higher concentrations it has either no effect or a mildly inhibitory effect on gastric acid secretions. The higher secretion of gastric acid following the consumption of alcoholic drinks having a lower level of alcohol, such as beer and wine, is attributed to the nonalcoholic contents (preliminarily identified as heat-stable, negatively charged substances) of these beverages.[6]

Ulcers are very common during the high tolerance phases of early- and middle-stage alcoholism and less frequent in the late stages of the disease when tolerance is lowered. Ulceration corresponds with an increased secretion of hydrochloric acid in the early- and middle-stage alcoholic. Late-stage alcoholics have lowered levels of hydrochloric acid secretion.

Respiratory Tract Diseases

In general, alcoholism causes damage to the lungs by interfering with the body's normal defense mechanisms and thereby making the alcoholic susceptible to respiratory infection and injury. Large doses of alcohol taken over long periods of time may block the formation of new cells, prevent living cells from destroying bacteria, and impair the lungs' ability to eliminate inhaled particles. This interference with normal functioning can lead to infections, tuberculosis, chronic bronchitis, emphysema, and lung abscess. Acute inflammation or infection of the lungs (pneumonia) is a frequent cause of death for late-stage alcoholics.

Recent research provides a more detailed picture of the complex, toxic effect of high alcohol consumption on the lungs. Chronic consumption of high levels of alcohol is a risk factor for acute respiratory distress syndrome (ARDS) and chronic obstructive pulmonary disease (COPD). Although ingested alcohol is metabolized mainly in the liver, a significant amount of the ingested alcohol, as well as its metabolic byproducts, such as acetaldehyde and/or reactive oxygen species (ROS), reach the airway passages of the lungs through the bronchial circulation, causing oxidative stress and suppressed immunity in the lungs. Such toxic, metabolic changes in the lungs caused by consumption of high levels of alcohol predisposes the individual to ARDS and COPD, lung diseases associated with high rates of mortality (depending on age and comorbidities, in the 30–45 percent range), including increased rate of mortality as a result of alcohol-induced lung damage.[7]

Cancer

For a long time, alcohol was not a widely accepted cancer-causing agent, even though there were strong indications that large amounts of alcohol taken over a prolonged period of time definitely contributed to or aggravated cancers throughout the body.[8] Alcoholics appeared to have an increased risk of head and neck, esophageal, lung, and liver cancers. For each of these cancers, it was thought that alcohol acted in a different way, sometimes directly affecting the cells, other times indirectly increasing the cells' susceptibility to cancer. There seemed to be a number of ways alcohol may have contributed to cancer:

- By directly irritating the cells, thus targeting an area that may then be more vulnerable to cancer.
- By damaging the liver so that the ability to break down and neutralize poisonous substances is greatly reduced. The accumulation of these substances in the blood may directly irritate the cells, increasing the likelihood of cancer.
- By causing nutritional deficiencies that may further weaken the cells' ability to withstand the toxic effects of large amounts of alcohol.
- By providing a vehicle for the chemical additives (congeners) that give alcoholic beverages their distinctive taste, smell, and color and which may be cancer-causing agents.
- By interacting with tobacco and increasing the risks of each taken separately. The effect may be synergistic, or multiplied, and therefore the risk of drinking and smoking at the same time may be much higher than that associated with doing either alone.
- By inhibiting salivation and thus interfering with the body's normal rinsing mechanisms. For alcoholics who are also heavy cigarette smokers, a buildup of tars in the saliva may contribute to the development of cancers of the head, neck, and esophagus.

Current research, as reported by the National Cancer Institute, confirms the association between alcohol consumption and the occurrence of some types of cancer. The increased risk of getting these types of cancers generally correlates with the amount of alcohol consumed and increases as the amount of alcohol consumed increases. Data from a 2009 epidemiological study estimated that 3.5 percent of cancer deaths in the United States (about 19,500 deaths) were alcohol-related.

For instance, the risk of getting head and neck cancers, including cancers of the oral cavity, increases fivefold in heavy drinkers (defined as having four or more drinks per day for women and five or more drinks per day for men). There is also a fivefold increase in the risk of getting esophageal cancer in heavy drinkers. There is a twofold increased risk of getting liver cancer in heavy drinkers. There is a 1.6-fold increase in the risk of getting breast cancer and a 1.2 to 1.5-fold increased risk of developing colon and rectal cancers in men and women who drink heavily.

Some evidence is accumulating to support an association between alcohol consumption and increased risks of getting melanoma, prostate cancer, and pancreatic cancer, while there is little or at best inconsistent evidence of an association between cancer risk and alcohol for cancers of the ovary, stomach, uterus, and bladder. Alcohol consumption has actually been associated with a decreased risk of non-Hodgkin lymphoma and kidney cancers.

Not surprisingly, epidemiological research indicates that the combined use of alcohol and tobacco results in a much greater risk of developing cancers of the oral cavity, throat, larynx, and esophagus than seen in people who use only alcohol or tobacco.

Finally, there is as yet no definitive evidence to support any protective benefit of drinking a moderate amount of red wine to reduce the occurrence of cancer, at least with respect to prostate or colorectal cancers.

The mechanisms by which alcohol consumption may increase

the risk of the occurrence of various cancers is still not yet fully understood, with researchers hypothesizing the following possible mechanisms:

- Increased levels of toxic metabolic breakdown products of alcohol, such as acetaldehyde and reactive oxygen species, capable of damaging the genetic material (such as DNA), proteins, and lipids in the human body
- Impairment of the body's ability to absorb nutrients that protect against cancer, such as vitamin A, B vitamins (such as folate), vitamin C, vitamin D, vitamin E, and the antioxidant carotenoids (plant pigments that produce the bright yellow, red, and orange colors in vegetables and fruits)
- Increasing blood levels of the sex hormone estrogen, which may increase the risk of breast cancer

It is also now understood that the risk of occurrence of an alcohol-related cancer can be influenced by genetic factors that affect alcohol metabolism. For instance, individuals of Japanese descent with the ADH1B*2 gene variant, which increases the conversion of alcohol to its toxic metabolite acetaldehyde, have a higher risk of pancreatic cancer than those with the more common, less active form of ADH.

The increased risk of cancer occurrence associated with alcohol consumption does not drop immediately once alcohol consumption stops, and in numerous cases it may take many years to drop to the level of those who never have consumed alcohol.[9]

Pancreatitis

Large and continuous doses of alcohol injure the pancreas, causing it to activate and release certain digestive enzymes that in turn aggravate the inflammation of this vital gland, located behind the stomach and liver. In extreme cases, the digestive enzymes may actually begin to digest the pancreas.

Pancreatitis usually develops after five to fifteen years of heavy drinking and is characterized by severe pain in the upper abdomen (often radiating to the back and lower chest), nausea, vomiting, constipation, increased heart rate, jaundice, and low-grade fever. The risk of repeated attacks leading to injury (atrophy, scarring) is 40 percent if the alcoholic continues to drink but drops to 14 percent with prolonged abstinence, although it's difficult if not impossible to reverse the damage to the pancreatic tissue.[10]

Malnutrition

All alcoholics suffer from malnutrition to some degree. A number of factors work together to make this condition almost synonymous with alcoholism. Large doses of alcohol interfere with digestion and passage of nutrients from the intestines into the bloodstream. The alcoholic's liver has a decreased ability to convert and release nutrients and make them available throughout the body. Without adequate nutrients, the cells, already weakened by long exposures to alcohol's toxic effects, are not able to create bone, tissue, blood, or energy. The sick and injured cells thus do not have the resources to repair themselves, and damage continues unchecked.

Even the alcoholic's earliest psychological and social problems stem from or are aggravated by nutritional deficiencies. For example, a thiamine deficiency (extremely common in alcoholics) can cause loss of mental alertness, easy fatigue, loss of appetite, irritability, and emotional instability. If the deficiency is allowed to continue, more severe mental confusion and loss of memory may develop.

In the later stages of alcoholism, the alcoholic is often so sick that he or she cannot eat, thus aggravating the already serious nutritional deficiencies. Massive vitamin or mineral deficiencies caused by long and heavy drinking may result in several unusual diseases of the central nervous system, including polyneuropathy, Wernicke's encephalopathy, Korsakoff's psychosis, and tobacco-alcohol amblyopia.

Polyneuropathy is a nutritional disorder generally associated with deficiencies of the B vitamins—including thiamine (B_1), pantothenic acid (B_5), niacin (B_3), and pyridoxine (B_6)—that weaken and eventually damage the peripheral nerves outside the brain and spinal cord. These nerves, which are similar to thin, elongated wires, carry electrical/chemical impulses that instruct the legs, arms, and torso to lift, move, run, walk, or feel warmth, cold, pain, and pressure. The strength of the current in the nerve depends on adequate food and nutrients for its power source. When the nerves are deprived of nutrients, the power of the sensory and motor impulses diminishes and weakens, and the nerves gradually lose their ability to transmit sensory and motor signals.

The first indications of polyneuropathy are numbness and tingling sensations ("pins and needles") in the extremities, usually the toes or fingers. As the condition progresses, the sensations occur higher in the limbs, affecting hands and arms, feet and legs. Polyneuropathy is reversible if arrested early enough. If the alcoholic stops drinking and continues to abstain from alcohol, and if they pay careful attention to their diet and vitamin and mineral intake (particularly the B vitamins), the nerves will heal themselves fairly quickly. If, however, the alcoholic continues to drink and malnutrition progresses unchecked, there will come a time when the damage is permanent and irreversible. Muscle tone will be lost, and the muscles will atrophy. Pain may be excruciating. Late-stage alcoholics with irreversible polyneuropathy may be able to walk only clumsily if at all.

Wernicke's encephalopathy, named after a nineteenth-century German psychiatrist and brain specialist, is a rare disease usually produced by a severe deficiency in vitamin B_1 (thiamine). The disease is marked by a rapid onset of headaches, double vision, abnormal eye movements, the tingling sensations and numbness associated with polyneuropathy, muscular incoordination, stupor, and brain hemorrhage. The condition is also frequently accompanied by the confusion, agitation, and hallucinations seen in delirium tremens, and the two conditions can be confused. In fact, Wernicke's encephalopathy is sometimes overlooked because the alcoholic appears drunk or in withdrawal. The "classic triad" symptoms of Wernicke's encephalopathy include altered mental state, an ataxic (stumbling, uncoordinated) gait, and paralysis or weakness of the eye muscles (ophthalmoplegia).

Until 1936, the prognosis invariably was death, but after the B vitamins were synthesized and readily available, significant improvement in the condition became possible and the symptoms are now largely reversible if treated promptly. Accurate diagnosis and immediate treatment are essential, however, because the condition can swiftly progress into the generally irreversible mental disorder called *Korsakoff's psychosis*. This condition, first described in 1890 by the Russian psychiatrist Sergei Sergeyevich Korsakoff, is caused in part by vitamin B_1 deficiencies, and it generally results in irreversible brain damage. The disorder has several striking characteristics, including hallucinations, the loss of short-term memory, and the consequent fabrication of stories to fill in the gaps (confabulation). The victim is often able to remember past events but is thoroughly confused as to present or recent events, such as where they are, why they happen to be there, what they have just eaten, or who may be sitting next to them.

Tobacco-alcohol amblyopia (TAA), another rare disease, occurs in approximately one in two hundred hospitalized alcoholics, most of whom are smokers and have a poor dietary history. It is characterized by progressive blurring or dimness of vision, difficulty reading small print, and in some cases difficulty distinguishing green from red. Although the specific nutritional deficiency responsible for this condition has not been identified, TAA is reversible with abstinence (from both alcohol and tobacco), improved nutrition, and large doses of the B vitamins.[11]

The Immune System

The adverse effect of alcohol consumption on the immune system is clear. Because the immune system is so complex and multilayered, however, the present state of research gives but a glimpse of the "highly variable and sometimes paradoxical influences" of alcohol consumption on immune system function.[12]

The immune system comprises two subsystems, the innate immune response and the adaptive immune response. Innate immunity provides an immediate, generalized defensive response to nonspecific pathogen and nonpathogen challenges not previously encountered by the human body. Adaptive immunity, in contrast, is a delayed immune response of the body to a specific pathogen or antigen. The body's innate immune response is a generalized inflammatory reaction that resolves once the pathogen is eliminated. The body's adaptive immunity response, in contrast, is the biosynthesis of antibodies designed to attack specific pathogens or antigens. The immune system is capable of "memorizing" this response to specific pathogens or antigens and can respond quickly with the specific antibodies upon a second exposure to the pathogen or antigen.

The regulation of normal immune function, including the innate and adaptive immune subsystems, is exceedingly complex, involving multiple layers of communication and regulation within the body. One aspect of this regulation is the bidirectional communication of immune cells with nonimmune cells at the local level within the body as well as "crosstalk" between the central nervous system and the peripheral systems of the body. These different layers of communication and regulation make it challenging to understand the mechanisms by which alcohol affects immune function.

The complexity of the immune system notwithstanding, current research delineates the undeniable damaging effect of alcohol consumption on immune function. For instance, excessive alcohol consumption impairs normal immune responses, increasing susceptibility to pneumonia, acute respiratory stress syndromes, sepsis, alcoholic liver disease, and certain cancers. Excessive alcohol consumption also results in a higher incidence of postoperative complications and slower and less complete recovery from infection and physical trauma, including poor wound healing—all immune-related health effects associated with excess alcohol consumption.

It is thus clear that alcohol's disruption of the body's normal immune pathways impairs the body's ability to defend against infection, contributes to organ damage associated with alcohol consumption, and impedes recovery from tissue injury by weakening both the innate and adaptive immune responses and significantly weakening the body's defenses against disease and injury.

Such damage is not limited to the alcoholic. Recent evidence shows that fetal alcohol exposure in utero can interfere with the developing immune system in the fetus, not only increasing the newborn's risk of infection and disease but also potentially causing impairment of the immune system of the newborn into adulthood.

Alcohol-induced damage to the immune system is not limited to the excessive consumption of alcohol. Recent studies show that acute binge drinking also affects the immune system, including impaired recovery from physical trauma.

Also emerging is a body of research indicating that immune signaling in the brain may contribute to alcohol use disorders. Specifically, there is evidence that binge drinking increases brain neuroimmune activation, which in turn may lead to persistent loss of the ability to adapt to changes (behavioral flexibility), an increase in risky decision-making, and an increase in alcohol consumption.[13]

NOW THAT THE early, middle, and late stages of the disease have been described from a technical standpoint, Chapter 7 describes the alcoholic. What are the psychological symptoms that alcoholics experience as they progress from the early to the late stages, and what are their reactions to these symptoms? Most important, why do they continue to drink when drinking is slowly but surely destroying them?

7

The Alcoholic

"Why are you drinking?" demanded the little prince.

"So that I may forget," replied the tippler.

"Forget what?" inquired the little prince, who already was sorry for him.

"Forget that I am ashamed," the tippler confessed, hanging his head.

"Ashamed of what?" insisted the little prince, who wanted to help him.

"Ashamed of drinking!" The tippler brought his speech to an end, and shut himself up in an impregnable silence.

—Antoine de Saint-Exupéry, *The Little Prince*

Once the disease of alcoholism is understood, the only remaining mystery is the victim—why do alcoholics continue to drink after it is evident that drinking is destroying them?

The answer is surprisingly simple: at every stage the disease itself prevents the alcoholic from realizing that they are addicted to alcohol. In the earliest stage, when the cells are adapting and tolerance is gradually increasing, the alcoholic does not consider giving up alcohol because nothing indicates that they are sick, and no one else suspects that they might be. In the middle stages, when their cells have become firmly dependent on alcohol for functioning, the alcoholic may be aware that they need alcohol more often and in greater quantities, but they do not know why. They do not know that their cells have been altered, nor do they know that their physical reaction to alcohol is drastically different from the nonalcoholic's. They only know that when they stop drinking, they suffer, and so their first priority is to get alcohol back in their system.

As the alcoholic drinks more and more often, alcohol's toxic effects disrupt the brain's chemical and electrical balances, causing profound psychological and emotional disturbances. Middle- and late-stage alcoholics are frequently irrational, deluded, irritable, unreasonable, and incapable of understanding what is happening inside them. They cannot see themselves as others see them. Their actions, thoughts, and emotions are warped by alcohol; their behavior is governed by the addiction.

To everyone else it may appear that alcoholics are somehow responsible for their disease, because they ignore all warnings and continue to drink. But—and this is a key to understanding alcoholism—they are already addicted to alcohol when their behavior and psychological stability first begin to deteriorate. The physical disease is already well established by the time the alcoholic begins to act like an alcoholic. In fact, the disease itself is responsible for most of the alcoholic's psychological problems, and as it progresses, the alcoholic's behavior becomes more bizarre and their psychological problems more profound.

Because the physical damage is not evident until the later stages of the disease, when the alcoholic is clearly addicted and can no longer reliably control their drinking, it is critically important that the early psychological and behavioral symptoms of alcoholism be recognized for what they are: the signs of an already established disease. Alcoholics should not have to wait until their lives are nearly destroyed by alcohol before their disease is recognized; they can be diagnosed in the early stages of the disease. An alcoholism specialist who knows what to look for and who understands that psychological and emotional problems are among the first symptoms of underlying alcoholism can make an accurate diagnosis after careful examination. A family history of alcoholism is one important clue; marital difficulties, problems at work, recurring bouts of depression and anxiety, suicidal thoughts or attempts, and changing drinking patterns are additional clues. A classic symptom of alcoholic drinking is a refusal to acknowledge or admit a drinking problem. Alcoholics often will deny or rationalize their drinking behavior because they are unaware of the addiction, believing that their drinking is merely a response to serious life problems.

The alcoholic's interaction with others can also provide telling clues. If their partner is worried; if they are frequently too busy to play with their children or are constantly irritated by their children's demands; if they would rather go drinking than stay at home; if they make new friends who happen to be heavy drinkers; if they keep a bottle in the office so that they and their friends can celebrate whenever the mood hits them—all these behaviors raise suspicions of alcoholism.

The alcoholic and others around them, however, usually have a difficult time determining whether alcoholism is at the root of their growing problems. In the later stages of the disease, when addiction is obvious and withdrawal symptoms provide an undeniable sign of physical dependence, the diagnosis is much easier to make. But in the early stages, alcoholic drinking can easily be confused with normal or problem drinking behavior. Simply because someone argues with their family members, stomps out of the house, and gets drunk at the corner tavern does not mean that they are an alcoholic. Relationship problems and job difficulties are not sufficient by themselves to indicate alcoholism. But add personality changes and a growing preoccupation with alcohol, and alcoholism is a very likely explanation.

Perhaps the strongest clue of all is the disease's progression. Alcoholism does not do a little damage and then suddenly stop its attack. If alcoholics continue to drink, they will not be able to reverse their psychological problems, which will only get worse. Alcoholics will be able to drink in a controlled way only temporarily; inevitably, alcohol will control them. They will drink more, and more often, in spite of the fact that alcohol is threatening their relationships, career, and health.

Every alcoholic, of course, experiences a slightly different progression of overt symptoms, and not every alcoholic experiences all symptoms. The "typical" alcoholic is therefore a summary of all, not necessarily a description of any individual alcoholic. Given that warning, a description follows of a "typical" progression of symptoms from the early stage through the middle stage and into the final stage of the disease.

The Early Stage

Jack is a forty-five-year-old engineer, popular with his friends and loved by his family. He has four children, lives in a comfortable suburban home, and enjoys golf and gardening.

Jack never drinks alone during the day, but at 5:00 p.m. sharp, he sits down in front of the TV and drinks three or four straight Scotches. He allows nothing to interfere with his "cocktail hour." He knows he drinks a lot, but many of his friends also drink heavily, and nobody seems to be worried about them. Besides, he never lets his drinking interfere with his job or family life, he rarely gets drunk, and alcohol always, without fail, makes him feel better.

The early alcoholic typically enjoys drinking, drinks whenever alcohol is offered, and often seeks out an occasion to drink. An afternoon baseball game may be organized with baseball as the secondary motive and drinking during the game or at a tavern after the game the primary motive. Drinking is fun, socially satisfying, and an important part of the early alcoholic's life.

Many nonalcoholics also drink whenever they have the chance, so the early alcoholic's drinking does not appear unusual or abnormal. Yet even in this early stage, there are symptoms that create a suspicion of alcoholism. The early alcoholic will typically have a *greater tolerance* for alcohol, drinking more than their friends, yet showing the effects less. Thus, they may be among the last to leave the party, and they may be the person who drives others home because they are least affected by alcohol.

Another early symptom is a *growing preoccupation* with alcohol. The early alcoholic rarely will be caught with a refrigerator or liquor cabinet empty of alcohol, and they will probably include wine or beer on their shopping list before the eggs, bread, and milk. Still, they do not necessarily drink every night, and when they do drink, they can usually control their intake, so they rarely get drunk. They believe they are in complete control of their drinking, and when they do drink too much, they insist that they were just "in the mood" to get drunk.

In short, the early alcoholic does not appear to suffer in any way from drinking. They usually feel happy and carefree when they drink. They may have frustrations but are not preoccupied by them, and anxiety or tensions do not appear to drive them to drink. They are, in most cases, psychologically and emotionally stable. Their childhood was normal, their family life comfortable; they are patient parents, loving spouses, and responsible employees.

If someone were to tell them that they were drinking too much, their reaction would be one of complete surprise. They are, after all, handling their liquor as well as or better than most of their friends; they rarely get drunk, usually drink at home with their partner or friends, and do not drink at lunch, in the morning, or even every day. On the surface, they seem to be like other people who happen to enjoy alcohol and thus seek the pleasure of its company more and more often. They see no reason to be ashamed or evasive about their drinking and may even brag about their drinking prowess. They can "take it or leave it," they insist, and it seems clear to them and others that although they like to drink, they certainly do not need to drink.

Their family and friends do not see anything unusual in their drinking because they do not deviate drastically from other people's patterns of drinking. The alcoholic may influence them to drink more, but they believe that the alcoholic simply likes to have a good time. The early alcoholic may be able to hold their liquor a little better than others, but that causes no alarm. They may look forward to drinking occasions, but that does not raise eyebrows either. Their ability to drink large amounts of alcohol without falling down drunk may, in fact, inspire affectionate pats on the back and a reputation as the life of the party.

If someone who knew the disease well and understood its earliest symptoms was closely watching the early alcoholic's behavior, they would probably suspect the gradual increase in tolerance, the growing preoccupation with alcohol, and the ability to function normally after drinking large amounts of alcohol as probable early symptoms of alcoholism. Most professionals, however, would hesitate to label this behavior "alcoholic drinking" because it just does not resemble the more blatant and obvious changes that occur later in the disease and are most often associated with alcoholism.

The Middle Stage

Over a period of several years, Jack began to drink more often and a little faster than his friends. Instead of waiting until 5 p.m., he began to drink at lunch, or sometimes left work early and had a few at the local bar. At parties he was the first to finish his drink, and he would quickly gulp down another. He rarely said no to an offer of a drink.

When his wife criticized him for drinking too much, he learned ways to disguise his intake. The bar became a regular stopover after work, and he kept a flask in his briefcase "just for emergencies." He also started drinking martinis because they had more impact than his regular Scotch.

He knew he was drinking too much, but he quickly dismissed the idea that he might be an alcoholic. After all, an alcoholic was someone who didn't care what he looked like, didn't care if he disgraced his family and friends—in fact, an alcoholic usually didn't have any family or friends! Jack knew he wasn't the type of person who could become an alcoholic. His upbringing had been normal and happy, his wife and children loved him, and his friends were respected members of the community. Nothing traumatic or unusual had ever happened to him.

As the cells of the central nervous system gradually become addicted to alcohol, alcoholics experience specific changes in their drinking behavior. They may begin *sneaking drinks,* which is one way of hiding their growing dependence on alcohol. On the way home from work, they may stop at a bar and quickly down one or two quick drinks; the stay-at-home parent may start drinking at 4 p.m. before their partner gets home. At a party, the alcoholic might go into the kitchen on the pretext of helping the cook and, not incidentally, stiffen up their drink while there.

The middle-stage alcoholic will often loosen up with a few drinks before the party begins. This is called *predrinking drinking,* and the goal is not just to get in the mood for a party but to help disguise their need to drink a lot of alcohol. The way they drink is also changing. The middle-stage alcoholic tends to *gulp the first drinks,* polishing off the first round and being ready for the next before anyone else has finished. Once they have started drinking, they want to continue—one or two drinks no longer satisfy them—and if others are showing signs of slowing down, they may order another round and attempt to liven up the conversation, hoping to prolong the drinking occasion. This behavior signifies the beginning of *loss of control.* The alcoholic may still be able to control when and where they begin drinking, but they cannot reliably count on being able to stop drinking once they have begun. With one or two drinks, the physical chain reaction begins that feels to the alcoholic and appears to others like a psychological demand for more alcohol. This inability to stop drinking once started does not occur every time they drink, but it will gradually increase in frequency as the disease progresses.

As the ability to control drinking gradually disintegrates, the alcoholic is placed in an extremely awkward position. They need to drink because of the growing addiction, but they must also try to avoid getting drunk in order to escape both the severe withdrawal symptoms and the censure of their family and friends. It becomes extremely important to the alcoholic to prove to themselves and others that they can still take alcohol or leave it alone. And so they develop their own unique *strategies of control*.

Alcoholics who discover that they regularly lose control with their first drink may go on the wagon for prolonged periods of time. Others may switch to beer or wine, drink only on weekends, only at taverns, or only after 5 p.m. Many middle-stage alcoholics can successfully control or appear to control their drinking throughout a period of probation set by a judge, employer, or spouse threatening separation or divorce. These temporary control strategies are often misinterpreted as evidence that the person is not addicted to alcohol and could control their drinking if they would only put their mind to it. Occasional "slips" are concealed or rationalized by the alcoholic and forgiven by the concerned nonalcoholic.

Thus, in the middle stage of alcoholism, the people who could exert pressure on the alcoholic to get help are instead blinded to the progression of the disease by the alcoholic's ability to control their drinking temporarily. Of course, most alcoholics will make a superhuman effort to control their drinking if a return to drinking out of control means jail, mandatory treatment, divorce, or loss of a job. In addition to keeping their marriage, career, and social status intact, however, the alcoholic's most important priority is protecting their continued freedom to drink, and they will cooperate with anyone who can make this possible.

Questions about their drinking cause the alcoholic concern and distress, and if anyone implies that they should stop drinking, their *defenses* slam shut around them. The middle-stage alcoholic will go to great lengths to avoid discussing their personal and drinking problems. If their partner or children ask them why they drink so much or plead with them to cut down, they may avoid an answer by changing the subject or may defend themselves by blaming their drinking on someone or something else. If their doctor happens to question them about their drinking, they may answer, "Oh, I drink moderately, just like my friends." If pressed, they often become more evasive or defensive.

When their drinking repeatedly begins to interfere with their responsibilities or otherwise is annoying to others, the all-important question is raised: "Why do they do it?" Most people look for the psychological motive or reason, believing that alcoholics drink too much because of stress, anxiety, insecurity, or profound unhappiness. "If you loved me, you wouldn't do this to me," the spouse complains. "Don't you care about your children [your job, your reputation]?" Alcoholics, feeling guilty and ashamed, ask themselves these same questions and agonize over their inability to control themselves. Knowing nothing of their addiction, they must come up with reasons for their excessive drinking and destructive behavior. And so they learn to explain and rationalize their drinking episodes. "I was tired and depressed, and the drinks just happened to hit me hard." "You've been nagging me all day, and I did the only possible thing I could do—drink to drown you out!" "We always get sloshed on Paul's birthday—you know that!" "They didn't serve dinner until 10 p.m.; how in the hell was I supposed to stay sober?"

Society mistakenly believes that alcoholic drinking is a response to stressful problems, and the alcoholic from the beginning shares this belief. Later on, this confusion of the consequences of drinking with the causes becomes the fortress of rationalization from which the alcoholic defends their drinking. To themselves they say, "My job is frustrating, my boss is unfair, my spouse nags and puts me down, my children are spoiled and disobedient. I'm frustrated, bored, depressed, trapped in a lousy job and marriage."

By rationalizing their drinking problems and pinning the blame on others, alcoholics are able to defend their integrity and self-respect and, of course, their right to drink. The drinking, they sincerely believe, is merely a response to far more serious life problems. They have become so totally wrapped up in what they see as acceptable reasons for their drinking behavior that they fail to notice that these have become mere excuses. They lose all ability to judge their own behavior accurately, and in their ignorance of their underlying physical disease, they know only that they must protect their freedom to drink.

At this point, they may *change drinking patterns* in the belief that the cause of their problems is the type of alcohol they drink, where they drink, or whom they drink with. They may change brands or switch from Scotch to gin or from bourbon to beer. They may stop seeing their nonalcoholic friends, convinced that their long faces and heart-to-heart talks are only making them drink more. They may try to drink only at home for a while in an attempt to get away from the "bad influences" at the tavern.

Changing jobs or moving to another town (known as *geographic cures* in Alcoholics Anonymous) represents another attempt to cope with growing problems. The alcoholic may decide that most of their troubles are related to their job ("It's demeaning," they complain bitterly, or "They expect too damn much of me"). They may blame the town they live in ("It's too small; everyone is always poking their nose into other people's personal business"). And so they move to another town, get another job, or arrange a new work assignment, preferably traveling much of the time so they are free to drink as much as they want.

The middle-stage alcoholic begins to experience frequent *mood swings* or *personality changes* when drinking. The quiet person may become obnoxious, the gentle person belligerent; the devoted wife or husband may begin to flirt with strangers; the carefree single person may become morose and disinterested in sex. As they continue to drink, they will begin to *lose their self-respect* and sense of personal integrity. They cannot find many reasons to like themselves. They make their family members miserable by continuing to drink, constantly complaining, and blaming them for their own unhappiness. Their remaining friends are fast losing patience; they look at the alcoholic with pity and disgust.

When the alcoholic wakes up after a drunk, they are overcome with *remorse* and *guilt*. Their efforts to control their drinking have clearly failed once again; their partners eye them with reproach, their children look at them with anger and bewilderment. "Why am I doing this to them?" they ask themselves. They cannot understand their own behavior, and they are frightened by the changes in their personality. "I'm just no damn good," they think, an opinion that only becomes more entrenched as they continue to drink.

Frightened and disgusted with themselves, alcoholics gradually turn inward, away from people. They spend *more and more time alone,* no longer able to cope with their family's anguished questions or their friends' reproaches. They are overwhelmed with *self-pity,* which intensifies as their isolation grows. Everyone is picking on them, they believe, and they know somehow that they are not completely at fault. On the other hand, they know they should stop drinking, but they cannot. And so they drink, risking everything else in their life for alcohol. To everyone else, their behavior seems self-destructive and suicidal, but for the alcoholic, drinking is self-preservation. They know what it feels like to wake up with the shakes, and they know the magic of alcohol in relieving them. They are trapped—more aware of the short-term torment of not drinking than of the long-term consequences of continuing to drink.

The middle-stage alcoholic's *emotions are strung tight.* They are usually tense and anxious unless they are drinking. One slighting remark or questioning glance, and they are immediately irritated. An unmade bed, a telephone call during the cocktail hour, a dirty bathtub, running out of ketchup, an unpaid bill, a driver honking the horn—any one event is enough to set them off. They explode, screaming at the kids, cursing their partners, humiliating their coworkers, and then they stomp off. Later they feel guilty and ashamed. These emotional outbursts occur most often when alcoholics are in withdrawal, only confirming to them their need for a drink. As soon as they take a drink, they calm down.

The alcoholic's interaction with others becomes increasingly tense and strained. At first, their career, their marriage, and their

personality flaws are blamed, and excuses are dredged up to rationalize their behavior. "It's probably my fault," the spouse worries.
"I should be more patient with them." "They'll get over it," friends
whisper. "It's just a phase they're going through."

But when it becomes obvious that the alcoholic's drinking is
not just a phase, their family and friends become more outspoken
in their concern. Because the middle-stage alcoholic's problems
seem mainly psychological, the family may suggest that they see a
psychotherapist or marriage counselor. Their personal physician is
just as likely to suggest psychiatric help because the signs of physical
deterioration or damage appear to be secondary to the emotional
problems and they may be unaware of the physiological basis of the
disease. If the alcoholic is referred to a psychiatrist for psychological
counseling, their guilt and self-loathing are likely to deepen. The
search for psychological causes of their drinking will only strengthen
their feeling that they are to blame somehow. Not only may psychiatric treatment fail to help, but it can actually be harmful, since
the search for psychological causes only reinforces the alcoholic's
rationalizations and diverts attention from the physiological causes
of the disease. Psychiatric exploration may go on for years, while
the alcoholic continues to drink and the physical disease goes on
unchecked.

The family attempts to cope with the alcoholic's behavior in
various ways. They may withdraw from all social occasions, embarrassed and ashamed for their alcoholic, or they may leave the house
whenever possible, letting the alcoholic "stew in their own juice."
Neither approach has any long-term effect, for the alcoholic continues to drink, and the psychological and behavioral problems worsen.

If the alcoholic does manage to go on the wagon or cut down,
the family is encouraged and hopeful. Eventually, however, the hope
turns to despair when the alcoholic returns to their old drinking
patterns. All the efforts to talk, to scream, or to love them until
the alcoholic realizes they have to stop drinking are of no avail; the
more drastic measures of pouring full bottles of alcohol down the

drain, booting the alcoholic out of the house, or calling the police also fail miserably. The drinking goes on, and in time it gets worse. Soon enough, any attempt by the alcoholic to change his or her ways is greeted with a tight-lipped nod and silence or a doubtful "We'll see." The family's existence is one of despair, a hanging-on filled with moments of fear and trepidation: "What will happen when I get home? Will she be drunk, passed out, or mean and sober? Will he be dead this time?"

After countless attempts to make the alcoholic stop drinking, the family may believe they have no options and no hope. Still, they may stick by the alcoholic, sensing that they are, at bottom, still the sensitive and loving person they knew before, someone who would not willingly hurt them—knowing, too, that something has taken over the alcoholic's mind and body. What it is, they cannot figure out; they only pray that it can be cured or fixed before it is too late.

The middle-stage alcoholic has probably been having *blackouts* from time to time.[1] The events that occur during a blackout are not forgotten; they are simply not stored or imperfectly stored in the brain. There is nothing there to be recalled later. During a blackout, the alcoholic may be functioning normally and aware of everything that is happening around them. They continue to talk, walk, eat, drive a car, conduct a business deal, or make love to their partner. Yet on sobering up, they have no memory trace of what occurred during a certain time period—it could be a minute, an hour, or even several days. In the early stages of the disease, blackouts are relatively infrequent, but as the disease progresses, they occur more often and last for longer periods.

Jack attended a series of weekend meetings held in a city ninety miles from his home. The last meeting ended in mid-afternoon, and Jack retired to the bar with several friends. It was happy hour, and the bartender announced a two-for-one special on martinis. Jack drank four specials and then decided to order dinner before he drove home. With dinner, he drank a bottle of wine. It was late when he started driving, but he remembered watching the moon rise over the low hills. The next thing he knew and could later recall, he was traveling 110 mph and was twenty-five miles past his exit. He had driven a hundred miles in a blackout.

It is not difficult to imagine how frightening blackouts can be. The alcoholic may wake up in the morning with no recall of the events of the previous evening. They get out of bed, afraid to inspect their clothes—did they get sick? Then the question occurs to them: "How did I get home?" They look out the window, fearful that the car will be missing. They do not remember driving home. The car is there, and they have another, even more frightening thought: "Did I hit something or someone?" They run outside and look at the front end. They search the seats for clues to help them piece back together the lost time. Humiliating thoughts race through their mind: "Did I disgrace myself? Will my friends talk to me? How can I find out what happened when I am too embarrassed to admit that I don't remember?"

Blackouts can be so frightening that they make alcoholics question their sanity. For the first time, they may realize that they are in deep trouble with alcohol. Despite their increasing problems, however, the middle-stage alcoholic rarely considers giving up drinking; they may believe a psychiatrist can help them sort out their "underlying psychological problems," but they cannot believe that drinking is responsible for those problems. It just does not make sense, because drinking makes them feel good, not bad. In fact, alcohol is the only thing they can count on to pull them through a tense day or a frustrating encounter. As a result, the alcoholic begins to *protect their supply*, always making certain that a bottle is hidden in the car, the house, or their desk at work—just in case they need it.

Of course they need it more, and more often. The withdrawal symptoms are becoming so severe that they drink frequently and are in extremely bad shape when they stop drinking. Whether they admit it or not, the alcoholic needs alcohol to function, and they are ingenious in discovering places to hide it. The toilet tank and glove compartment are classic hiding places; more innovative caches include the steam compartment in an iron or the windshield washer compartment in a car. W. C. Fields allegedly kept a hidden supply of alcohol in his walking cane.

Soon enough the alcoholic is in *trouble at work*. Mondays are frequently missed because of weekend binges; lunches may last for two or three hours; colleagues who are tired of covering for the alcoholic and assuming that person's workload complain; rumors of bottles in their desk and whiskey on their breath filter through the office. Employers may shut their eyes, hoping the problem will go away by itself, but at some point they will be forced to do something about their alcoholic employee. They may fire them based on the accumulated evidence, or they may give the alcoholic the choice between treatment or being fired. This last option may finally make the alcoholic realize how serious the problem is. Alcoholic drinking takes a lot of money. The alcoholic's job feeds his or her family, pays the bills, gives them an identity, supports what is left of their self-respect, and holds together their fragile lifestyle. To lose their job would be a financial and emotional disaster. No matter how sick they are, that fact will usually register—if only for the reason that, without a job, they will no longer be able to afford alcohol.

Toward the end of the middle stage of alcoholism, alcoholics often *neglect eating* because their inflamed digestive system rejects food. They keep going instead on the easy energy of alcohol, which also temporarily alleviates the symptoms of gas, bloating, nausea, and heartburn. They may also experience a *decrease in sexual performance*. As Shakespeare wrote, drink "provokes the desire, but it takes away the performance" (*Macbeth*, act II, scene iii).

Numerous *doctors' visits*, referrals to psychiatrists, and *hospitalizations* may take place toward the end of the middle stage of the disease. *Psychiatric treatment* or counseling may continue for many years, but as long as the drinking continues, the alcoholic's marital, work, and personal problems can only get worse. As this happens, the alcoholic is frequently given *prescriptions* for sedatives, tranquilizers, anxiolytics, or sleeping pills to relieve their mental and physical misery. These substitute drugs are harmful to the alcoholic even if taken as prescribed. As with alcohol itself, the superficial benefits only mask deeper penalties. At best, the alcoholic will switch and become addicted to the prescription drug and continue to deteriorate. But because of cross-tolerance, they will typically increase the dosage in an attempt to get the desired effect.* Since the drugs lack calories and are a poor substitute for alcohol, the alcoholic is very likely to switch back to alcohol or to drink while taking the drugs, a practice that complicates and aggravates their symptoms and increases the risk of accidents and potentially fatal overdoses.

The Deteriorative Stage

Jack knew that something was seriously wrong. He couldn't sleep, and he was constantly nervous and tense. Any little annoyance or disruption of his routine made him irritable.

He finally agreed to see a doctor, who prescribed tranquilizers for his tension, told him he was working too hard, and advised him to slow down. But the irritability and tension persisted, and in fact, Jack began to feel worse. He stopped taking the pills because they weren't helping anymore. Alcohol worked better and faster. At least when he was drinking, he felt in control again.

He was drinking every day now, and most of the day. His wife threatened to leave him if he didn't quit drinking or get help. Finally she filed for divorce. Everything fell apart after that. He lost his job and most of his friends. He had recurring thoughts of suicide, but they only intensified his drinking. His wife got the house, and he spent his last months in a cheap

---

* See Chapter 10 for a discussion of cross-tolerance.

rooming house. One evening after drinking a quart of whiskey, Jack passed out with a lighted cigarette in his hand. He
died in the fire.

Morning drinks become a habit in the final stages of alcoholism.
At first the alcoholic starts to drink in the morning to silence the
withdrawal symptoms. They cannot hold a pencil without drop-
ping it. The coffee cup shakes in their hand until they spill half the
contents on their lap. Their heart feels as if it would hammer right
out of their chest. They are queasy, nauseated, paranoid, and terrified. They must drink if they are to stop the shakes, and they drink
in the morning before they allow themselves to see anyone; they
drink again in the car on the way to work; and they nip at the bottle
in their desk until it is time to go to lunch, where they throw back
a few more.

Soon enough the alcoholic is not able to keep up this charade, for
they too often *drink beyond their tolerance* and get drunk. They can
no longer choose when or where they drink; they must drink all the
time, wherever they happen to be. The ever-impending withdrawal
symptoms have become so excruciating that the alcoholic is com-
pelled to drink just to delay them. They have no choice but to drink,
because alcohol is the only cure for their physical and mental torment. Loss of control is complete. The late-stage alcoholic escapes
the overwhelming need to drink only when unconscious, but the
blessed relief of unconsciousness is only temporary. As the alcohol
is eliminated from their body, the withdrawal symptoms build up,
and the alcoholic awakens to an overpowering need for a drink.

Soon there is no distinction between morning, noon, and evening; only the time of drinking and the time of unconsciousness
or exhausting nausea exist. The cycle continues around the clock.
Prolonged binges are now the rule, and the alcoholic drinks continuously for days or weeks until they become so sick that they must
stop. *Hospitalizations, suicide attempts,* and *arrests* for driving while

intoxicated or public drunkenness are frequent consequences of these binges.

By this time, the late-stage alcoholic has probably lost their job and is *financially dependent* on their family or the welfare system. Their habit is expensive, but they have no money to pay for it, and so they do anything they must to get alcohol. They borrow from friends, steal from their spouse's wallet, smash their children's piggy banks. If the money situation gets too desperate, they may resort to drinking anything that contains alcohol, including vanilla extract, canned heat, shaving lotion, cough syrup, or rubbing alcohol. This practice may also land them in the emergency room or mental ward.

They begin to *drink alone or with inferiors* in seedy taverns or in the hallways of dilapidated rooming houses. They avoid previous haunts because they are terrified of meeting someone who might recognize them. They cannot even wind their watch or unzip their fly, and their shame locks them inside the four walls of their room, alone with their only remaining friend, alcohol. They are incapable of thinking rationally both when they are drinking and when they are in withdrawal. Their attention span is short, they cannot follow a conversation, and they have difficulty speaking clearly.

Paranoia and *vague fears* begin to haunt the late-stage alcoholic's waking hours. The slightest noise—a telephone ringing, the door-bell, a person's voice, a child's shout, a faucet dripping—makes them jump and stare wild-eyed. They are terrified of strangers and may be convinced that people are talking about them or planning to lock them up. Their fears are magnified during withdrawal, and the only cure for them is more alcohol. Even alcohol, however, has lost much of its magic. Now it doesn't really make them feel good; it only eases the shakes and the pain. After just a few drinks, they are either drunk or violently ill.

Eventually the reality of what the alcoholic's life has become can no longer be ignored. The rationalizations, denials, and excuses crumble, and the alcoholic is left with the spectacle of a wasted and broken life. They may seek permanent and immediate escape from this crushing knowledge through *suicide;* they may fear both death and life without alcohol and so continue to drink until death puts an end to their misery; they may experience *vague religious or spiritual desires,* hoping for a miracle to pull them out of the mess of their life and return their sanity and self-respect; they may begin to look for help. Tragically, help usually consists of a brief drying-out period, after which they simply return to their old lifestyle. They may be given pills or told to report to an outpatient counseling program. With this minimum level of help and support, the late-stage alcoholic has only a slim chance of starting a recovery from the disease.

The alcoholic's addiction is now obvious to even the most casual observer. They are the classic picture of the skid row bum.* All the family's efforts appear to have ended in failure, and failure breeds fear, frustration, and resentment. The alcoholic's spouse and children may lash back at them; screaming, hysterical battles may rock the household and destroy any remaining hope of an end to the long and bitter tragedy. The family may suddenly stop fighting and simply give up, convinced that they can only provide the alcoholic with a warm place to sleep and food to eat. Or, having lost all hope, they may pack up and leave the alcoholic to their misery.

Whatever course the family takes, they are usually as emotionally sick as the alcoholic. The spouse may feel responsible; they may also feel worthless, incompetent, useless, and unloved, and suffer from crippling guilt and self-pity. The alcoholic's children are battle-scarred as well. All the solid foundations of love, security, and predictability have been knocked out from underneath them, and they are frightened and torn apart with doubts and fears: "Will he die? Does she hate me? Is it my fault? Why can't I do something?"

The late-stage alcoholic is isolated from friends and relatives. Social contacts have disintegrated. Neighbors lower their eyes.

---

* As A.A. members say, skid row is not a geographic location, but a condition between the ears.

Relatives may be so paralyzed by anger or grief that they, too, stop trying. The alcoholic "problem" is ignored, put out of mind, locked away where it cannot hurt so much. Late-stage alcoholics are not totally alone, however, for they are in frequent contact with the caretakers of our society—police officers, social workers, doctors, emergency room personnel, and public health workers. These are the people who will either refer them for effective help or finally pull the sheet over their head.

Help must come fast for the late-stage alcoholic, but it must be the right kind of help. With effective intervention and treatment, even the most advanced, deathly ill alcoholic may recover. The human organism has extraordinary abilities to restore or compensate for damaged tissues. The surviving cells can regenerate, poisons can be flushed out, and the body can begin the slow process of healing itself. Most alcoholics now sober were once considered "hopeless" by the people close to them.

8

Getting the Alcoholic into Treatment

I doubt if any alcoholic ever wakes up, looks out the window, and says, "This would be a nice day to go for rehabilitation. I think I'll call the doctor." He may not see the gun, but some type of pressure—outside forces or his health—motivates him.

—Thomas Fleming, M.D.[1]

Without help, most alcoholics cannot permanently quit drinking. A combination of factors works to imprison the alcoholic within the addiction. In the early, adaptive stage, before social and psychological problems develop, neither the alcoholic nor those around them see any reason why they should stop drinking. As problems do begin to develop, the heavy drinking is generally seen as merely a symptom, and the alcoholic may be advised to get help with their "underlying problems." Later, when the heavy drinking itself is clearly contributing to their problems, alcoholics and others are more likely to conclude that they should cut down on their drinking, not that they should quit altogether.

Typically, only when the more blatant symptoms of alcoholism develop does anyone suggest that the alcoholic ought to stop drinking completely. By this time, the alcoholic's mental processes are firmly under the influence of the addiction, and their need to drink pushes aside all rational concerns about the harmful consequences of continuing to drink. They may come to realize that they should stop drinking, and under pressure they may even go on the wagon for a while. But without a new perspective on the problem and a sustaining force powerful enough to override the addiction, all such periods of abstinence are temporary.

More often, alcoholics will reject any idea that they should stop drinking. Dimly they may realize that their problems are connected with drinking, but the addiction blinds them to the fact that alcohol is causing those problems. Alcohol is their first aid and their medicine. It is the effective remedy for the psychological and physical pain that ails them, immediately relieving their anguish and tension, stopping their hands from shaking and their stomach from heaving, allowing them to think more clearly and act more normally, and, particularly in the later stages of the disease, providing the only moments when they are released from suffering. When they stop drinking, the real trouble begins. The tension, frustrations, tremors, irritability, and nausea finally become so unbearable that they have to drink because alcohol is the quickest way to relieve the pain.

Alcoholics need help, and they need it as early in their disease as possible. The widely accepted belief that alcoholics have to "hit bottom" before they can be helped has been completely discredited in recent years. Waiting for the alcoholic to realize they need treatment is simply a mistake, for if they are left to their own devices, they are likely to become less willing to seek treatment, not more willing. If treatment is delayed until alcoholics are so ravaged by their disease that their liver and brain are permanently damaged, their family members have given up on them, their employer has fired them, and they are living on welfare, it may have been delayed too long.

Alcoholics who can stand on their feet, who still hold a job, and whose relationships are intact may insist that they do not have a problem and stubbornly refuse to get help. They may lie, steal, and cheat to protect their right to drink. But their deceptions and refusals are no indication that treatment will fail. No matter how fiercely the alcoholic fights those who want to help them stop drinking, they can be helped more often than not.

While many people fear that forcing alcoholics into treatment is demoralizing, challenging self-sufficiency and undermining the possibility of a stable, long-term recovery, recent research shows that while "involuntary" patients might appear less ready or willing to change, their motivation when admitted to treatment is "unexpectedly high" and similar to that of alcoholics who voluntarily enter treatment. Six months after treatment, 75 percent of involuntary patients acknowledged that they needed treatment and expressed gratitude for the experience. The researchers conclude that patients who are mandated or involuntarily admitted to treatment have "as good or better outcomes" as patients who are voluntarily admitted.[2]

Well over half of the alcoholics now being treated successfully were forced into treatment against their will; they did not want to stop drinking, but certain crises in their lives backed them into a corner and forced them to seek help. For one alcoholic, the motivating force may have been her husband's threat to pack up and leave if she did not get help; another alcoholic may have finally agreed to enter treatment after getting drunk and smashing his car into a bridge abutment. Early- and middle-stage alcoholics have been pushed into treatment by spouses planning divorce, employers threatening loss of jobs, judges offering the choice of treatment or jail, landlords threatening eviction, and doctors warning of fatal consequences if drinking continues.

Guidelines for Helping

Rather than waiting for such a crisis to occur, strategies have been developed in recent years to use the involvement of those closest to the alcoholic to convince them to accept treatment. Anyone who hopes to help an alcoholic should follow five basic guidelines.

Learn About the Disease

Understand the nature of the chemical alcohol, how alcohol affects the alcoholic and the nonalcoholic in different ways, and why alcoholics continue to drink when drinking is obviously harming them.

Learn about the early-, middle-, and late-stage symptoms of the disease and how these symptoms change as the alcoholic continues to drink. Learn about the underlying physiological changes, including adaptation, tolerance, physical dependence, and the withdrawal syndrome, all of which have a profound effect on the alcoholic's behavior. Finally, learn why the alcoholic needs to drink, why they become irritable, frustrated, and depressed when they are not drinking, and why their sincere promises to stop drinking are washed away like writing on sand.

Avoid Moral Judgment

The alcoholic is a sick person, not a bad person. Alcoholics need compassion and understanding, not anger and indifference. Moral judgment and condescending attitudes only make them defensive and hostile and push them even further away from treatment.

Develop an Emotional Detachment

The person trying to help must understand that the alcoholic is both physically and psychologically sick and that their behavior is governed by their addiction. When drinking or between drunks, the alcoholic acts in bizarre and unpredictable ways. At one moment, they may be consumed with self-pity and sincere promises to change their ways; moments later, they may angrily deny that they have a drinking problem and become belligerent or indignant when anyone suggests that they do. Remember that the alcoholic believes what he or she has been taught—that alcoholism is a symptom of underlying psychological and social problems. They interpret the facts as evidence that their drinking is caused by events outside their control.

If the alcoholic's family or friends become emotionally embroiled in these excuses and denials or believe that they are somehow responsible for causing the alcoholic's unhappiness, the real problem—the physical addiction—will get sidetracked, and the psychological symptoms will be mistaken as the source of all the trouble. The helper must remember that their first and most important priority is to get the alcoholic into treatment and off alcohol. Only after the alcoholic's body has a chance to recover from its long, poisonous alcohol bath can there be a return to psychological and emotional stability.

Pick a Specific Treatment Program

Not all treatment programs are the same, and some treatment programs are simply not effective in helping alcoholics recover. Those who are trying to help the alcoholic into treatment should understand the limitations of various treatment programs. Outpatient programs, for example, offer counseling services but have no inpatient medical facilities. Most general hospitals provide brief inpatient detoxification but offer little or no intensive alcoholism treatment as such. Alcoholics Anonymous (A.A.) is not really a treatment program, as it provides no detoxification facilities, medical support, or professional counseling services—but as a program for helping the alcoholic to maintain sobriety after treatment, A.A. is the best there is.*

The early-, middle-, and late-stage alcoholic will have the best chance of long-term recovery if they are treated in a comprehensive, disciplined program that includes the following:

- Inpatient medical detoxification
- A four-week minimum of inpatient care
- Educational programs that stress the physical basis of the disease and its role in causing psychological and social symptoms
- Intensive nutritional therapy and education

---

*See Chapter 9 for a detailed discussion of Alcoholics Anonymous and recent research demonstrating its effectiveness in helping alcoholics get and remain sober over the long term. The features of an effective, comprehensive treatment program are also more fully discussed in Chapter 9.

- Strong emphasis on A.A. and/or other mutual recovery support groups for long-term sobriety and fellowship
- Thorough follow-up care and continuing care over the long term (as is routinely offered with other chronic, progressive diseases such as diabetes and heart disease)
- Involvement of the family in treatment and follow-up care

If possible, the family, employer, or friend should select an inpatient program that comes as close to meeting these criteria as possible. Not every alcoholic can attend such a program, due to limited availability of quality programs, lack of financial resources, or insufficient or inappropriate guidance from knowledgeable healthcare professionals. However, if the only ready options are outpatient programs or A.A., they should by all means be tried. Just one warning, however: If the alcoholic returns to drinking, the family and friends should not give up, saying, "We tried treatment, and it didn't work." They should instead try to find a program that gives the alcoholic a better chance of recovery, and if that treatment fails, they should try again and again. While relapses are discouraging, they are not the end of the road. In fact, most alcoholics now sober have had at least one relapse on the way to lasting sobriety.

Finally, if left to their own devices, alcoholics will likely select a program that provides the least interference with their drinking. An outpatient program that requires only an hour a day with a counselor or a weekly A.A. meeting would be more to the alcoholic's liking than a four-week-minimum inpatient program, which would completely cut off their access to alcohol. Their primary reason for rejecting inpatient treatment will be denied and masked by the argument that they can't afford the program or that they can't take the necessary time off from work. It is thus important that people closest to the alcoholic, including family, friends, and knowledgeable healthcare providers, intervene in the choice of a rigorous, high-quality program that maximizes the likelihood of the alcoholic's recovery.

Get Help

A careful intervention strategy must be worked out in advance. Years ago when First Lady Betty Ford showed signs and symptoms of alcoholism and prescription drug addiction, her family sat her down and outlined why they thought she had a drinking problem. Their words were carefully rehearsed. Under the guidance of a physician and nurse from a successful treatment program, the family members had prepared what they were going to say. Mrs. Ford's excuses, denials, anger, and tears were all expected, and the family knew how to use the intervention to force her to a realization of her addiction.

Those who hope to help alcoholics into treatment will need help themselves. Among the many website offerings for families, www.gethelpgivehelp.info and www.drugfree.org are among the best, offering comprehensive, up-to-date, easy-to-use information with no commercial ties to specific agencies or programs. An online search for "alcoholism agencies" or "alcoholism treatment programs" offers dozens of leads to helpful resources. Talk to counselors and treatment staff, ask specific questions, and press for specific answers: "What do I do if he ignores me, becomes angry, or refuses to talk?" "How do I convince her that she needs treatment?" Books on intervention are listed in the Suggested Reading List.[*] Helpful, unbiased resources are available through government agencies, including NIAAA and the Substance Abuse and Mental Health Services Administration (SAMHSA).

Individuals can also learn a great deal by attending some A.A. and Al-Anon meetings. A.A. has open meetings that anyone can attend; just call the local A.A. number listed online and ask for specific times and meeting places. Al-Anon is an organization patterned after A.A. but specifically designed for the concerned nonalcoholic. Both A.A. and Al-Anon offer the family and friends of alcoholics the solace of

---

[*] More than forty-five years ago Vernon Johnson first detailed the concept and process of intervention in his classic book *I'll Quit Tomorrow*.

knowing that they are not alone and that others have been through similar or worse ordeals.

Who Can Help?
The Family

Of all the people who can help the alcoholic into treatment and support their recovery after treatment, the alcoholic's spouse and children may be the most effective. The family has firsthand experience with the alcoholic, they know how serious the drinking problem is and how far it has progressed, and they often have the emotional power to compel the alcoholic to seek treatment.

The family's deep emotional involvement with the alcoholic can also be a burden, however. The family may be so desolated by the alcoholic's behavior that they are paralyzed with grief and guilt and unable to help. They may be so filled with shame that they hide the problem and refuse to discuss it with anyone. Or they may be so familiar with the alcoholic's suffering when they stop drinking that they are reluctant to ask them to stop.

In order to help the alcoholic, the family must learn as much as they can about this disease and understand that they are not responsible for the alcoholic's behavior. Nothing they have said or done has caused the alcoholic to act the way they do. The disease itself is responsible for the alcoholic's behavior and personality changes. By learning about the disease, the family can keep an emotional distance from the problems and understand why alcoholics think and behave in characteristic ways, and what they can do to help them.

The family must also understand that the alcoholic has to stop drinking or they will continue to get worse. Waiting until the alcoholic realizes the extent of the problem is waiting too long, for the family itself may be destroyed by their involvement, and without the family's involvement, participation, and support the alcoholic is less likely to get help.

The family can let the alcoholic's physician know the extent of the problem and enlist their help in getting the alcoholic into treatment. The spouse can explain the facts of the disease to the children so that they understand their alcoholic parent's behavior and what must be done to make them well again. The family can also talk to friends and relatives, outline the problems at home, and make sure that they, too, understand the seriousness of the alcoholic's continued drinking.

A major problem at this point may be one of misguided loyalty. The family may feel disloyal when they reveal confidences or begin planning interventions behind the alcoholic's back, and the alcoholic, of course, will cry "traitor" if they get wind of their family's plans. But families cannot rely on alcoholics to help themselves. Family members demonstrate their true loyalty when they do everything in their power to help the alcoholic get well.

When devising an intervention strategy, the family should seek enlightened professional counsel. Intervention specialists, addiction medicine specialists, specialized treatment staff, A.A. members, physicians, clergy members, and community alcoholism counselors may all be of help in choosing the best available treatment program and planning the intervention.

Finally, having enlisted the help of the alcoholic's friends, relatives, and physician, armed with knowledge about the disease and how it can best be treated, and backed by professional advice and counsel, the family can squarely confront the drinking problem. Refusing to accept the alcoholic's denials and evasions, the family members can calmly and firmly tell them that they have a disease, they need help, and help is available. The alcoholic must know that the family is not bluffing, and the family should therefore be prepared to follow through on appropriate boundaries or consequences.

This road is not an easy one. Alcoholics may deny their problems, throw tantrums, or weep with self-pity. There may be ugly quarrels and moments when hope and optimism are just too painful to hold on to. Friends and relatives who do not understand the disease may believe the family is overreacting. Encounters with unenlightened physicians, psychiatrists, and other professionals who insist that the alcoholic is psychologically or emotionally disturbed rather than suffering from a physiological addiction may be frustrating and confusing.

Once the alcoholic's family know the facts of the disease, however, they can do something about it, and doing something for the alcoholic is, however difficult, less painful than continuing to be involved in their slow death. Covering up, ignoring, or denying the disease is a sure way to prolong the agony. If the alcoholic keeps drinking, the disease cannot get better—it can only get worse.

The Employer

The employer can wield enormous influence over the alcoholic's decision to enter treatment. It is the employer who can pose the critical choice: enter treatment or lose their job. As former congressperson and recovering alcoholic Wilbur Mills once said, "An alcoholic may be insane, but he's not crazy. He'll go to a facility any time rather than lose his job. He has to have money to finance his habit."[3]

In order to exercise their power over the alcoholic, employers must understand the disease, gather the evidence carefully, and then, preferably with the family's knowledge and consent, clearly explain the facts to the alcoholic. These interventions are most effective when they are conducted by several people the alcoholic knows and respects and when the evidence is presented clearly and without moral condescension or judgment. For example, the employer might say:

John, last Friday a group of your fellow employees picked you up off the floor of the bar next door and deposited you in a taxicab. You cursed and attacked the driver, who immediately opened the door and kicked you out. You went back into the bar, where you took a swing at your coworker and accused him of trying to steal your job, punched an innocent bystander in the jaw, and then passed out on the table. Three weeks ago, the janitor found an empty whiskey bottle under your desk. Another employee tells me you insulted a customer at lunch last week and told him to take his "filthy business" elsewhere; he called me today and canceled his account. Last month you were out sick five days; last year you took forty sick days. I have reports here from your supervisors, complaints from the people who work with you, customer complaints, and a list of your sick days and accident reports—and they all add up to a serious problem. We believe you have a chronic and progressive disease, and we want you to get well. You are a valued and respected employee. But we cannot allow this to continue any longer. For your sake and for the sake of this company, we must offer you a choice: either go for treatment, or you are fired. I'm afraid that is all there is to it.

Such a factual presentation squarely backs the alcoholic into a corner. They are no longer able to pretend that their life is normal or that their drinking does not interfere with their work. The hard evidence is there, and the boss is not backing down.

The employer's emotional distance from the alcoholic is another powerful weapon. The alcoholic's family will frequently accept the blame for the alcoholic's drinking and suffer from confused feelings of guilt, inadequacy, and shame. Many families are unwilling or unable to leave the alcoholic or force them out of the house because they fear that will destroy rather than help them. The employer, on the other hand, has a business relationship with the alcoholic and is usually able to maintain a professional detachment. Unlike the family members, the employer is specifically concerned with the economics of the situation, and they can verify their observations with facts from the personnel record or written reports from other employees. The employer can document hours of work missed, sick days, complaints, and supervisor comments and then clearly and unemotionally present these facts to the alcoholic.

Employer interventions are successful also because the employer is dealing with an alcoholic who is still able to come to work and at least keep up a semblance of normal behavior. If the alcoholic is still working, he or she is probably in the early or middle stages of their disease. They still have some pride and sense of personal integrity, their physical and mental health is not too impaired, and their job is usually extremely important to them. All these factors help fuel the alcoholic's motivation to get and stay sober.

The Physician

The family physician can be pivotal in alcoholism treatment, helping the alcoholic to realize the serious medical consequences of drinking, providing information and referral to an effective treatment program, and supporting the alcoholic's sobriety after the specialized treatment. The strictly medical aspects of their role are quickly learned. Effective patient management, however, requires much more than mere relief of acute medical symptoms. In order to be really helpful, the physician must acquire special knowledge of the disease, its causes, and progressive symptoms, and learn how to guide the patient into treatment. Because few medical schools include any significant education or training in alcoholism, the average physician needs to do some self-education. Reading alcoholism literature and attending some A.A. meetings are good places to start.* Most physicians soon learn, however, that they can make the most effective use of their time and talent by working closely with an addiction medicine specialist, preferably one who is an alcoholic in long-term recovery and who is active both in a professional role and in A.A. Through these relationships, physicians can soon familiarize themselves with the various treatment programs, costs, admission procedures, and staff liaisons so that they can advise the alcoholic about specialized treatment.

* See the Suggested Reading List, page 243.

Once educated about the disease, the physician is in a position to be particularly helpful. They can:

- Diagnose the disease in its early stages, recognizing the psychological symptoms of depression, irritability, moodiness, and anxiety for what they are—evidence of the underlying physiological disease of alcoholism
- Go beyond halfhearted warnings such as "You should cut down on your drinking" and instead outline exactly what will happen medically to the alcoholic if he or she continues to drink
- Recommend specific treatment options and explain the advantages and disadvantages of each
- Maintain regular contact with the alcoholic, following up on the referral to make sure that the alcoholic gets into treatment once they are diagnosed
- Involve the family in helping to motivate the alcoholic into treatment and then help the family to deal with any problems that may arise after treatment
- Encourage the alcoholic's attendance at A.A. meetings or other mutual support groups
- Warn the alcoholic about the risks of taking drugs of any kind—particularly sedatives, tranquilizers, and painkillers, which are addictive and interfere with alcoholism recovery
- Warn the alcoholic about taking any medication or foods that contain alcohol*

Alcoholics must almost inevitably go through a series of crises before they are able to recognize the seriousness of their disease. The physician can speed this process along by helping their alcoholic patients face the realities of their drinking behavior and, at the same time, by letting them know that help is available. Most important, the physician can refuse to give up on the alcoholic. Alcoholics can

---

* See Appendix A for a list of such medications.

often miss appointments, stubbornly deny drinking problems, and continue to drink despite serious warnings. The physician must understand that the alcoholic's behavior is governed by their addiction and that they are incapable of acting in a normal, responsible fashion, whether they are drinking or between drunks.

Police Officers, Judges, and Attorneys

Police officers are in constant contact with alcoholics, picking them up for drunk driving, car accidents, vagrancy, street fights, theft, assault, disorderly conduct, and public drunkenness. The police officer is not a diagnostician or a social worker, but given appropriate training, they can learn that alcoholics are not primarily criminals or mentally disturbed individuals but victims of an addiction they are helpless to control. The police officer's response can then be one of compassionate discipline rather than hostility or disgust. They will understand that the alcoholic's problems cannot be solved either by punishment or by a hot meal and a place to sleep. Instead, the alcoholic may need medical care to help them through withdrawal or for other complications associated with alcoholism. In both subtle and obvious ways, the police officer can influence the alcoholic to see themselves as a sick person who needs special help.

Judges know well that people with legal troubles often also have drinking problems. A person with a history of DUI (driving under the influence) arrests, car accidents, divorce, and financial problems is very likely an alcoholic in need of specialized help. If the judge suspects alcoholism, they can require the offender to be diagnosed and evaluated by a competent alcoholism specialist. If the diagnosis is alcoholism, judges can then use their full powers to get the alcoholic into the recommended treatment program.

Whenever possible, judges should require an effective inpatient program. But if outpatient treatment is the choice, the alcoholic should be put on notice that if they return to drinking they will be immediately remanded to inpatient treatment. A minimum two-year probation period should be established, and the alcoholic's sobriety should be monitored closely during probation. The most effective treatment programs are those requiring A.A. or other mutual support group attendance during probation.

Enlightened attorneys are also in a position to identify alcoholic clients and motivate them toward effective treatment. The alert attorney knows that legal problems and alcohol problems go hand in hand. They can ask detailed, personal questions of their client, and since the client usually expects these questions, they answer them freely. They listen to the attorney's advice because they need to have their problems solved, they are dependent on the attorney to help them, and they know that if they refuse to heed the advice, severe legal penalties may await them.

Again, the attorney is not a trained diagnostician or alcoholism counselor, but they can learn the symptoms of alcoholism, and they can refer their clients to an alcoholism specialist for diagnosis and recommendation. Attorneys can then use every weapon in their arsenal, including their powers of argument, patience, and perseverance, their familiarity with the painful consequences of repeat offenses, and their knowledge of available treatment programs to direct the alcoholic into effective treatment.

Alcoholics Anonymous

Alcoholics Anonymous is the best program in existence for helping alcoholics to stay sober, but it is not a particularly effective vehicle for getting the alcoholic sober in the first place. A.A. is not a treatment program because it has no detoxification facilities or staff, no twenty-four-hour medical care, no professional counseling services, and no authority to ensure patient compliance with a treatment regimen. Alcoholics who attempt to get sober through A.A. must detoxify themselves, a difficult and painful process that only a minority of alcoholics can endure without resorting to alcohol for relief from withdrawal.

In the past, many A.A. members were wary of formal treatment programs, and therefore did not advise alcoholics struggling to get sober on their own to seek inpatient treatment. Historically, there are understandable reasons for this distrust. A.A. members were all too aware of the condescension and judgmental attitudes about alcoholism that pervaded conventional health agencies. They may have been drugged with tranquilizers and sedatives, have spent years in expensive and fruitless psychotherapy, and have endured indifferent and even hostile professional attitudes toward them and their disease. Many of these early A.A. members came to believe that only an alcoholic can help another alcoholic, which is the basis of the belief that only alcoholics can lead alcoholics to sobriety. These beliefs were founded in experience, for not until they came into A.A. did many alcoholics find others who really understood their problems and could help them to accept the disease and stop drinking. The long-standing antagonism to alcoholism treatment programs appears to be lessening, however, as programs emerge that are based on an understanding of the addiction, are staffed by recovering alcoholics, and emphasize A.A. attendance for staying sober. But some degree of distrust lingers on.

Another tenet of A.A. philosophy that works against early treatment is the idea of "hitting bottom," generally expressed as the belief that alcoholics can be helped only when they realize the hopelessness of their condition and are willing to accept help. This belief, too, has changed over the years, but A.A. is generally a self-help organization, and many members still cling to the idea that alcoholics must first come to grips with their problems and then get themselves into treatment.

Finally, A.A. is of limited help in getting the alcoholic into treatment because it lacks potent leverage. Unlike the spouse, the employer, the physician, or the attorney, A.A. does not have the power or influence necessary to pressure the alcoholic into treatment by threatening an even less attractive alternative.

A.A. members do, however, have the wisdom of experience.

They have suffered through the disease, and with the wisdom of their own experience they can tell the alcoholic what to expect if he or she continues to drink. As more and more individuals find their way into A.A. and encourage friends and family members to intervene and help alcoholics into treatment before they hit bottom, countless numbers are being spared the suffering and humiliation of the later stages of the disease.

Friends

Friends can do more to hurt than help the alcoholic. They are frequently guided by the misconception that alcoholism is an emotional weakness and are therefore unwilling to attach the label "alcoholic" to someone they love and respect. They are also accustomed to defending their friend against criticism because "that is what a friend should do." By failing to recognize that the alcoholic has a serious and potentially fatal illness, a friend may actually be placing subtle pressure on the alcoholic to keep drinking in order to prove that they are indeed a "normal" drinker.

Even if friends want to help, they often feel frustrated and helpless. They may make tentative advances, only to have the alcoholic become hostile and defensive. "What can I do?" they may ask. "It's not my place to tell them to stop drinking!"

Yet the alcoholic's friends can help. Armed with correct information, a friend can help the alcoholic realize their problem and confront it. The friend must also learn, however, how to approach the alcoholic. If they attack, the alcoholic will defend, and no good will come of the encounter; if they approach with understanding and compassion, the chances that the alcoholic will listen and act are much greater.

Friends can also talk to the alcoholic's family and encourage them to seek help. They can refuse to be manipulated by the alcoholic's rationalizations and denials and make clear to the alcoholic that they have a problem and need help. The alcoholic may simply ignore the friend's advice, or they may be so furious with their friend for threatening their continued freedom to drink that the friendship may not survive. But the risk is worth it. Friends who refuse to support the alcoholic's continued drinking are expressing their concern for the alcoholic's life. This concern may make a profound difference.

Acquaintances and Associates

The person motivating the alcoholic to seek help need not be an intimate friend, family member, or someone with formal or tacit authority over the alcoholic such as a judge or physician. Many alcoholics have been guided into treatment by casual acquaintances or associates such as teachers, taxi drivers, hospital orderlies, or landlords.

The critical determinant of whether an individual can help is not who they are but how well they understand the disease. Their attitude toward the alcoholic will also affect the alcoholic's willingness to listen and respond to advice. A sympathetic and knowledgeable taxi driver can be more help to a drinking alcoholic than an uninformed physician who refers the alcoholic to a psychiatrist to "work out their underlying emotional problems" or gives them tranquilizers and sends them home. A landlord who serves a tenant with a court order offering the choice of eviction or treatment does more to force recognition of the problem than the man who buys his wife alcohol every day because he knows she feels better when she is drinking.

The point is that anyone can help push the alcoholic toward treatment. The basic tools needed are a comprehensive knowledge of the disease, an understanding that alcoholics are physically and emotionally sick and that their behavior is governed by their addiction, a recognition of the fact that in many if not most cases they are unable to help themselves, an ability to be emotionally detached, and a refusal to participate in fear, guilt, shame, anger, or pity.

9

A Guide to Treatment

It's a long road to a good sobriety. But I can wait. I can put one foot in front of the other. Life has meaning if not perfection. I'll be with my family tonight and find joy in being with them. I'll get up tomorrow and go to work—without cold sweat, headache, and misery in just the thought of another day of exertion with another hangover. I don't have life all worked out—I never will, or there would be no challenge to it. But working on the mystery of it has its own rare rewards. There's a chance for happiness now. I didn't have that before.

—A recovered alcoholic

Historical Perspective

In 1804 Thomas Trotter, an Edinburgh physician, wrote a paper stating his belief that habitual drunkenness was a disease:

In medical language, I consider drunkenness, strictly speaking, to be a disease, produced by a remote cause, and giving birth to actions and movements in the living body that disorder the functions of health.[1]

Trotter's essay provoked an explosive controversy that continues to this day. In one sentence, he challenged the moral code of a society, threatened a basic tenet of the Christian church, and questioned the medical profession's traditional lack of involvement with the drunkard. Ever since Trotter, society has been deeply divided over the question: Is alcoholism primarily a physiological disease, or is it, after all, a symptom of character inadequacy and emotional weakness? This is still the root of conflict and confusion in the alcoholism field today.*

The church's vehement opposition to Trotter's essay was based on several points. By elevating "depravity" to the status of "disease" and insisting that the victim was not responsible for his actions, Trotter threatened society's moral code, over which the church stood guardian. Throughout history, the habitual drunkard was considered a sinful and pitiful creature who, preferring vice to virtue, was responsible for their many troubles. This was part of the moral code, which proclaimed that drunkenness is bad, moderation is good; that drunkards are to be pitied and despised, abstainers are virtuous and admirable.

If excessive drinking is a disease, as Trotter proclaimed, the drinker cannot be held responsible for their own actions and are thus protected from moral condemnation and judgment. By shifting the blame from the alcoholic's character to a "remote cause" outside the alcoholic's control, Trotter's new theory confused the lines between "good" (that is, willpower, self-control, and moderation) and "evil" (that is, weakness of character, gluttony, and intemperance).

The medical profession was equally upset by Trotter's essay, which suggested that the treatment of this "disease" was mainly their responsibility. The physician's involvement with the drunkard had been limited to treating the physical complications accompanying excessive drinking, performing autopsies, and signing death certificates. The average physician viewed alcoholics with the same mixture of fear and disgust expressed by the rest of society, and most had no desire to spend their time ministering to men and women who presumably lacked motivation and ambition, consorted with unsavory characters, and carelessly threw their lives away in pursuit of debauchery.

---

* For the most comprehensive and enlightening look at the history of treatment and recovery in the United States, read *Slaying the Dragon: The History of Addiction Treatment and Recovery in America* by William L. White.

Without the moral approval of the church or the professional cooperation of the physician, the fledgling "disease concept" did not catch on. In fact, the first attempts to treat alcoholism as something other than a mental or social aberration encountered fierce and effective opposition. Almost a quarter century after Trotter's essay appeared, Eli Todd, medical superintendent of the Hartford Retreat for the Insane, suggested that it might be better to give "inebriates" a separate retreat rather than lump them with the insane and mentally incompetent. His indignant colleagues forced him to abandon the idea. A similar suggestion by the Connecticut State Medical Society two years later was also hastily scrapped for lack of support.

Not until 1841, when the Washington Home first opened in Boston, was an "institution for inebriates" able to withstand public disapproval and keep its doors open. The next sixty years witnessed an age of enlightenment in the study and treatment of inebriates; by 1900, over fifty public and private facilities had opened for the sole purpose of treating inebriates. In 1870, the American Association for the Cure of Inebriates (soon renamed the Association for the Study of Inebriety) was founded by a group of physicians and superintendents of inebriate asylums. In 1876, the association launched the *Quarterly Journal of Inebriety,* which, until it ceased publication in 1914, stimulated research and discussion by publishing hundreds of articles on alcohol-related issues.

Yet despite these significant advances, most people continued to view alcoholics as moral degenerates rather than the innocent and unwilling victims of a disease. The church insisted that the chronic inebriate was responsible for their unhappy state and needed the church's moral guidance to be reformed. The belief that alcoholism was a disease failed to ignite the interest of most physicians, and their acceptance of this revolutionary concept was half hearted at best.

Almost one hundred years after Trotter's essay first generated heated controversy, the moral and religious attitudes toward drunkards and drunkenness were, if anything, even more intense and intolerant. By the end of the nineteenth century, the burgeoning temperance movement had organized a crusade against alcohol at the national level, launching attacks from the pulpit with Bibles in hand and hymns of salvation. The Volstead Act, establishing national Prohibition in 1919, effectively eclipsed further study of alcoholism as a disease. Although Prohibition did reduce total alcohol consumption in the country, it had no long-term effect on alcoholism and thus missed its mark. As typically happens with misguided attempts to legislate morality, Prohibition not only failed to curb the original problem but added a host of others. Bootlegging, hijacking, and syndicated crime became so widespread that the whole experiment had to be abandoned.

Shortly after the repeal of Prohibition in 1933, an event occurred that reinstated alcoholism as a subject worthy of scientific interest. In 1935 the fellowship of Alcoholics Anonymous was begun by two men who had been given up as "hopeless" drunkards by their physicians. Both men were able to stay sober, and they went on to help thousands of other alcoholics recover in a program that relied on simple spiritual principles and the compassion and understanding of fellow sufferers to achieve total abstinence from alcohol. A.A. demonstrated for the first time that alcoholics in significant numbers could recover and return to productive, useful lives. Most important, it proved that alcoholics, when they stayed sober, were decent, normal human beings and not hopeless degenerates.

The significance of these insights was undermined, however, for A.A. had also embraced the moral attitudes of the day: while asserting that alcoholism is a disease, the program fixed the blame for contracting the disease squarely on the victim. In the books *Alcoholics Anonymous* (A.A.'s "bible") and *Twelve Steps and Twelve Traditions,* A.A.'s cofounder Bill Wilson refers repeatedly to "glaring personality defects" and "character flaws" that caused excessive drinking and thus alcoholism:

We reluctantly come to grips with those serious character flaws that made problem drinkers of us in the first place, flaws which must be dealt with to prevent a retreat into alcoholism once again.[2]

Thus, from its inception, A.A., like the rest of society, has mistaken the psychological consequences of alcoholism for its causes, and the moral approach of the program followed logically. The Christian formula of sin, repentance, and redemption can be clearly seen in A.A.'s Twelve Steps, especially Steps 4 through 7:

Step 4: Made a searching and fearless moral inventory of
    ourselves.

Step 5: Admitted to God, to ourselves, and to another human
    being, the exact nature of our wrongs.

Step 6: Were entirely ready to have God remove all these
    defects of character.

Step 7: Humbly asked Him to remove our shortcomings.[3]

Despite its moralistic foundation, however, A.A. worked as no other approach to alcoholism had before, and as a long-term sobriety maintenance program, there still is not even a distant rival. Thus A.A. stands as a colossal paradox. The fellowship has undoubtedly been the most powerful force in getting society to accept alcoholism as a treatable disease. Yet at the same time, it has become a powerful obstacle to accepting the otherwise overwhelming evidence that biological factors, not psychological or emotional factors, usher in the disease.

Nevertheless, A.A. has helped millions of alcoholics to get and stay sober. Inspired by A.A.'s early success, several major developments followed; like A.A., they moved the disease concept forward but also retained the belief that the onset of the disease is caused by defects of character. In 1940, the *Quarterly Journal of Studies on Alcohol* was established within the Laboratory of Applied Physiology at Yale University. Now titled the *Journal of Studies on Alcohol* and published by the Rutgers Center of Alcohol and Substance Use

Studies at Rutgers University, this publication renewed scientific interest in the physiological and biological aspects of alcoholism and reestablished alcoholism as a field worthy of scientific research. Once again, however, this influential effort was undermined by the age-old assumption that the cause of the disease was to be found in some mysterious character flaw or personality defect.

Having encouraged the development of the *Quarterly Journal* at Yale, Marty Mann, one of the first women members of A.A., also founded the voluntary lay organization that was later to become the National Council on Alcoholism (NCA). Along with A.A., NCA has helped to spread the idea that alcoholism is a treatable disease, while also maintaining the belief that psychological problems are the primary predisposing factors.

The impact of these developments was enormous, and the church and medical profession were finally forced to modify their positions. One hundred forty-two years after Trotter's essay, the Presbyterian Church became the first religious organization to acknowledge formally alcoholism's status as a disease. Note, however, the allowance for moral censure in the qualifying phrase of the proposition accepted at the church's 158th Assembly, in 1946: "*Once drinking has passed a certain point,* alcoholism is a disease; that is, the drinking cannot be stopped by a mere resolution on the part of the drinker" (italics added).

The medical profession shuffled its feet for another ten years until the American Medical Association (AMA) finally "voted" alcoholism a disease in 1956. Yet even here the disease concept was seriously compromised, for the main body of the medical profession continued to view alcoholism as a self-inflicted symptom of an underlying psychological inadequacy and relegated treatment of the disease to its psychiatric branch. More than thirty years would pass before the AMA granted the American Society of Addiction Medicine (ASAM) a seat and a vote in the AMA House of Delegates and agreed to recognize addiction as a "self-designated specialty." ASAM now has two seats and functions as a powerful advocate for state and national policy solutions, physician education, addiction treatment research, and access to high-quality, evidence-based treatment.

FROM THIS BRIEF history, it should be clear why alcoholism continues to be the arena of such intense conflict and emotional turmoil. Students of the disease have tried to have it both ways, proclaiming loudly that alcoholism is a treatable disease and at the same time continuing to affix the blame and stigma for contracting the disease on the character of the unwitting victim. Both scientists and treatment professionals striving to advance the disease concept of alcoholism defeat their own aims by continuing to believe, or condoning the belief, that alcoholism is caused by heavy drinking (pejoratively labeled alcohol "abuse"), which in turn is caused by defects in the drinker's psychological, social, and cultural fabric. This is the belief that keeps alive all the age-old myths and misconceptions and the stigma, shame, and contempt for the alcoholic that continue to cloud the field of alcoholism research.

Failure to recognize and dispose of this cancerous root results in a host of conflicts. Since the parties to the conflict are not dealing with the real problem, they end up fighting and arguing about superficial or irrelevant issues. Thus, even as scientific information accumulates explaining the hereditary physiological causes of alcoholism, professional attitudes remain mired in myth and misconception. In Henrik Wallgren and Herbert Barry's encyclopedic *Actions of Alcohol,* the authors comment:

> It is difficult to develop understanding of a subject which arouses strong emotions and deep prejudices. The large amount of information available about alcohol is mingled with a great deal of misinformation, and much of the literature is distorted by emotion and burdened with an evaluative purpose, either to attack or to defend the social use of the beverage. Most facts are used to support the evaluative conclusion that "alcohol is evil" or "alcohol is innocuous."

Accordingly, most of the literature on alcohol has little scientific value.[4] (Italics added)

While confusion about effective treatments for alcoholism still abounds in the professional arena, grassroots movements inspired by A.A. have given rise to a proliferation of treatment options. Today, there are more than eighteen thousand "substance abuse" treatment programs, and they come in a bewildering variety of philosophies and practices—inpatient and outpatient, public and private, hospital-based and non-hospital-based, long-term and short-term, medical and nonmedical, intensive and less so, and, more to the point, effective and ineffective.

Virtually all the effective programs have in common the understanding that alcoholism is a disease that can be treated, that it can be arrested but not cured, and that the cornerstone of full recovery must be continuous total abstinence from alcohol and substitute drugs. Many of these programs also usher their patients into A.A. for long-term sobriety maintenance after treatment. There are still programs, however, even those that are relatively successful in the short term, that base their treatment philosophies and strategies on the belief that alcoholism begins with a character flaw or other psychological inadequacy, and this belief is the major shortcoming among otherwise effective treatment programs everywhere.

By treating the psychological problems as primary rather than the physical disease and addiction, programs that could otherwise help more than 80 percent of their patients make lasting, high-quality recoveries instead can only claim recovery rates half that high and a relatively poorer quality of sobriety for their patients. These programs typically underestimate or miss completely the long-term effects of toxicity, malnutrition, hypoglycemia, and even the post-acute withdrawal syndrome in causing or aggravating the alcoholic's psychological problems. Instead, the recurring psychological problems are mistaken as evidence that the alcoholic is, at bottom, an inadequate, depressed, anxious, and self-destructive personality. As stressed throughout this book, such a view of the alcoholic's character and personality reinforces the sick alcoholic's belief that they are responsible for their disease, increases their guilt and shame, intensifies their anxiety and resentments, and stiffens their defensiveness against both the diagnosis of alcoholism and the proposed treatment. These aggravated symptoms then loom as the major problems to be "diagnosed" and treated rather than as the symptoms of an underlying physical disease.

A high proportion of treatment programs, especially outpatient programs, rely on "cold turkey" withdrawal—that is, withdrawal without benefit of medical care. Nearly half of the eighteen thousand treatment programs in this country do not have a physician available to their patients, with publicly funded programs most often lacking access to medical care and physician-directed diagnosis, treatment, and recovery planning. Of the treatment programs that do provide medical management of withdrawal, only a small minority provide intensive nutritional analysis and therapy.

Regardless of the treatment method, the majority of alcoholics have not had adequate diagnostic evaluations or treatment for their primary disease and its complications, for hypoglycemia, or for other nutritional complications. The most noticeable lingering symptoms of this neglect are chronic psychological problems. It is fair to conclude that the quality of their sobriety when treated in such settings is not high. In fact, it has been seriously compromised by their treatment.

More than 1.4 million people are admitted into addiction treatment programs every year, and only 43 percent complete treatment. When patients do not complete treatment, most programs offer no follow-up care in an effort to reengage the patient in treatment and recovery programs. Fifty-eight percent of people admitted to treatment programs have had at least one prior admission, yet they are once more offered the same treatment, or treatment that is even less effective, again with no offer of alternative or more intensive programs.

Also discouraging is the fact that every year more than 126,000 alcoholics are administratively discharged from treatment prior to achieving at least preliminary, stable sobriety due to the very symptoms of the disease of alcoholism, such as missed counseling sessions or relapse to alcohol consumption.[5] In contrast, premature discharge is rare or nonexistent for other diseases such as diabetes, cancer, or heart disease.

This relatively low quality of treatment, recovery support, and sobriety has been the only general norm available to researchers. It has therefore become the standard for evaluating alcoholics who have been through treatment and for comparing various treatment alternatives. To be more specific, if treatment programs are not based on a real understanding of alcoholism as a physical disease, if the medical and nutritional needs of patients are neglected, and if follow-up, family programs, and continuing care are unavailable, then it does not really matter whether treatment occurs in an inpatient or outpatient setting. If all an inpatient program has to offer is "cold turkey" withdrawal and A.A. orientation, then the staff will probably find it hard to justify holding the patient for longer than two or three weeks. And since the success rate (30 to 40 percent) and quality of sobriety (seriously flawed) of such a program can also be achieved in a purely outpatient setting, then many would argue, with some justification, that the outpatient form should be favored for economic reasons.*

So long as arguments about the type and duration of treatment are based on a lack of understanding of alcoholism as a physical disease and on low standards of success, treatment programs are not likely to improve. Unfortunately, both public policies and decisions by insurance companies concerning the funding of alcoholism treatment are presently being based on norms from these inadequate treatment programs.

* For "alcohol use disorders" of less severity and complexity, outpatient programs (including "virtual" options) may be successful. Essential elements of these programs, however, are access to physicians for diagnosis and ongoing medical care and assertive post-treatment monitoring and support.

Because of the controversy in the clinical world and the wide-spread limitations on the quality of treatment available, a word of advice is in order for the reader who is an alcoholic in need of treatment. First, rule out any program that does not at least have total abstinence as a treatment goal and also any program that pre-scribes substitute drugs beyond the acute withdrawal period. With these exceptions, go ahead and try the treatment available. Don't jeopardize your recovery by criticizing the program while you are still in it. Concentrate instead on the options offered that will help you to stay sober. A.A., for example, is in nearly every community, and attending their meetings will be most helpful.

The important point is that sobriety has to have first priority, for without it no other significant life improvements are possible. If you do stay sober, you will have plenty of time in the future to find ways to improve on nutrition and otherwise enhance the quality of life in sobriety. You are not alone, and you will find many other recovered alcoholics seeking the same objective.

Clearly, however, it is time to establish a higher standard of treatment based on an awareness of the physiological basis of the disease as presented in this book. A program that treats the disease of alcoholism as a primary, physiological disorder will view the patient's psychological complaints and disturbances as symptoms of the disease the alcoholic is living with and of the desperate state they are in. The staff will know that the disease has created a grotesque caricature of the underlying person. The alcoholic's anger, fear, depression, immaturity, and defensiveness will be treated for what they are: the outpourings of a sick brain. By consistently treating the patient's negative behavior as a symp-tom of their disease, the staff will let the alcoholic know that their condition is thoroughly understood. This approach will be enor-mously reassuring to sick alcoholics as they come to realize that not they but the illness is being blamed for their behavior and that their treatment is aimed at relieving their suffering and treating the underlying disease. The entire treatment sequence and the attitude of the staff toward the patients will be shaped by this understanding.

Such high-quality treatment programs are increasingly available in the United States and other countries. In 1970, the Alcenas Hospital program was founded expressly as a demonstration model of the understanding of alcoholism presented in this book, and although Alcenas no longer exists, the fundamental principles of its highly successful program still serve as a gold standard for other programs.[6] Except for the nutritional components, the Alcenas program may outwardly sound like many others—a private inpatient treatment program exclusively for alcoholics, a twenty-four-hour medical staff to help with detoxification and continuing medical care, a four-week minimum of inpatient treatment, lectures, films, tapes, group and individual counseling, group and individual family therapy, twelve weekly follow-up group counseling sessions, and A.A. participation during and after treatment.* What made the Alcenas program (and others today like it) unique, however, is the nutritional element and the fact that the *content* of the lectures and all other communications with the patients are expressions of the revolutionary understanding of alcoholism presented in this book.

The optimal treatment sequence as dictated by the disease itself and as tried and proven in more than eleven years of practical application at Alcenas Hospital is described in the remainder of this chapter.

A Model Treatment Program

Phase I: Getting Started

The first treatment priorities are to gain control of the addiction and to assess for any underlying medical conditions or complications.

* The nutritional program at Alcenas included nutritional analysis (laboratory workup, five-hour glucose tolerance test, skilled staff evaluation) and intensive nutritional therapy.

The best way to achieve these objectives is to get the alcoholic into a hospital or other inpatient treatment center with a medical staff and modern medical facilities. Alcoholics simply have a better chance of recovery if they are placed in a controlled medical setting where their drinking can be stopped with certainty, medication can be used to control the withdrawal symptoms, laboratory workups can be conducted to assess complications and nutritional needs, diet and nutritional supplements can be fully controlled, and a competent medical staff can be on hand twenty-four hours a day to handle any emergencies and to monitor progress.

Alcoholics detoxified in a nonmedical setting suffer unnecessarily and may be in grave physical danger. An untrained, nonmedical staff may inaccurately diagnose the alcoholic's complaints and neglect underlying medical problems such as pneumonia or infections. Without adequate laboratory procedures, the alcoholic's physical health cannot be effectively assessed and monitored. Inpatient medical care, on the other hand, provides priceless insurance against medical complications and severe withdrawal symptoms and gives alcoholics the comfort and security they need during the sometimes traumatic first days of treatment.

Effective treatment includes a thorough medical examination, bed rest, fluids as indicated, medication to prevent the more serious withdrawal reactions, and a balanced diet with vitamin and mineral supplements as individually indicated. Injectable supplements should be available and used in the first few days of treatment or until the patient is able to absorb and utilize oral supplements. With this care, the withdrawal syndrome presents no serious problems for the majority of alcoholics.

Some alcoholics will be prone to grand mal convulsions, hallucinations, extreme mental confusion, or dangerous fluctuations in blood pressure, temperature, and pulse rate during withdrawal. These symptoms typically occur in more advanced alcoholics, or in patients with major medical complications such as liver disease, hemorrhage, pneumonia, heart disease, and gastrointestinal disturbances. An alcoholic who has been drinking the equivalent of a fifth of whiskey daily for several weeks is also a likely candidate for these major withdrawal symptoms. With intensive medical care, however, even the most severe withdrawal symptoms can be prevented or minimized.

Because histories taken at the time of admission are notoriously unreliable, it is sometimes difficult to determine which patients are at risk for the more serious withdrawal reactions. Therefore, all severely ill patients should be given a controlling level of tranquilizing medication as a preventive safety measure. The drug dosage should then be decreased each day and typically discontinued after a few days of treatment. After the acute withdrawal period, no tranquilizers or sedatives should be used. However, other medications necessary for the control of heart disease, diabetes, or epilepsy may be used as required.

After a few days in detoxification, the crisis is over for most patients. The acute withdrawal symptoms fade, and the alcoholic feels better and can begin to think more clearly. Some treatment programs, notably state or county detoxification centers, release alcoholics at this point, when they are "dry" and the worst of the withdrawal symptoms appear to be over. Unfortunately, the addiction is still strongly in control during this period, and too often the first thing the alcoholic does after leaving the treatment center is find a drink. Thus, the alcoholic who is hospitalized for three or four days, detoxified, given a bottle of vitamins and/or antidepressant drugs, and then released has not been adequately treated. Their hands will shake, their body's cells will cry out for alcohol, and they will continue to be confused, depressed, and fearful. They will almost invariably drink again as soon as they leave the protection of the treatment center, because they do not yet have the ability to choose not to drink.

Treatment must be more than an interlude between binges. It must do more than get alcoholics dry and back on their feet. It must go on to get them started in a new life of sobriety.

Phase II: Into a New Lifestyle

After a few days of good food, nutritional supplements, rest, medical attention, and abstinence from alcohol, most patients experience a noticeable transformation. Clouded eyes clear, hands stop shaking, posture straightens, thinking becomes more rational, and depression, insomnia, and paranoia begin to fade. At this point, most patients are ready to begin the second phase of treatment: learning about their disease and what they must do to cope with it.

Some alcoholics—particularly late-stage, severely malnourished alcoholics with medical complications such as cirrhosis or gastritis—may require a longer time in detox and may not be able to absorb new information as quickly or completely as the relatively healthier patients. The treatment program should recognize that every patient is different despite the fact that they all suffer from the same basic disease, and it should allow extra time for those patients who are having difficulty thinking clearly, concentrating, remembering, or relating to other people.

Educating alcoholics about their illness would not be such an important or difficult part of treatment if everyone in society understood the disease and why certain people cannot drink "normally." But misunderstandings abound, and alcoholics themselves are always confused about their disease. They must be reeducated—told why they are an alcoholic, what they must do to get well, and how they can protect themselves against internal and external pressures to drink when they leave treatment. Information and education alone cannot keep an alcoholic sober, but they are essential to the patient's motivation and ability to learn the lifestyle that will protect their sobriety. The three main elements of this protective system are understanding the nature of the disease, nutritional discipline, and A.A. participation.

Understanding the Nature of the Disease.   The alcoholic must fully and completely understand the disease—how it occurs, how it has affected their personality and behavior, why they are depressed when they stop drinking, why alcohol makes them feel better, why they experience the urge to drink, why they cannot ever safely take a drink, why they will return to drinking if they are not protected. All of these questions must be confronted and answered. Once alcoholics understand the disease, they will also understand what they must do to control it.

Alcoholics must also understand that they are not responsible for the things they said or did when they were drinking. The physical addiction controlled their behavior, and because they are powerless over the addiction, they cannot be held responsible for it. When alcoholics look back at their lives as drinking alcoholics, they should learn to say, "That's what alcohol did to me," not "That's what I did." Saying the words "I am an alcoholic" should convey the same moral overtones as the words "I am allergic to pollen."

In counseling sessions, alcoholics should be encouraged to confront their drinking life, but there should be no attempt to analyze their behavior or dig down and uproot past traumas, psychological problems, or conscious or unconscious conflicts. Efforts to analyze the alcoholic's drinking behavior in these terms only heighten their guilt, shame, resentments, and frustrations. The purpose of counseling in treatment during the acute and post-withdrawal period should instead be to build up their self-confidence and self-respect and to encourage normal interactions with other patients and the treatment staff. The emphasis should be on the present and the future, not the past, and alcoholics should be taught to disown their past behavior as foreign to their true nature, as actions dictated by a sick and poisoned brain. They must come to believe that they could no more control their reaction to alcohol than an epileptic could control the electrical activity in their brain causing seizures.

Once the alcoholic understands the disease and what it takes to stay sober, however, a moral obligation does enter the picture. *Now they know:* if they follow the sobriety maintenance program, they will stay sober; if they willfully or carelessly deviate from the program, they will drink again and inflict the illness on themselves and others. They have a clear choice now, and they should feel the moral imperative to make the right choice.

Nutritional Discipline.   Nutritional therapy is critical to successful treatment, and yet it is a neglected or slighted feature of almost every treatment program in this country. The alcoholic must receive vitamin and mineral supplements in order to repair the cellular damage caused by years of drinking. Given proteins, vitamins, and minerals in correct amounts and proportions, the body will be able to generate new cells, repair injured cells, and strengthen its defenses against other diseases. Also important is a high-protein, low-carbohydrate diet, which will control the alcoholic's chronic low blood sugar and prevent the symptoms associated with this condition, including depression, irritability, anxiety, shakiness, headaches, and mental confusion. If, after treatment, the alcoholic maintains a lifelong dietary regime with appropriate vitamin and mineral supplements, the addiction will remain dormant, and they will not be threatened by the craving for alcohol that plagues so many alcoholics for months and years after their last drink.

Why, then, do so many treatment programs ignore or downplay the powers of good nutrition? Physicians, who typically receive little or no training in nutrition in medical school, are often wary of nutritional "cures" and extravagant claims about the powers of vitamins and minerals to restore physical and mental health. While their skepticism is sometimes warranted, there is no question that what we eat profoundly affects our emotions and other psychological processes. Furthermore, when a patient is chronically malnourished, as most alcoholics are, long-term nutritional therapy is obviously required to restore physical and mental health, and ignoring patients' nutritional needs is simply inadequate treatment.

Hypoglycemia sparks even more controversy in the medical profession. A number of books published in the 1960s and 1970s made sweeping claims that hypoglycemia is a disease of epidemic proportions and the cause of disorders as varied as schizophrenia, suicide, drug addiction, divorce, crime, apathy, family disintegration, and moral decay.* Recently published books also make exaggerated claims about the "epidemic" of hypoglycemia in North America. Aware of the lack of documentation and research to support these claims and the swelling numbers of patients who diagnose themselves as hypoglycemic, many healthcare practitioners have gone to the other extreme, claiming that hypoglycemia is actually a rare condition and that most patients who believe they are hypoglycemic are actually suffering from purely psychological problems.

While the diagnosis of hypoglycemia may mistakenly be used by people to explain unrelated psychological and emotional problems, there is no question that the great majority of alcoholics suffer from chronic low blood sugar. When given the five-hour glucose tolerance test, over 95 percent of both early- and late-stage alcoholics experience a spike in blood sugar level after intake of sugar and then a rapid plunge. If their erratic blood sugar level is not controlled, alcoholics suffer chronic symptoms of depression, irritability, anguish, fatigue, insomnia, headaches, and mental confusion. Worst of all, low blood sugar causes a craving for substances that can quickly raise the blood sugar and relieve the symptoms, such as alcohol and sweets. Sober alcoholics, therefore, must learn to control their sugar intake in order to avoid mood fluctuations, anxiety, depression, and recurring impulses to drink.

Some treatment programs do emphasize a high-protein, low-carbohydrate diet during treatment but assume that once alcoholics stop drinking and stay sober for several weeks or months, their nutritional problems are solved. The healing process can take several years, however, and if alcoholics neglect their diet after months—or even years—of sobriety, their bodies will have a difficult time

---

* See the Suggested Reading List under "Nutrition" for several works taking a measured view of hypoglycemia and the role of nutrition.

completing the repair work.* Because some of the damage—in the liver and elsewhere—is often permanent, continued supplementation will be needed to offset continued deficiencies. Low blood sugar also will remain a chronic condition that will surface continually unless it is controlled through diet.

For all these reasons, nutrition should be emphasized from the start of treatment. Under medical supervision, the patient should be given a complete lab workup to assess specific vitamin and mineral deficiencies and a five-hour glucose tolerance test to determine their sensitivity to sugar. Coffee (and other caffeinated drinks) and refined carbohydrates (including pastries, desserts, and candies) should be strictly avoided because they cause abrupt changes in blood sugar levels and aggravate hypoglycemic symptoms.[†]

During treatment alcoholics should be informed about their need for specific vitamin and mineral supplements and taught how to plan their diet and read labels to determine the sugar content of various foods. The treatment program should emphasize the critical importance of continuing the hypoglycemic diet and supplements after discharge. Assertive follow-up care should reinforce the need for dietary and nutritional vigilance. The alcoholic must learn that this nutritional program is an integral part of a lifelong sobriety maintenance regime that will protect them against a craving for alcohol and the depression, irritability, and anxiety associated with hypoglycemia.

Alcoholics Anonymous Participation.   A.A. is far and away the most effective program in the world for helping alcoholics stay sober and recent research proves it.[8] In fact, helping alcoholics to stay sober is the primary purpose of A.A. Most recovering alcoholics, however, have the same reservations about A.A. that nonalcoholics

---

* Recent research indicates that four to five years of stable abstinence is required before the lifetime risk of recurrence (return to alcoholic drinking) drops below 15 percent.[7]

[†] See Appendix C for a sample hypoglycemic diet.

have, envisioning A.A. members as a group of losers and scruffy fanatics speaking a mumbo jumbo of love, spiritual renewal, and brotherhood. With this image in mind, most alcoholics shun the thought of A.A. meetings, whether because the fellowship frightens or repulses them or because they believe that they do not need it and can stay sober on their own. Left to their own devices, then, most alcoholics will not become involved in A.A.

The treatment program should therefore routinely do everything possible to increase the alcoholic's familiarity with A.A., requiring patients to attend meetings while in treatment and encouraging them to discuss their reactions to A.A. Most alcoholics need to attend twenty or thirty meetings before they feel at home in the fellowship and fully appreciate the need for it. Many treatment and recovery experts encourage the "90-90 formula"—ninety meetings in ninety days—as a solid base for long-term recovery.

A.A.'s strengths are, of course, formidable. Most alcoholics need protection against the permanent threat of their addiction; A.A. offers shared experience, strength, and hope. Most alcoholics flinch from looking at their past; A.A. helps them to face their lives as alcoholics, accept their disease, and keep in touch with it so as not to lapse into wishful thinking that they can drink again. Most alcoholics have some difficulties getting started on a sober life; A.A. offers guidance, support, and discipline.

Yet for all its strengths, A.A. is not perfect, and the recovering alcoholic should be warned of A.A.'s shortcomings. First, A.A. is not a treatment program, and alcoholics who walk in off the street have a very rough time trying to stay sober. The alcoholic who is just starting a new life of sobriety should realize this fact and not be disheartened by those A.A. members who stop attending meetings and start drinking again.

The recovering alcoholic should also beware of the A.A. belief that character flaws or personality defects cause alcoholics to get into trouble with alcohol, a belief that simply has no basis in fact. In his book *Educating Yourself About Alcohol and Drugs: A People's Primer*, psychiatrist and researcher Marc Schuckit summarizes the extensive research into the connection between psychological problems and alcoholism:

> There is no evidence that people who later go on to develop severe alcohol and drug problems are more likely than others in the general population to have had severe depressions, severe anxiety conditions, or psychotic conditions prior to the development of their alcohol and drug disorders.[9]

The alcoholic should be assured throughout treatment that their personality did not cause their disease and that they are in no way responsible for it. This assurance will rid them of years of accumulated guilt and shame and help them to understand that abstinence is essential for the simple but very real reason that they are physically incapable of processing alcohol in a normal way. If they believe that their personality caused their disease, they may then believe that once their personality problems are fixed, they can return to normal drinking. Furthermore, an alcoholic who feels guilty and ashamed may rebel against a program that aggravates these feelings, and forfeit their sobriety in the process.

Patients should be taught never to base Step 4—"Made a searching and fearless moral inventory"—on a review of their past drinking behavior. Instead, the inventory should be based on their conduct *after* detoxification and enlightenment about their disease and the recovery process. A helpful way to take the inventory during the first weeks and months of sobriety is to answer the following question: "Now that I have a chance to start a full recovery, am I doing all in my power to comply with the program, to fulfill my moral obligation to stay sober, and to increase the quality of my sobriety?" As time goes by and the alcoholic gets a clearer, more complete picture of who and what they are in sobriety, they can add other guidelines and questions to this original one and update the inventory at intervals to ensure continuing personal growth and progress in sobriety.

Finally, the alcoholic should understand the flaw in the once-cherished A.A. advice that it is acceptable and even beneficial to drink coffee or tea and to eat foods high in sugar such as candies or ice cream when depressed, anxious, irritable, or feeling the need for a drink. This is dangerous first aid, for while caffeine and sweets have the immediate effect of elevating the alcoholic's low blood sugar, their use is followed soon after by a sharp drop in blood sugar, thus intensifying the hypoglycemic symptoms. Worst of all for the alcoholic, an unstable blood sugar level often leads to an impulse to drink if not an outright conscious craving for alcohol.

Phase III: Staying the Course

Over a period of years, alcoholism has a devastating effect on all aspects of the victim's life. Although only the alcoholic has the primary disease, family members become participants in the illness and often become as emotionally sick as the alcoholic. They need to recover, too, if they are to adapt to the alcoholic's new sober lifestyle. The alcoholic may be compulsive about A.A. attendance, leading the family to believe that they care more about A.A. friends than them. On the other hand, they will be alarmed if the alcoholic stops attending A.A. meetings or gets off their nutritional program. How do they cope when the alcoholic has spells of depression or irritability? They may even come to believe that it was easier to live with the alcoholic when they were drinking.

If the family members are to understand the problems that can arise during recovery and how they can help solve them rather than contribute to them, they must learn about the disease, the importance of diet and nutritional supplements, and the value of A.A. and/or other mutual support groups in helping the alcoholic to stay sober. At the same time, they must know and accept the fact that the alcoholic has the primary responsibility for their sobriety maintenance program. Whenever possible, the family should be involved in the treatment program and in follow-up sessions after treatment. Family members can also take advantage of programs like Al-Anon, Alateen, and Structured Family Recovery so they can accompany their loved one on the journey of recovery.

While sobriety requires adjustments and compromises from the family as well as the alcoholic, it need not be a time of constant depression, frustration, or fears that it may not last. The alcoholic must understand that doubts and fears are normal but that all problems can be resolved without resorting to alcohol. Because they cannot turn to alcohol or drugs for relief of tension and frustration, they will have to learn how to deal with life's inevitable blows without giving in to resentments, self-pity, envy, or anger. Just trying to be normal is not good enough; they must reach for a higher level of maturity and self-knowledge than most nonalcoholics achieve, for they must cope with greater difficulties without resorting to chemical relief.

As sobriety continues, everything else will gradually improve. The alcoholic will soon learn that anything they could accomplish with alcohol they can do better, and enjoy more, without it. They will remember their drinking past for the hell it really was and understand that there is no problem that drinking would not make worse. At first, as they watch others drink and enjoy themselves, they will feel deprived of something good. Later, they will feel gratefully rid of something bad. They will be able to say to themselves, "Thank God I don't ever have to go through that again."

The Patient's Response to Treatment

The success of treatment is a function not only of what is done for the alcoholic patient but also of what alcoholics do for themselves in response to treatment. The patient's attitude and behavior toward their disease, their family, the treatment staff, and fellow alcoholics must undergo fundamental transformations if treatment is to be successful and sobriety secure. These transformations occur in three basic stages: submission, understanding, and commitment.

Submission

The first significant change required in the alcoholic's attitude toward treatment is the willingness to submit to the illness and the treatment program. Submission does not require that the patient be enthusiastic or even motivated when they begin treatment. In fact, most alcoholics initially fight the diagnosis and the need for treatment, and they may resent anyone who helped to put them there. If treatment is to progress and be successful, however, the alcoholic must at least comply with the rules of the program and submit to the authority of the treatment staff.

When alcoholics first start treatment, they are, with rare exceptions, often confused, frightened, and clearly in deteriorated mental and physical health. Their brain is fogged by long-term exposure to large amounts of alcohol, and they have difficulty thinking or reasoning clearly. They may be hostile and defensive. Nevertheless, something has forced them into treatment—marital difficulties, a car accident, hospitalization, a court mandate, or a suicide attempt—and they are probably very aware that they are desperately sick and need help.

As they accept the competent help provided, they begin to realize that they have come to the right place. They do not need to defend themselves, because they are not being attacked. They are not being punished or made to feel ashamed of themselves. Their suffering is minimal, as the staff does everything possible to make them comfortable. With these newly ignited feelings of hope and health, the alcoholic can submit to the treatment program, and the process of recovery can begin.

Barbara, age fifty, a dance teacher and mother of two teenage children, finally entered treatment when her husband threatened to leave her if she did not get help. He had threatened separation before, but Barbara realized he was deadly serious this time. During her last drinking binge, she had swallowed a handful of sleeping pills. She was drunk when she took them, and she still did not know whether she had intended to kill herself or just get a good night's sleep. But her good or bad intentions did not affect her husband's decision to solve the problem in one way or another. He had had it, and he offered her the final choice: treatment or divorce.

On the drive to the treatment center, Barbara drank from a pint of whiskey, and on arrival she was feeling angry and belligerent. "Alcoholics," she sniffed, looking with distaste at the staff members and other patients. "These people may be alcoholics, but I'm not one of them. What the hell am I doing here? I don't belong in this place!"

The image of a skid row alcoholic flashed in her mind, and she shuddered. She was not old and decrepit, her brain full of water, her eyes clouded, a stinking old bum. She was attractive, slender, wealthy, and middle-aged. "Why am I here?" she asked herself again.

She was escorted to the medical wing, where she glumly answered the nurse's questions and passively submitted to a physician's examination. She was then given a hospital gown and instructed to wear it until she was released from "detox."

Despite the gown and the outer trappings of a hospital, Barbara was surprised how liberal the rules were. After a day of laboratory tests and stabilization, she was encouraged to walk around, go to meetings, read, and talk to the other patients. The afternoon of her second day, she walked into the patient lounge to get some fruit juice. A man in the corner of the room watched her silently and, trying to be friendly, said "Welcome to the club."

"Some club," she thought, marching out of the room.

She thought a lot about drinking that first week. She did not want to stop. She liked to drink, and sometimes it seemed that a drink was the only friend she had. Her children lived their own lives, her husband worked late, the dance classes were often frustrating, and the students were frequently inept and clumsy. "Anyway," she reasoned, "alcohol makes me feel good. Maybe I was drinking too much and too often, but I can cut down. As soon as I get out of this place, I'll prove it to them all that I can drink like everyone else."

Yet despite her anger at being in treatment and her fear of living without alcohol, Barbara knew she had no choice. She was stuck here, for better or worse. Her husband was going to leave her if she didn't stop drinking, and he meant it this time. She did not believe that much could come from this treatment, but she was trapped and knew she had to give it a try.

Understanding

After several days of rest, good nutrition, and medical attention, the withdrawal symptoms subside in intensity, and the patients become accustomed to the treatment center and staff. They are sleeping better, they are able to think more clearly, and their hands have stopped shaking. The daily lectures begin to make some sense, counselors and staff are seen not to be such ogres after all, and other patients actually begin to look human.

Scattered pieces seem to come together. In the daily lectures, the emphasis is on the fact that alcoholism is a disease with certain identifiable symptoms. These symptoms are all familiar: the frustrations, unbearable tensions, vague fears, and problems at home and at work. As they relate the lectures and discussions to their own life, the description of the disease begins to make some sense, and they begin to understand why they acted the way they did. They understand that they are not a self-destructive or suicidal personality; they simply cannot process alcohol in the same way the majority of people can.

As their understanding of the disease grows, they finally realize how sick they were before they made it into treatment. They understand that their depression, anxiety, and irritability, the fights with their partner, and the fears of insanity were all the results of a brain poisoned by alcohol. As they begin to feel better, they also understand how close they were to losing everything—their family, their job, their health, and their life.

At this point, the recovering alcoholic may feel an urgent need to completely reorder their life and try to fix everything that was destroyed when they were drinking. They want to apologize to all the people they hurt in the past, and they feel a need to get right to work on their many problems. The relief of finally understanding what happened to them and the camaraderie of being with a group of people who have been through the same experiences fill them with hope and energy. Their self-esteem increases and their enthusiasms multiply. For the first time in years, everything seems to be clear and sensible.

After two weeks or so in treatment, the alcoholic often appears to be healed and ready to be released. They understand their disease, they finally admit how sick they were when they were drinking, and they experience a surge of self-confidence. They want to get out and prove to everyone that they can stay sober. This euphoric stage is dangerous, however, for the alcoholic's understanding of the disease is still somewhat superficial and unstable. If they are released now, they will probably return to drinking. They must go through one final stage if they are to achieve a secure and unshakable sobriety.

After detox, Barbara was transferred to a room that she shared with two other women. Marie was only thirty-five and a vice president of a downtown bank. She voluntarily entered treatment when her boss, an alcoholic in long-term recovery, gave her the choice of treatment or losing her job. Joan was a middle-aged special education teacher, obviously in bad physical and mental shape. Her hands shook constantly and uncontrollably, she talked to herself when she was awake and asleep, and she cried off and on, day and night.

After hearing her roommates' drinking histories, Barbara

still could not accept the fact that she was an alcoholic like them. She looked in the mirror, and there was the proof that she was better off than most everyone else in the treatment center. She looked healthy, perhaps a bit thin with the skin stretched tight over her cheekbones, but she was not anything like Joan, who shook all day and all night, or Bob, the man across the hall who was up every night yelling into the phone to his business partner that they should buy new trucks because the lettuce crop was so successful this year. Barbara told herself that she was not physically impaired, and she was not mentally fogged. She was just not like the rest of them, she decided.

As the days went by and she began to think more clearly and rationally, Barbara began to examine her past in more detail. She told her counseling group about her suicide attempts, about the psychiatrist who gave her Valium for her anxiety, about her dance classes and how she would have to cancel them when she was drinking too much. She thought about her children and the many times they had tried to talk to her about her drinking; after a while, she had stopped talking to them and tried harder to conceal her drinking. She remembered the night her fifteen-year-old daughter had found her in the closet, an empty vodka bottle in her hand and vomit all over her clothes.

She remembered all the parties when she'd embarrassed her husband by drinking too much. She remembered that she had stopped going to social gatherings and then drank only at home; she remembered the endless talks when her husband would break down and cry, begging her to stop drinking. She also remembered the last time when he was so cold and stern, and she knew that he meant it when he offered her one last chance.

As she remembered, she slowly accepted the truth. She knew that she could not control her drinking. She realized that alcohol was not her friend but her enemy. Gradually she realized how lucky she was. She had lost almost everything that mattered to her. The realization frightened her, because she had never understood it before. In the past, she had thought only of drinking and resented anyone who prevented her from drinking the way she wanted to drink.

She saw the improvement in her roommates. Joan's hands stopped shaking, and Marie stopped blaming everyone for her problems and began to let go of her resentments toward her boss and co-workers. Bob laughed at himself now for his crazy nightly phone calls and nearly cried with relief that his partner had not kicked him out of the business.

She saw the look in her children's eyes when they came to visit her, and she knew in a way that she would never know by looking in the mirror how changed she really was.

She was slowly filled with enthusiasm and hope. She understood her disease, she accepted it, and she actually wanted to live without alcohol. She wanted to stay sane and sober and healthy. She knew she could make it through; she was certain she had the disease licked.

Commitment

Understanding alone cannot reliably keep the alcoholic sober for the long term. Understanding the disease is helpful only if it guides alcoholics to live differently than they used to live. "You have to walk the walk, not just talk the talk," said alcoholic expert Father Joseph Martin, referring to the fact that alcoholics must do more than talk about their disease and decide to stay sober—they must commit their thoughts and actions to living a life without alcohol.[10] This commitment signifies a total acceptance of the disease and the lifestyle necessary to staying sober.

In this last stage of treatment, the enthusiasm reached during the stage of understanding becomes a committed determination.

The belief that "this is going to be a snap" slowly evolves into the knowledge that sobriety is not easily won but requires a new lifestyle with built-in vigilance and protection. Complacency can ruin sobriety, for when the alcoholic is feeling confident and certain of their ability to stay sober, they may loosen their controls, relax their vigilance, and allow themselves to "cheat" just a little. They may give in to a craving for sweets; they may work too hard and forget to eat as they should; they may miss A.A. meetings because they do not feel they need them anymore; they may think that after months or years of sobriety they can experiment with a drink or two every once in a while; or because they feel completely normal and don't crave alcohol, they may decide that they aren't really an alcoholic after all.

The disease may not look so dangerous now that they have been sober for a while. Strict controls may seem unnecessary. They may believe that a few weeks or months of sobriety have proved their ability to resist temptation. Whatever the reason, if the alcoholic is feeling complacent, their recovery is in danger, and they must renew their commitment to their program of lifelong sobriety.

Most important of all, alcoholics must accept the responsibility for their own recovery. If they say, "It is going to be really easy for me to stick to my diet because my wife won't let me get away with cheating," or "I won't have any choice but to attend A.A. meetings because my kids will drop me off and wait until the meeting is over," they are placing responsibility for the future of their sobriety on someone else rather than taking the primary responsibility themselves. Whenever an alcoholic's sobriety is dependent on another human being, it is a temporary sobriety because human beings get sick, die, lose patience, fall out of love, or move out of town. Alcoholics who place the responsibility for their sobriety on someone else are jeopardizing their lives.

To stay sober, alcoholics must understand that their susceptibility to addiction will never go away; they must accept the fact that they can never safely take a drink. They must learn everything they can about the disease and then incorporate this knowledge into their life, making a profound, deeply felt commitment to living without alcohol. If they avoid this commitment and hope that someday they might be able to drink again, they will.

Barbara was ready to be discharged. The fourth and last week in treatment had been difficult and demanding, and she felt a little shaky about being on her own and away from the protection of the treatment center. She was afraid she might fail, for she realized now how easy it would be to take a drink.

Her counselor assured her that her fears were a good sign: they showed that she was being realistic about the problems she might face in the immediate future. "Sobriety is like learning to ride a bicycle," the counselor explained. "At first, it is scary and easy to fall off. Yet, after a short while, riding a bike is as easy as walking. But you have to keep going forward, or you will fall over. The trick, then, is not to become complacent and think you are invulnerable. Don't take chances; don't play games. Above all, get to your follow-up meetings, attend your support groups, and stay on your nutritional program."

Barbara realized that she was learning to take responsibility for her own behavior and that this responsibility carried a heavy weight. She understood her disease. She knew that living the program was her protection.

One day shortly before her release, Barbara remembered a teenage incident involving her diabetic grandmother. She had walked into her grandmother's kitchen to find her nibbling on cookies just from the oven. "Nanny, you're not allowed to eat those!" she cried. Her grandmother's eyes grew wide, and her mouth trembled in anger. "How can I cook without taking a sample to see if it's good enough for everyone else to eat?" she asked angrily. "Now get out of my kitchen!"

Barbara realized now that her grandmother never completely accepted the chronic and progressive nature of her disease. In the kitchen she cheated whenever she wanted, and her rationalizations and denials made everyone in the family so uncomfortable that they ignored her nibbling. But diabetes, like alcoholism, can be lethal, and cheating can be fatal. Barbara's grandmother died in a diabetic coma at the age of sixty-five.

Barbara knew that staying sober would sometimes be difficult, but she also understood one other fact—her life depended on her staying sober. She also knew, through the example of hundreds of thousands of recovering alcoholics, that she could do it. And more than anything else in the world, she wanted to stay sober.

"My life began during treatment," Barbara told her counselor the day she left the program. "Before treatment, I was someone else, ruled and controlled by alcohol. But during treatment I saw miracles worked with the other patients, and I realized that the change in my life was also something of a miracle. Now nothing is more important to me than my sobriety—not my husband, my children, or my career—because I would not have them if I started to drink again. If I lose my sobriety, I lose everything."

10

Drugs and the Alcoholic

A high percentage of alcoholics—some of whom are aware of their drinking problem and try to hide it, and some of whom are not able to recognize it—visit their doctors for tranquilizer prescriptions because their complaints mirror the symptoms of anxiety or stress for which tranquilizers are promoted. These complaints—nervousness, anxiety, insomnia, and so on—sound to some doctors like a classic case of anxiety when they are, in fact, a reflection of the early stages of alcoholism. Doctors are too quick to reach for the prescription pad when they hear such complaints.

—Richard Hughes and Robert Brewin, *The Tranquilizing of America*[1]

Alcohol in combination with other drugs can be deadly. The case of Karen Ann Quinlan offers a dramatic example of the killing power of combined drugs. One night in 1975, the twenty-one-year-old Quinlan drank several gin and tonics and took some Valium pills. She lapsed into a coma. Years later, with all life-support equipment removed, she continued to lie unconscious and unknowing in a New Jersey nursing home. She never regained consciousness, and she died ten years later.[*]

Few people today have heard about Karen Ann Quinlan, but cases of drug addiction and overdose among the famous are reported frequently in the news. In 1969, Rolling Stones musician Brian Jones, twenty-five, drowned in his swimming pool with a combination

---

[*] Karen Ann Quinlan's tragedy had significant effect on our healthcare system, resulting in the development of advance health directives and formal ethics committees in hospitals and nursing homes.

of alcohol, amphetamines, and sleeping pills in his bloodstream—a death labeled at the inquest as a "misadventure." In 2011, singer/songwriter Amy Winehouse, twenty-seven, died of acute alcohol poisoning (another "death by misadventure," according to the coroner's report) with traces of Librium, a sedative prescribed for anxiety and withdrawal relief, in her blood. In 2012, singer Whitney Houston, forty-eight, drowned in her bathtub; she'd been drinking champagne and beer, and the toxicology report noted "acute cocaine intoxication." In 2014, actor Philip Seymour Hoffman, forty-six, a recovering alcoholic with twenty-three years of stable recovery, died of "acute mixed drug intoxication" including heroin, cocaine, benzodiazepines, and amphetamine. In 2018, rapper Mac Miller, twenty-six, died of "mixed toxicity," according to the coroner's report, with alcohol, cocaine, and fentanyl in his system.

When celebrities get in trouble with drugs or die of drug-alcohol interactions, the story hits the front page. For each celebrity, however, there are thousands of cases that are never reported or are noted only on the obituary page. Anyone who drinks and takes tranquilizers, sedatives, hypnotics, prescription painkillers, or illegal drugs (heroin, fentanyl, cocaine) at the same time is toying with a chemical time bomb that could explode into multiple addictions, multiple withdrawal syndromes, convulsions, coma, brain damage, and death. One drink plus one pill does not equal the effect of two drinks or two pills. Instead, the potency of the drugs is multiplied three times, four times, or even more.

Pioneering research first published by Charles Lieber provides at least a partial explanation of why these explosive interactions occur.[2] Lieber found, and dozens of other researchers in recent years have confirmed, that alcohol and other drugs compete for the same enzyme processing system in the liver. This is the system that metabolizes drugs, eventually inactivating them and eliminating them through the bloodstream. When alcohol is taken in combination with tranquilizers, sedatives, painkillers, or other drugs (including over-the-counter drugs such as acetaminophen), the enzymes are unable to work on both drugs at the same time. Alcohol is always given first priority, and the other drug must, in effect, wait for its turn to be processed and eliminated. This delay in normal processing causes the other drug's effects to be magnified, since the drug is allowed to build up and remain active for a longer time. The synergistic (multiplied) effects of drugs that impact the central nervous system—alcohol, tranquilizers, sedatives, painkillers—can cause increased sedation, euphoria, agitation, confusion, increased risk of falls, memory defects, breathing problems, and overdoses.

Alcoholics are in particular danger when combining various drugs because their cells are already chemically altered by long exposure to large doses of alcohol, and these adaptations affect the cells' reactions to other drugs. As one researcher explains, the normal drug interactions are changed because the person taking the drugs is changed: "The interaction is not so much between two drugs as between an organism modified by exposure to one of these drugs (ethanol) and the subsequent modification in the reaction of that organism to some other drug."[3]

This altered interaction is particularly noticeable with tranquilizers, sedatives, prescription painkillers, and all other drugs that act as central nervous system depressants. When the alcoholic takes these prescription drugs, they experience an unusual effect—the prescribed drug dose is simply not strong enough. The alcoholic is instantly tolerant to central nervous system depressants because their central nervous system cells are already tolerant to alcohol. Having adapted to one drug, their cells are also adapted to similar drugs, and in order to get the intended effect, an alcoholic must take more pills than prescribed.

The instantaneous ability to withstand the effects of drugs pharmacologically similar to alcohol is termed *cross-tolerance*. It accounts for the alcoholic's ability to continue to function with tranquilizer or sedative doses, for example, that would be incapacitating or even lethal for nonalcoholics.

The dangers of cross-tolerance are obvious. Because of their increased tolerance, the alcoholics have to drink more to experience the desired effects of alcohol; if they are taking prescription pills, they will also have to increase the dosage to get the intended effect. Combined, these large drug doses are extremely dangerous, even for the alcoholic who can tolerate large doses of each drug individually. As the research demonstrates, the effects of the tranquilizer or sedative are magnified because alcohol always wins the competition for the enzyme-processing system. The other drug then builds up in the bloodstream and can cause toxic reactions including convulsions, coma, and respiratory failure.

Furthermore, a drinking alcoholic on pills is often too befuddled to use medications according to directions. They may forget when or if they took their last pill, or they may double or triple the prescribed dose in an attempt to forestall the inevitable withdrawal symptoms. Accidental overdoses are frequent because the alcoholic simply loses track of their intake of pills and alcohol.

For late-stage alcoholics, the dangers of combining pills and alcohol are intensified. As described in Chapter 4, chronic exposure to large doses of alcohol weakens the cell membranes and enlarges and distorts the energy-producing cell parts, the mitochondria. As the cells progressively become weaker, they are no longer able to function normally with large doses of alcohol, and the alcoholic's tolerance for alcohol gradually decreases. At the same time, the alcoholic's tolerance for tranquilizers and sedatives decreases as well. The alcoholic is now in an extremely precarious situation if they combine alcohol and prescription drugs, for their tolerance is lessening and yet their withdrawal symptoms are increasing in frequency and intensity as the addiction strengthens. They must continually medicate themselves with alcohol and/or pills, yet their weakened cells can no longer tolerate the amounts necessary to stop the physical and mental anguish of withdrawal. Once again, the dangers of accidental overdose are very real.

Disease further weakens the alcoholic's ability to withstand the combined effects of alcohol and prescription pills. An injured liver is incapable of eliminating drugs at a normal rate, and the drug's effects will be enhanced and prolonged. Other alcohol-related diseases including kidney disease, pancreatitis, and gastrointestinal disorders contribute to the body's inability to metabolize and eliminate various drugs.

Not the least of the late-stage alcoholic's problems is the constant mental confusion and emotional distress associated with drinking a lot of alcohol over a long period of time. When the alcoholic is drinking, their brain is saturated with alcohol, and they cannot think straight or reason rationally. When they are not drinking, they are in acute or post-acute withdrawal, and their thoughts are equally jumbled. As a result, they spend most of their waking hours confused, in pain from withdrawal, overwhelmed with self-pity and despair, and often depressed beyond all caring. Swallowing a bottle of pills may seem the only way to escape a hopeless, miserable existence.

WHILE THE PHENOMENON of cross-tolerance helps explain some of the dangers associated with combining alcohol and prescription drugs, it does not explain why hundreds of thousands of alcoholics become addicted to prescription drugs. Are these alcoholics, in fact, addictive personalities, or is there some physiological explanation for the alcoholic's increased susceptibility to multiple addictions?

As with most of the mysteries in alcoholism, the explanation is physiological, not psychological. Addiction to alcohol ensures that the alcoholic will quickly become addicted to pharmacologically similar drugs, a process called *cross-addiction*. Tranquilizers and sedatives are addictive for anyone who uses them over a long period of time, even if they are taken as prescribed. For alcoholics, however, the drug addiction process is speeded up. Since the alcoholic's cells are already physically addicted to alcohol, the cellular equipment necessary for addiction to tranquilizers and sedatives is, in a sense, already established.

Because these drugs can partially substitute for alcohol in relieving withdrawal symptoms, because the symptoms of alcoholism mirror emotional disorders, and because many physicians are not aware of the cross-addiction process in alcoholics, sedatives, tranquilizers, and painkilling drugs are often prescribed for alcoholics, with instructions to use them whenever they feel shaky, nervous, or anxious. While the alcoholic may feel better temporarily after taking a sedative or tranquilizer, they will rapidly become addicted to these drugs if they continue to take them.

Once addicted to both alcohol and prescription drugs, the alcoholic experiences a complex combination of withdrawal symptoms, and their mental and physical torment multiplies. The polydrug-addicted alcoholic is caught in a brutal cycle of increasing pain and decreasing benefits, as they must step up their use of alcohol or pills to medicate themselves against the ever-impending and increasingly severe withdrawal symptoms. Blackouts, mental confusion, and suicidal depressions intensify with multiple addictions, and the possibility of overdose dramatically increases.

A critical and dangerously overlooked aspect of addiction to alcohol and/or drugs is its permanence. Once established, the addiction can be reactivated by using either alcohol or prescription drugs, even after prolonged periods of abstinence. Tranquilizers and sedatives, for example, because of their similar effects to alcohol on the central nervous system, can reactivate the physical addiction to alcohol, causing a craving for alcohol that leads to a return to drinking.[4] Many sober alcoholics given medication for tension, pain, or insomnia have relapsed and started drinking again. Over-the-counter medications containing alcohol, such as cough syrup, also can and do trigger the addiction and start a sober alcoholic drinking again.

MORE THAN FOUR decades ago First Lady Betty Ford, a moderate social drinker for most of her life, became addicted to both alcohol and drugs prescribed by her doctors for a pinched nerve and arthritis. As her ordeal demonstrates, even moderate nonalcoholic drinkers can become addicted to alcohol if they are simultaneously taking prescription drugs. For years, she had been a social drinker who was also taking pills prescribed by her doctors for pain and stress. "I had never been without my drugs," she confides in her autobiography, *The Times of My Life*. "I took pills for pain, I took pills to sleep, I took mild tranquilizers."[5] At some point, however, her body was no longer able to tolerate the combination of prescription drugs and alcohol. She began to slur her words, stumble on the stairs, and behave in ways totally unlike herself. With no warning, she had become addicted to both pills and alcohol.

In actuality, the addiction process had probably been established years before, but her doctors never detected the addiction, and she therefore had no reason to suspect it. The pills were prescribed for legitimate complaints, and she took them as directed—how could they be dangerous? She drank alcohol, but no one ever warned her not to, and she rarely drank to excess—how could she be an alcoholic? Her bewilderment is reflected in the following passage from her autobiography:

The reason I rejected the idea that I was an alcoholic was that my addiction wasn't dramatic. So I forgot a few telephone calls. So I fell in the bathroom and cracked three ribs. But I never drank for a hangover, and in fact, I used to criticize people who did. At house parties, I would look at friends who knocked back Bloody Marys in the morning, and I would think, isn't that pathetic?

I hadn't been a solitary drinker, either; I'd never hidden bottles in the chandeliers or the toilet tanks. When Jerry [President Ford] was away, there had always been neighbors to have cocktails with, either at their houses or at our house, and at Washington luncheons I'd never touched anything but an occasional glass of sherry. There had been no broken promises (my husband never came to me and said, "Please quit") and no drunken driving. I worried about my children too much to risk taking them anywhere in a car when I'd been drinking.

And I never wound up in jail, or in a strange part of town with a bunch of sailors.[6]

Yet Betty Ford was addicted to pills and alcohol. Millions of Americans have suffered the same fate. In the 1980s, alcoholic treatment centers throughout the country reported that over half of their patients were addicted to both alcohol and one or more prescription drugs. What can only be termed a multiple-addiction epidemic had swept the country, and it hit women particularly hard. The National Institute on Drug Abuse (NIDA) estimated that 32 million women—or 42 percent of the adult female population—had taken tranquilizers at some time in their lives, 21 percent (16 million) had used other prescription sedatives, and 16 percent (12 million) had used stimulants. One of every five women, or 16 million women eighteen years and older, were reported to have taken tranquilizers in any given year; of these women, the Food and Drug Administration estimated that two in five, or 6.5 million, were regular users of alcohol and one in five, or more than 3.2 million, was a heavy user.[7]

Prescription drug use and addiction have increased dramatically since Betty Ford entered treatment in 1978. The opioid epidemic—which is directly related to dramatically increasing prescription rates of opioid medications, stronger prescription medications such as oxycodone and fentanyl, and patients receiving long-term opioid therapy for chronic pain—has led to untold misery. Between 1999 and 2018 more than 232,000 Americans died from overdoses involving prescription drugs. Emergency departments have seen an 84 percent increase in visits related to adverse drug effects. Every year 18 million people, or more than 6 percent of Americans over age twelve, are described as having "misused" prescription drugs at least once. Five percent of these "misusers" are youth between ages twelve and seventeen, and 14.4 percent are young adults ages eighteen to twenty-five.[8]

Combining alcohol with prescription drugs is common. More than half of these described "misusers" of prescription drugs reportedly also binge-drink, according to a 2019 press release from the Centers for Disease Control. Two studies conducted by University of Michigan researchers showed that "alcohol-dependent" (i.e., alcoholic) men and women are eighteen times more likely to report "misuse" (nonmedical use) of prescription drugs than those who don't drink at all. Young adults between the ages of eighteen and twenty-four are the most at risk, leading researchers to urge clinicians to "conduct thorough drug use histories, particularly when working with young adults."[9]

Like Betty Ford, most "prescription junkies," as they are sometimes pejoratively called, are normal and healthy before they start taking pills. Their complaints are minor or temporary, and time alone would probably straighten out most of their problems. But physicians give them drugs, they willingly follow doctor's orders and the directions on the pill bottle, and they innocently get hooked. Thus, many people are destroyed not by any primary illness but by their treatment.

When a patient requests medication, even the knowledgeable and aware physician is presented with a dilemma. Should they probe into the patient's reasons for wanting a tranquilizer or sedative and take a detailed medical history to ensure that the patient is not taking or addicted to other medications or alcohol, and should they then spend ten to fifteen minutes explaining the various drug interactions? Or should they simply comply with their patient's request, trusting them to know about the hazards of drug interactions? This dilemma is summed up by addiction medicine specialist Dr. Joseph Cruse, founding medical director of the Betty Ford Center:

> I'm amazed at how often I go through the questioning, the examination, and treatment program for the chief complaint, and just before leaving, the patient says "Oh, by the way, Dr. Brown gives me Valium, but he's out of town. Would you write me a prescription for 100?" She is as uncomfortable

about asking as I am about refusing. It takes 30 seconds to write the prescription and 30 minutes not to. Now I have to make a hard choice on a busy afternoon when I'm already behind schedule.[10]

When alcoholics visit a doctor, their complaints frequently appear to be psychological. They can't sleep; their marriage seems to be falling apart; they no longer care about their work; they are depressed, easily frustrated, and constantly tense. Unless the physician is familiar with the disease of alcoholism and the early, often confusing psychological symptoms, they may not even guess that there is an underlying physical disease that is causing these complaints. The patient is complaining of relatively minor problems that appear to be signs of some kind of temporary difficulty in their social life or career, and the physician may easily misinterpret the symptoms as evidence of a purely emotional or psychological disturbance. The most logical therapy will therefore often appear to be prescription drugs.

When the symptoms persist and increase in intensity—which they will if the alcoholic continues to drink and/or take pills—the physician may increase the dosage or switch the patient to a stronger tranquilizer or sedative. Even with intensified symptoms, there may still be no direct evidence of serious damage to the patient's physical health. In fact, the early alcoholic often appears to be in good physical condition, and a brief medical examination will detect no evidence of organ or tissue damage. Bloodwork looks normal. Without this evidence, prescription pills again may seem to be the most logical method of treatment.

Even physicians who know a patient's history of heavy drinking may prescribe drugs as part of treatment on the premise that alcoholism is essentially an emotional illness and that prescription drugs are more effective and safer than alcohol in relieving emotional problems. The physician may also hope that their patient can be helped to switch from excessive, uncontrolled drinking to a medically controlled program of drug treatment. The physician may reason that if the alcoholic continues to drink to excess, they will inevitably deteriorate, ending up in prison, the emergency room, or the morgue. If, on the other hand, the patient can be persuaded to switch to prescription drugs, the dosage can at least be controlled.

All these reasons for using drug therapy are misguided and based on ignorance of both alcoholism and the complex interactions of various drugs. Tranquilizers, sedatives, and painkillers may temporarily alleviate the alcoholic's discomfort, but they will not halt the addiction to alcohol. In fact, they aggravate the addiction and make it even more difficult for the alcoholic to recover. As discussed earlier in this chapter, these drugs speed up the addictive process, increase the risk of accidental overdose and toxic reactions, intensify the alcoholic's emotional and psychological problems, and cause multiple addictions and multiple withdrawal syndromes. When physicians write prescriptions for tranquilizers, sedatives, or painkillers for their alcoholic patients, they may, in effect, be signing the patients' death certificate.

Writing a prescription for any patient is a heavy responsibility. The physician should, of course, take a detailed medical history before they prescribe drugs, and they should expend some time and energy trying to determine the precise causes of the patient's anxiety or depression. If they decide to prescribe, they should inform the patient about the known and suspected risks associated with taking the drug. They can help protect their patients by giving them a form that lists the common interactions of drugs and alcohol. The National Institute on Alcohol Abuse and Alcoholism offers a detailed listing online titled "Harmful Interactions Mixing Alcohol with Medicines" (see also Appendix D).[11]

For alcoholic patients, the physician's responsibilities are even clearer and more straightforward: *Tranquilizers, sedatives, and opioid painkillers should never be prescribed for a known or suspected alcoholic.*

What About Medications?

F. Scott Fitzgerald, who died at age forty-four of an alcohol-induced heart attack after numerous hospitalizations and incarcerations, once complained that he could never stay sober long enough to tolerate sobriety. Researchers familiar with this common complaint have long been inspired to search for a substance that would discourage spontaneous drinking and force the alcoholic to stay sober long enough to let rationality prevail. There is such a substance, but it is a decidedly mixed blessing.

Antabuse (disulfiram) was accidentally discovered when workers in a rubber factory found that they could not drink without becoming violently ill. Shortly after World War II, Danish researchers traced the source of the trouble to tetraethylthiuram disulfide, a chemical used in the processing of rubber. In the late 1940s, the chemical was first introduced for use in treating alcoholism.

Antabuse works by interfering with the metabolism of alcohol in the liver. The medication stalls metabolism at the acetaldehyde stage so that acetaldehyde accumulates in the body, producing the violent symptoms of the reaction. Because Antabuse is slowly absorbed and excreted, a single dose will "protect" the alcoholic for five to seven days. As long as the alcoholic abstains from drinking, Antabuse has no apparent side effects. Just a few minutes after ingesting even small amounts of alcohol, however, Antabuse causes a violent reaction to the alcohol. The amount of alcohol in a dose of cough syrup or an alcohol rubdown is enough to initiate this reaction. As described in the *Physicians Desk Reference,* this reaction

"produces flushing, throbbing in head and neck, throbbing headache, respiratory difficulty, nausea, copious vomiting, sweating, thirst, chest pain, palpitation, dyspnea [labored or difficult breathing], hyperventilation, tachycardia [abnormally rapid heart rate], hypotension [low blood pressure], syncope [sudden loss of strength], marked uneasiness, weakness, vertigo, blurred vision and confusion. In severe reactions there may be respiratory depression, cardiovascular collapse, arrhythmias, myocardial infarction, acute congestive heart failure, unconsciousness, convulsions, and death.

The intensity of the reaction varies with each individual, but is generally proportional to the amounts of Antabuse and alcohol ingested."[12]

Clearly, Antabuse is a medication that must be used with extreme caution. The alcoholic's medical history must be taken in detail, and the risks associated with using the medication should be thoroughly outlined. The patient must be made aware of all medications and foods to avoid, and their physician should regularly monitor them for adverse reactions. Alcoholics with a history of congestive heart failure, liver and kidney disorders, diabetes, thyroid problems, brain damage, polyneuropathy, psychosis, or suicidal tendencies should not be given Antabuse.

It is also important to note that while researchers now understand the basics of Antabuse's activities in the body, when the chemical was first used in the 1940s research on its side effects was almost nonexistent. The side effects were noted as they occurred, and dosage was adjusted through trial and error. Decades later, the experimentation continues with recent studies showing that daily doses of Antabuse can have profound effects on the physical and mental health of even the abstinent alcoholic, ranging from mental health issues to metabolic aberrations that may result in toxicity and damage to the body's organs.[13]

The fundamental question, of course, is this: are the benefits worth the risks? On the positive side, the urge to drink can come over a sober alcoholic suddenly and sweepingly; with Antabuse they have a means to combat this urge and to give themselves time to think rationally. Antabuse can buy precious time.

Yet while Antabuse may temporarily deter some alcoholics from impulse drinking, it does little or nothing to ensure or promote lifelong sobriety. Antabuse cannot control or eliminate the physical addiction to alcohol, a fact underscored by the many patients who simply stop taking their daily Antabuse when the craving for alcohol asserts itself. Antabuse is "aversive" rather than "corrective," meaning that while taking the drug makes the drinking experience distinctly unpleasant, it doesn't target the neurological adaptations underlying addiction. Tragically, the physical imperative to drink may be much more powerful than fear of the Antabuse reaction, and the alcoholic may then drink while taking Antabuse and suffer the dangerous and sometimes fatal consequences.

More recently developed medications, now approved by the Food and Drug Administration (FDA), appear to directly target the brain's opiate receptors, thought to underlie the craving for reward and / or relief, to restore the natural balance of chemicals in the brain. *Naltrexone* (sold under the brand name ReVia in pill form and Vivitrol as a once-monthly injection) is an opioid antagonist that binds to the brain's opioid receptors, blocking the high of pleasure and reward that people experience when drinking, that may eventually reduce the urge to consume alcohol.[14] Recent systematic reviews of more than a hundred randomized trials including nearly seventeen thousand patients found that naltrexone increased abstinence rates and decreased heavy drinking.[15]

Acamprosate (sold under the brand name Campral) also reduces craving, most likely by restoring chemical balances in the brain associated with relief and thereby reducing anxiety and depression.[16] Studies indicate that acamprosate promotes abstinence but is most effective when abstinence is required before treatment begins.[17]

Finally, care should be taken that the use of Antabuse—or any medication—does not distract the alcoholic from assuming responsibility for staying sober. Thus, whatever medication may be used to try to help alcoholics abstain from consuming alcohol, the alcoholic's continued sobriety depends to a large extent on the ability to come to grips with the progressive, chronic nature of the disease. They must understand that their vulnerability to alcohol's harmful effects will not go away with time, and they must therefore continually guard against potential obstacles or hazards to their sobriety. With effective treatment, this need not be a grim and constant struggle. When alcoholics learn the facts of their disease, they will know why they cannot drink and what to do to protect their sobriety. When the deficiencies in their nutrition have been corrected, the recurring bouts of depression, anxiety, and craving for alcohol will subside. The power to say no to alcohol will come from within.

Medication-assisted treatment is one of many pathways to recovery. Both researchers and clinicians are careful to warn, however, that no medication is a panacea, and that the standards of care, developed and honed over more than fifty years, continue to be abstinence, diet and nutritional therapy, long-term recovery support, and involvement in A.A. or other mutual support groups. These are the proven strategies and practices that help alcoholics achieve not only sobriety but long-term recovery.

11

Beyond Prejudice and Misconception

He that is possessed with a prejudice is possessed with a devil, and one of the worst kind of devils, for it shuts out the truth, and often leads to grievous error.

—Tryon Edwards

It is never too late to give up your prejudices.

—Henry David Thoreau, *Walden*

The information in this book can save millions of lives and billions of dollars, but first, two types of prejudice must be destroyed. Prejudice born of ignorance is fairly easily eliminated once the facts are made available and people are given accurate information. Prejudice born of interest is not so easily destroyed, however, for the facts can be misinterpreted, denied, or covered up. Those who have a professional or economic need to view alcoholism as a mental health problem will cling stubbornly to their prejudices, ignoring or slanting the evidence. They will not be able to see the facts or accept them, for the facts disorder their particular view of the world.

The prejudice of vested interests is epidemic in the field of alcoholism. The federal government supplies millions of dollars every year for alcoholism research, treatment, education, and prevention. The competition for these funds is stiff, and the stakes are high—an atmosphere perfectly suited to the breeding of hostility, jealousy, and carefully guarded self-interest.

The battle against the prejudices of ignorance and interest will eventually be won—the facts themselves will tip the scales—but it will not happen overnight. It may take years for society to slough off the myths and misconceptions concerning alcoholism that have governed thought for centuries. But it will happen. Every recovering alcoholic adds fuel to the fire of this movement forward. Doctors who are trained and educated in early diagnosis and treatment, employers who offer the alcoholic the choice of treatment instead of automatically firing them, family members who witness and participate in the recovery process, and police officers, attorneys, judges, and mental health providers who come in contact with recovered alcoholics and effective treatment programs all help to advance the new understanding of alcoholism. As researchers contribute to the already substantial body of evidence, as effective treatment programs replace ineffective ones, and as the number of recovering alcoholics enjoying lasting sobriety continues to grow, this movement will gain a momentum that cannot be stopped.

It can—and must—be accelerated, however. Major overhauls must take place in all areas of alcoholism research and treatment. These changes cannot be superficial but must be deep, massive alterations in the social, political, and economic fabric of this country and every country as it relates to alcoholism. The changes required are so sweeping that an entire book could be devoted solely to outlining and exploring them. The following survey is therefore intended only to highlight those areas that require immediate and significant change.

The Need for Definitions

Each of us has his private view and private meaning attached to the words that are used in the alcohol field.[1]

For a very long time, universally accepted definitions did not exist in the alcoholism field. As the researcher just quoted acknowledged, everyone involved in the field had his or her own private view of the disease. The professionals believed they were entitled to their own opinions about alcoholism because there was no clear picture of what alcoholism is, what causes it, how it progresses, and why certain people become addicted while others do not.

And yet, as this book makes clear, there is a firm basis of research evidence, amassed over many decades, for understanding the disease. The disease itself is understandable and definable; the victim's behavior is understandable and definable; and the recovery process is understandable and definable. Research in the last forty years has exploded, adding depth and breadth to the facts originally presented in this book and opening up fascinating new areas of interest and inquiry.

Opinions must no longer be allowed to overshadow facts. The language we use—and the words and phrases we discard—can go a long way to combating the still pervasive stigma of the disease. An example of the dangers inherent in allowing researchers to interpret the data according to their own private meanings is contained in a 1976 RAND report. In this government-funded study, which assessed the effectiveness of forty-four federal government treatment programs, the term *recovery* was replaced with a broader term, *remission*. Remission included the category "normal drinking," defined by the authors as drinking less than 3 ounces of pure alcohol every day.[2] An alcoholic was considered to be in remission, then, if he or she was drinking the equivalent of 6 ounces or less of 100 proof whiskey every day. Thus, treatment centers that embraced this definition of remission could claim up to 80 percent success rates—even though most of the alcoholics so labeled were still drinking.

The word *remission* by itself is not offensive, but when it is used to describe acceptable "normal drinking" in alcoholics, the dangers are very real. The RAND report created an uproar in the field of alcoholism when it was published, with some professionals insisting that the report provided evidence that some alcoholics could return to normal drinking, and others condemning the study as dangerous and irresponsible since it might encourage alcoholics to believe that they could control their drinking permanently.

Four years later, the RAND researchers backed away from their original conclusions. A follow-up study found that the so-called normal alcoholic drinkers had nearly three times the relapse rate of long-term abstainers when they tried to stop drinking. "Normal drinking" is clearly a dangerous and potentially fatal goal for alcoholics, for while they may be able to control their intake for a period of months or even years, if they continue to drink, their disease will steadily progress until eventually the addiction overpowers their best efforts to control it.

One important and lingering example of the power of words to promote misconception is the use of the terms *alcohol abuse* and *alcohol abuser* as synonyms for *alcoholism* and *alcoholic*. *Alcohol abuse* identifies alcoholism as a compulsion, and puts the onus on the person who allegedly abuses the substance. Instead, the emphasis should be where it belongs—on the drug, the addiction, the disease. Because the word *abuse* cannot encompass the ideas that alcoholism is a disease and that alcoholics are innocent victims, the result for a long while was the development of a theory that two types of alcoholism existed: one a compulsive, psychologically caused abuse of alcohol and the other a physical disease most likely caused by such "abuse." The very name of the National Institute on Alcohol Abuse and Alcoholism gives support to this contradictory view of alcoholism. It is long past time that the National Institute on Drug Abuse, the Center for Substance Abuse Treatment, the Substance Abuse and Mental Health Services Administration, the *Journal of Substance Abuse Treatment,* and so on abandon the word *abuse* in the titles of their agencies and in their press releases, public information campaigns, and research.

Relatedly, *responsible drinking,* a favorite alcohol industry term today, is linked to the word *abuse* because, according to the liquor industry, "irresponsible" drinkers who "abuse" alcohol cause all the problems and give beer, wine, and hard liquor a bad name. The advice to "drink responsibly" makes no more sense for those genetically predisposed to alcohol addiction than "shoot up responsibly" makes for heroin users.

The need for precise definitions should be obvious. The following definitions, based on the facts already established in the scientific literature, are central to any attempt to communicate clearly about alcoholism.

Alcoholism.   A chronic, primary, hereditary disease that progresses from an early, physiological susceptibility into an addiction characterized by tolerance changes, physiological dependence, and loss of control over drinking. Psychological symptoms are secondary to the physiological disease and not relevant to its onset.

Recovery.   A return to normal functioning—physical, psychological, and social well-being—based on total, continuous abstinence from alcohol and substitute drugs, on corrective nutrition, and on an accurate understanding of the disease. The word *cure* should not be used because it implies that the alcoholic can engage in "normal" drinking after their "problem" has been corrected.

Problem Drinker.   A person who is not an alcoholic but whose alcohol use creates psychological and social problems for themselves and/or others.

Heavy Drinker.   Anyone who drinks frequently or in large amounts. A heavy drinker may be a problem drinker, an alcoholic, or a normal drinker with a high tolerance for alcohol.

Alcoholic.   An alcoholic is a person with the disease of alcoholism regardless of whether they are initially a heavy drinker, a problem drinker, or a light or moderate drinker. The alcoholic's increasing problems and heavier drinking stem from the underlying addiction process and should not be confused with problem drinking or heavy drinking in the nonalcoholic.

Recovering Alcoholic.   The alcoholic who maintains continuous, total abstinence from alcohol and substitute drugs and who has returned to a healthy, sober lifestyle. The term *reformed alcoholic* implies that the alcoholic has been "bad" and is now being "good"—a reflection of the moralistic approach to alcoholism, which has no basis in fact. The term *ex-alcoholic* should not be used either, for it implies a cure rather than a recovery.

Relapse ("Slip" in A.A. Language).   Use of the word *relapse* to describe a recurrence of alcohol consumption by a recovering alcoholic can imply some type of moral failing. As such, use of *relapse* or *slip* is preferably replaced with a morally neutral term, such as "an individual *resumed* consuming alcohol" or "an individual experienced a *recurrence* of symptoms."

The words we use matter. For an A–Z look at the language used to describe addiction and recovery, complete with "stigma alerts" to identify outdated or inaccurate terms that stigmatize the disease and its victims, visit the "Addictionary," put out by the Recovery Research Institute, at https://www.recoveryanswers.org/addiction-ary.

Research Priorities

In the last seventy to eighty years, researchers have provided an abundance of knowledge about the disease of alcoholism, including its onset, underlying mechanisms, predisposing factors, symptoms, and progression. In particular, the work of Charles Lieber on the metabolism of alcohol, Benjamin Kissin on the causes and progression of the disease, Roger Williams on hypoglycemia and nutrition, Donald Goodwin on heredity, and Bert Vallee on liver enzyme activities have provided notable initial milestones in understanding alcoholism. Because so much of the major, groundbreaking work had been accomplished when this book was first written, researchers have had the opportunity to add important knowledge to this framework.

It remains particularly important that researchers be precise about what they are studying and measuring. For example, they should be sure to make these distinctions: Is the drinker an alcoholic, a heavy drinker, or a problem drinker? Is the alcoholic in the early, middle, or late stage of the disease? Is the alcoholic in acute withdrawal or protracted withdrawal? Is alcohol responsible for the effect observed, is acetaldehyde responsible, or are both substances contributing?

At the time this book was originally published, the research areas below were, and remain, exciting opportunities for further refinement:

Nutrition.   The role of nutrition in the onset and progression of alcoholism, the withdrawal syndrome, and the treatment and recovery process has been neglected, and the whole range of disciplines—biochemistry, pharmacology, physiology—should thoroughly explore this clinically important area.

Drug interactions.   Another fertile area for research by the life scientists is drug interactions. Particular areas of interest are the addictive properties of drugs in alcoholics whether or not they are drinking, the long-term or cumulative effects of taking various drugs, the special problems created by polydrug addiction, and so on.

Heredity.   The evidence is overwhelming that alcoholism is a hereditary disease. Replication and extension of research findings should continue, particularly in the area of identifying the specific genetic factors that predispose individuals and racial and ethnic groups to alcoholism.

Enzyme abnormalities.   Numerous competent researchers are advancing knowledge in this area, further clarifying the specific liver enzymes involved in alcoholism. The potential significance of this research is enormous and should be encouraged by both public and private funding.

Acetaldehyde.   The complex relationships between alcohol, acetaldehyde, and other breakdown products in the liver, brain, and other organ systems deserve continued attention.

Protracted withdrawal syndrome.   Pioneering researchers Henri Begleiter, Bernice Porjesz, Benjamin Kissin, and others laid the

groundwork for understanding the source of the recovering alcoholic's continued psychological and social problems. The linkage
between both short- and long-term psychological problems and
their physiological causes is a key area in the study of alcoholism
and should receive continued strong support.

Fetal alcohol syndrome disorders.   Diagnosing and treating FASDs
remains a challenge, but researchers are hard at work identifying distinctive biomarkers, subtle physical and behavioral characteristics, and specific targets—nutritional, environmental,
pharmaceutical—for interventions.

In the years to come, there are obviously many new critical areas
to explore, spanning approaches to the complex issues of education,
prevention, intervention, treatment, and recovery for the disease of
alcoholism.

Education and Prevention

Education and prevention efforts in the past were hampered by the
prevailing psychological theories about the causes of alcoholism,
ongoing debates about the disease concept, and contradictory and
often conflicting approaches to diagnosis, intervention, and treatment. When this book was first published, the federal government
was spending millions of dollars on a "responsible drinking" campaign, promoting the idea that alcohol "abuse" causes alcoholism
and that responsible drinking will prevent it. This "responsible drinking" campaign only served to validate the prevailing misconception
that alcoholism is a symptom of psychological and social problems
rather than a physiological disease.

Another controversial issue involved the need for warning labels
on alcoholic beverages. Proponents insisted that labeling is both useful and cost effective. The issue is complicated, however, because as
numerous studies conducted in the past forty years show, the health

hazards vary from mild to moderate to severe depending on the population. Most people, for example, can have an occasional drink without experiencing any negative effects. For others the risks can be severe, even life-threatening. Alcohol is an addictive drug that is especially perilous for adolescents, whose brains are still developing, and for those with a family history of alcoholism. Recent research shows that even very low levels of daily alcohol consumption (less than one drink) increase the risk of some cancers.[3] Binge drinking greatly increases the risk of car crashes, violence, and suicide. Alcohol can cause miscarriages and birth defects in the developing fetus. Taking alcohol with certain medications increases the risk of addiction, overdose, and death.

The current federal warning labels state only that pregnant women should not drink alcohol and that drinking alcohol impairs the ability to drive a car or operate machinery. This feeble "warning" misses the main target—the biologically susceptible individual whose drinking is regulated by their addiction—and completely overlooks the fact that heavy drinkers (alcoholics and binge drinkers) consume nearly sixty percent of all alcohol sold.[4]

Future education efforts must shift focus and concentrate on identifying those individuals who should temporarily avoid or cut down on their alcohol consumption (pregnant women, for example) and those individuals who are at higher risk for alcoholism and alcohol-related problems (such as those taking medications or from families with a high incidence of alcoholism). Educational efforts should then be directed to explaining why these individuals are at risk and precisely what the risks are. Low-risk individuals—the majority of drinkers—should also be educated about the disease and its early symptoms so that they can make informed decisions about their own consumption of alcohol or when confronted with alcoholics at home or at work.

Factual knowledge about alcoholism must be the foundation of any prevention effort. Prevention efforts in the past were often weak or even counterproductive, as they, too, were based on the misconception that alcoholism is a behavior-based problem with psychological, social, and cultural roots. One example of a misguided prevention effort was the approval of a $1.5 million federal grant to Inuit villages where alcoholism rates ran as high as 70 percent.[5] The money was earmarked to build village recreational centers, which would, it was hoped, ease the villagers' boredom and isolation and thus cut down on the amount they drink. But boredom is not a cause of alcoholism, and while the Inuit villagers may have needed and used the recreation centers, these centers did not have any significant impact on alcoholism rates. What the villagers really needed was accurate information about the disease and comprehensive treatment.

Alcoholism prevention programs should be directed at attacking and halting the physical disease. Comprehensive educational programs and effective treatment centers clearly must be the cornerstones of these programs. The National Institute on Alcohol Abuse and Alcoholism's 2017–2021 Strategic Plan clearly recognizes this need; in his introduction to the plan, director George F. Koob, Ph.D., states that NIAAA's mission is "to generate and disseminate fundamental knowledge about the effects of alcohol on health and well-being and apply that knowledge to improve the diagnosis, prevention, and treatment of alcohol-related problems, including alcohol use disorder, across the lifespan." The five primary goals of the NIAAA's mission are:

- *Basic science,* with the objectives of identifying mechanisms underlying alcoholism and co-occurring mental health conditions, identifying the ways in which alcohol impacts health and disease across the lifespan, and advancing research on alcohol's effect on the adolescent brain
- *Diagnostics and epidemiology,* focusing on improving the diagnosis of alcohol use disorders, developing new approaches for diagnosing and early interventions for fetal alcohol syndrome disorders, and improving the diagnosis of alcohol-related organ damage
- *Prevention,* to promote universal screening and brief interventions

for alcohol and other substance use problems, with emphasis on adolescence as a time of extreme vulnerability to alcohol's harmful effects and addiction potential

- *Treatment,* recognizing that less than 10 percent of people in the United States with alcoholism or other alcohol-related problems receive treatment or help, and thus devoting resources to evaluating the effectiveness, accessibility, and affordability of alcoholism treatments and recovery models, identifying obstacles, and advancing individualized medical interventions and individualized care
- *Public health measures,* to improve public awareness of the effects of alcohol on health and well-being and options for prevention and treatment, in addition to developing resources for healthcare professionals, researchers, and policymakers.[6]

The New Professionals

Aside from research, credit for most of the progress in the field of alcoholism belongs to the people, many with specialized education and training, who are dedicated to helping the alcoholic recover.

Tens of thousands of these new professionals, like an underground army, have manned the battle stations on all fronts and at all echelons in the fight against alcoholism. In the 1970s and 1980s, these dedicated professionals worked endless hours for a pittance, as Mel Schulstad put it,[7] at detox centers, hospitals, and inpatient and outpatient treatment programs, giving help and hope through their own lived experience to alcoholics desperate for knowledge about their disease.* With the advent of managed care in the 1990s and the move to professionally directed treatment services, a new age of recovery-focused efforts began. Grassroots advocacy groups redirected their

---

*Mel Schulstad was the cofounder and first president of the National Association of Alcoholism Counselors, formed in 1982, which in 1984 became the National Association of Alcoholism and Drug Abuse Counselors (NAADAC).

energies, shifting attention from the all-encompassing focus on treatment and endless arguments about whether or not treatment works to highlight the reality of recovery in the lives of millions of people and their family members.

This important move found an organizing voice in the nonprofit organization Faces and Voices of Recovery, founded in 2001. This group is dedicated to mobilizing and organizing community efforts to provide recovery support services and promote the fact that recovery is a reality in the lives of an estimated 22.35 million adults—9.1 percent of the U.S. population.[8] Hundreds of recovery community organizations all over this country (and around the globe) are currently focusing attention on education and employment needs, housing stability, improved health, and social connectedness for people in recovery, with the overall goal of improving quality of life.

Over the years, people in recovery have spearheaded important federal and state legislation, staffed the burgeoning treatment and rehabilitation programs, and provided the primary liaison between the established agencies and professions and the still sick alcoholic. Their efforts have helped reduce the stigma and discrimination that prevents millions of people from seeking help and focused attention on the full range of services they need to move on to rich, full lives in recovery.

Physician Education and Training

Even today, most physicians have received little or no education or training in alcoholism in medical school; most do not have the experience or the skills to recognize or diagnose alcoholism in its early stages; and the majority have scant familiarity with available treatment methods, with A.A. and other mutual support groups, with recovery support systems, or with the current scientific literature on the subject.

The primary reason for this neglect is that the medical profession, along with the rest of society, has classified alcoholism as a psychological disorder. Physicians routinely treat the more serious physical consequences of alcoholism (that is, liver, heart, and respiratory disease), but they often miss the underlying cause—the disease itself. To the extent that physicians do recognize alcoholism, it is usually as a symptom of psychological and social problems beyond their area of expertise and responsibility.

Four decades ago, Joseph Pursch, an outspoken critic of the medical profession and a physician himself, forcefully insisted that physician ignorance about alcoholism and prejudice toward alcoholics are the major obstacles to effective treatment. At the August 1978 meeting of the National Association of Alcoholism Counselors (NAAC), Dr. Pursch emphasized the importance of educating the physician. "The best thing you can do," he told the counselors, "is to decrease the ignorance and increase the awareness and knowledge of physicians." One of the most effective means of changing the physician's attitude toward the alcoholic, Pursch continued, is to emphasize the fact that alcoholism is a treatable disease and that alcoholics by the thousands get well every year. "It's quite remarkable that the healers of the country don't know anyone who is getting well from alcoholism—which means that they only know those who are dying." Pursch went on to explain that this continuing view of alcoholics as hopeless and their disease as inevitably fatal helps to prejudice the doctor's view and reinforce their desire not to treat alcoholics.[9]

Pursch's plea for increased physician awareness and knowledge finds a modern voice in Stanford University Medical School professor Keith Humphreys, Ph.D. "One of the fundamental barriers to providing effective treatment is the fact that addiction is not integrated into medical practice," says Humphreys. "And a lot of medical people like and want it that way; they do not want to deal with addiction; they do not like to deal with the people and they do not feel effective addressing the problem."[10]

In recent years, several professional societies and associations, including the American Society of Addiction Medicine (ASAM), the American Board of Addiction Medicine (ABAM), the American Academy of Addiction Psychiatry (AAAP), and the International Society of Addiction Medicine (ISAM), have emphasized the importance of the education and training of physicians and other health professionals in understanding and treating the disease of addiction.

To be maximally effective, the content of physician, physician assistant, and nurse practitioner education and training programs must be based on the understanding that alcoholism is a physiological disease and not a symptom of psychological, social, or cultural problems. Once the medical profession accepts this basic point, they can very quickly understand the techniques and skills appropriate to their role in helping alcoholics recover.

The Role of Mental Health Providers

Psychiatrists virtually controlled the alcoholism field for many years, holding the top posts in NIAAA and other funding agencies, receiving major research grants, and helping to shape the general public opinion of alcoholism as a mental health problem with psychological and emotional roots.

As the "mental health" view of alcoholism came under increasing pressure, psychiatrists were gradually phased out of positions of leadership in federal, state, and local alcoholism programs, and larger chunks of the available research money were funneled from psychiatry into the biological and neurophysiological sciences. New leaders in the field, influenced by the abundance of research showing that alcoholism is a physiological disease, suggested that psychiatry, by ignoring or downplaying the physiological aspects and concentrating instead on the secondary psychological symptoms, may even harm the patient by delaying treatment, increasing the patient's guilt and shame, and allowing them to deny their drinking problem or blame it on someone or something else.

The following comments by pioneering psychiatrists in the 1970s predicted the transformation that would occur in the field of addiction medicine as it shifted from a mental health perspective to a physiological approach:

- In 1973, NIAAA deputy director Kenneth Eaton told a special task force that alcoholism is "not a mental health problem," adding that the psychiatric approach to alcoholism is "not only the most expensive, but probably the least effective."

- Peter Bourne, M.D., President Jimmy Carter's special assistant for health issues and a psychiatrist himself, told a December 9, 1977, board meeting of the Alcohol and Drug Problems Association that "one of the big battles you are going to face in the next few years is whether psychiatrists should have any involvement at all in treating people with alcoholism problems." He predicted that this battle would be resolved in favor of the "non-psychiatric position as the primary treatment persons for the alcoholic."

- In January 1978, Peter Brock, then director of education and research for the Group Health Association of America, reported to the President's Commission on Mental Health: "Too frequently in the past, the mental health professionals have approached the alcoholic patient with the idea that if his aberrational behavior were corrected, his drinking would go away. They have not addressed the underlying problem, and have struck out."

- Psychiatrist David Ohlms gave a pointed warning to psychiatrists and mental health practitioners at the June 8, 1979, Midcentral Regional meeting of the National Association of Alcoholism Counselors: "As long as the mental health field insists on viewing alcoholism as a symptom rather than a primary disease that creates its own symptoms, it should keep its nose out of this [alcoholism] field."[11]

Underlying the revolt against psychiatric treatment of alcoholism was the accumulation of evidence that it simply did not work. Research reports attested to psychiatry's failure, and many individual psychiatrists openly admitted to it. In a 1956 survey of members of the Southern California Psychiatric Association, for example, over one-half of the psychiatrists who treated alcoholics reported no success with any of their alcoholic patients; for the remainder, success occurred in only 10 percent of their cases.[12] The reason that psychotherapy as a primary form of treatment did not work then and does not work today, of course, is that alcoholism is not primarily a psychological disease. Without attention to the underlying physiological addiction, the alcoholic continues to struggle with the disease of alcoholism. In a 2005 interview in *Addiction* magazine, psychiatrist George Vaillant offers a modern perspective: "I think almost everything psychoanalysis has said about alcoholism has been (180 degrees) wrong."[13]

The pioneering efforts of individual psychiatrists such as David Ohlms, Peter Bourne, Joseph Pursch, and George Vaillant helped to create a transformation in the field that has proven enormously productive for both patients and psychiatrists. With the advent of addiction psychiatry as a medical specialty, trained and educated psychiatrists have contributed steadily and consistently to the science of alcoholism and addiction and become leading advocates for effective, appropriate treatment for alcohol dependence and any co-occurring psychological symptoms.

Alcoholics Anonymous

The worldwide organization of A.A. has saved hundreds of thousands of lives, spurred research, and given hope where there was none. The 2020 Cochrane Review based on twenty-seven studies including 10,565 people found that 42 percent of people participating in A.A. remained abstinent one year later compared to 35 percent of those who received psychological treatments such as cognitive behavioral therapy (CBT). Clinically delivered Twelve-Step Facilitation (TSF) programs designed to increase A.A. participation led to better outcomes, "producing higher rates of continuous abstinence."[14] But even this remarkable fellowship can improve. In the past, A.A. has been able to change and adapt with the times, a quality that has allowed the organization to expand and grow, reaching ever-increasing numbers of alcoholics. As professionals correct their understanding of alcoholism with factual knowledge, A.A. can be expected to adapt its philosophy as well.

A redefinition of the disease, as suggested in this book, will have a profound effect on the A.A. understanding of alcoholism. As a result, character flaws and personality defects will be seen as symptoms of the disease rather than causes, the use of sweets as a substitute for alcohol will be discontinued, and individual A.A. members will be able to work even more effectively with an enlightened professional community. The goal, of course, is not to change the basic structure of A.A. but to expand its unquestionable strengths.

Legal System

In the absence of a uniform understanding of alcoholism, the fifty states initially went in fifty different directions. A clearer understanding of the disease of alcoholism and addictive behavior has led to more rational legal codes and procedures. For instance, many courts have established diagnosis and referral systems for alcoholics that allow them to avoid the "revolving door" of legal and social agencies and instead help them get into effective treatment. Juvenile laws are being adapted to recognize that delinquent behavior, including drinking, is often an indication of an underlying alcohol-related problem rather than a symptom of innate criminality or psychological deviance. When the cause is identified, court services personnel work together to refer the juvenile offender to effective treatment and support services. Adult offenders must also be helped. With 50 percent of the adults who are in prison because of alcohol-related crimes, the need for accurate diagnosis and appropriate treatment is obvious. Yet, historically, these offenders were rarely diagnosed as alcoholics and received little or no treatment for their disease.

A truly effective criminal justice system must move beyond mere punishment and make effective alcoholism treatment a requirement of parole or probation.

Over the past several years, inspired by advances in our understanding of addiction and the need for ongoing recovery support, there have been significant strides in reforming the justice system. The "get-tough" policies of the 1980s and 1990s are being replaced by "smart on crime" policies and programs that address underlying issues such as addiction, holding offenders accountable while simultaneously providing treatment and recovery support.

Industry

One interesting area of activity in alcoholism treatment today is Employee Assistance Programs (EAPs). Of course, the same old problem initially plagued this area as well—namely, the mistaking of alcoholism as a symptom of psychological and social problems. As a consequence, alcoholics were often misdiagnosed and referred to psychological counseling as a treatment option or offered otherwise inappropriate or ineffective treatment options. With a new understanding of alcoholism and a thoughtful and personalized approach, however, the EAPs could become far more effective, with the potential to reach millions of alcoholics.

Insurance

Many insurance policies cover inpatient treatment for alcoholics. However, treatment is a $35 billion industry in the United States. *Industry* is the key word, for as insurance coverage is increasingly restricted by an aggressive managed care system that mandates shorter durations of stay, even for the most severe cases, many if not most treatment centers have chosen to focus on budgets rather than best practices. This trend toward briefer inpatient stays and low-quality treatment should be discouraged. Alcoholism is not a self-inflicted illness deserving only minimum care, but a very serious physiological disease fully deserving the best in medical protection and treatment. With improvements in the quality of treatment, it should become clear that effective inpatient treatment is far and away the most cost-effective approach to our number one public health problem.

The National Institute on Alcohol Abuse and Alcoholism (NIAAA)

In 1970, the National Institute on Alcohol Abuse and Alcoholism was established in the federal government as a separate agency on the same level as the National Institute of Mental Health and the National Institute on Drug Abuse. It is important to understand, however, that NIAAA was originally established not to recognize alcoholism as a separate, primary disease but merely to give alcoholism "more visibility" in the competition for funds.

Because it has been the greatest source of funds in the alcoholism field, NIAAA historically also had the most powerful role in shaping programs, public policies, and opinion. Unfortunately, this agency originally viewed alcoholism not as a primary disease but as a symptom of psychological inadequacy. In the name of preventive education, for example, NIAAA widely promoted and disseminated in the schools and in other community organizations the idea that irresponsible drinking causes alcoholism and that alcoholism can be prevented by learning to drink responsibly. Consistent with this philosophy, NIAAA turned over the accreditation of all alcoholism programs to a panel of psychiatrists in the Joint Commission on Accreditation of Hospitals.

The issue that the federal government in general and NIAAA in particular must tackle and have increasingly focused on in the ensuing years is this: is alcoholism a physiological disease, or is it a symptom of psychological and social problems? As NIAAA shifted from its original mental health view of alcoholism to, more recently, seeing alcoholism as a disease with complex genetic and biological underpinnings, the agency has become increasingly important in funding and supporting the search for understanding the disease of alcoholism and efficacious treatments for this disease.

The Individual

Alcoholics and their families cannot afford to wait for physicians to be educated, federal government programs to be realigned, treatment programs to be modified, and laws to be changed. Rather than wait in the hope that someone or something else will protect them, they should instead take responsibility and protect themselves. Having read this book, they will be armed with the basic facts about the disease. They will know that alcoholics are not morally or psychologically defective people, but innocent victims of a chronic and progressive disease. They will know the warning signs of alcoholism, and they will know how to get into treatment. All who understand the disease can join forces to enlighten others. They can insist on change in all areas of community involvement, including health and social service agencies, the judicial system, and federal, state, and local programs.

Each person's role in the movement toward a complete and unprejudiced understanding of alcoholism may seem small and insignificant. And yet individuals can truly move mountains. Society is not a solid block with one mind and heart, but a changing and shifting collection of millions of different people. When enough people devote their energies to eliminating the myths and misconceptions surrounding alcoholism, they will be able to build on this scientific understanding and create a new era of enlightenment for the alcoholic, those who love them, and all the rest of us whose lives are affected by their disease.

ACKNOWLEDGMENTS

We are especially grateful to Mrs. Dorris M. Hutchison, cofounder and for eleven years executive director of Alcenas Hospital. More than any other individual she is responsible for exploring and demonstrating the validity of this new approach to alcoholism treatment.

Special thanks go to Patrick Spencer, Fisher Howe, Elizabeth Howe, Kathe Monroe, Bill Asbury, and Mel Schulstad for their advice and support. For their expert guidance and encouragement with the revised edition of this book, deep gratitude is extended to John Kelly, Ph.D.; William L. White; Marvin Seppala, M.D.; Debra Jay; Jeff Jay; Arthur Cederbaum, Ph.D.; William Billica, M.D.; Marc Schuckit, M.D.; Joel Gelernter, M.D.; Howard Becker, Ph.D; Michael W. King, Ph.D; Susan Broderick, J.D.; and William Cope Moyers.

Thanks to Jane Dystel and the talented team at Dystel, Goderich, & Bourret literary agency for championing the need for a revised edition of this book; to Kathryn M. Milam, Ph.D., J.D., for her expertise and dedication to continuing her Father's legacy; and to editor Erin Kane, for her keen and thoughtful feedback, steady encouragement, and unending patience.

Our greatest acknowledgment must always be a tribute to Alcoholics Anonymous, the inspiration and guiding force of the reform movement in alcoholism since 1935.

There are many anonymous human beings to whom this book refers only by pronouns. The book, however, is dedicated to all who suffer from the disease of alcoholism.

APPENDIX A

MEDICATIONS CONTAINING ALCOHOL:
A RESOURCE SHEET

The Health Professionals' Services Program thanks Pappy Corbitt, R.Ph., Recovery Support Liaison at Serenity Lane, for letting us share this document.

Licensees who are in the Health Professionals' Services Program should be aware of the products that contain alcohol, especially if the licensee is in the toxicology testing program and subject to ethyl glucuronide (EtG) testing. The following list is not a comprehensive list of all medications containing alcohol; it merely serves as a basic reference. Medications listed may differ from those produced in countries other than the United States and labels should always be read to ensure compliance and safety.

Alcohol in pharmaceutical products acts as a preservative and/or promotes sedation, depending on the agents listed, and the responsibility lies with the consumer of knowing what is in medications that are taken. Therefore, prior to administration consult with your physician or pharmacist to avoid untoward reactions with other medications you may be taking or preexisting medical conditions.

Medications included in this list may contain addictive substances such as opiates, barbiturates, etc. Therefore, prior to administration, consult your healthcare professional. Fact: If it has "-lixir" in the name, it has alcohol in the product. Example: Tylenol Elixir.

See products that are also available as alcohol-free on pages 211–212.

Read the label prior to administration; product ingredients may change over time.

Medications with % of Alcohol Content

ANTI-DIARRHEAL MEDICATIONS

Tincture of Paregoric 45%

Paregoric (corrective
  mixtures) 2%

DiaGuell 10%

Donnagel 3.8%

Donnagel PG 5%

Lomotil Liquid 15%

Parepectolin 0.6%

LAXATIVES

Cascara Products as much
  as 18%

Dr. Caldwell's Senna Laxative
  4.5%

Fletchers Castoria 3.5%

Senecot Syrup 7%

Black Draught 5%

ANTI-EMETIC (NAUSEA/VOMITING)

Dramamine Liquid 5%

COMMONLY DISPENSED PRESCRIPTION AND OTC MEDICATIONS

Actonel Expectorant 12.8%

Asbron Elixir 15%

Anahist 0.5%

Ambenyl Expectorant 5%

Anti-Tuss DM Expectorant
  1.4%

Atarax Syrup 0.5%

Bactrim Suspension 0.3%

Benedryl Decongestant 5%

Benedryl Elixir 14%

Bentyl PB 19%

Benylin 5%

Benylin DM 5%

Black Draught 5%

Breacol 10%

Bronkelixir 19%

Calcidrine 6%

Creose 2.5%

Creose DM 2.5%

Cheracol 3%

Cheracol D 3%

Chlortrimeton Expectorant
  7%

Codimal DM 4%

Coldene Cough Syrup 15%

Coltrex 4.5%

Coltrex Expectorant 4.7%

Conar Expectorant 5%

Contact Severe Cold 25%

Consutuss 10%

Contrex 20%

Coryban-D 7.5%

Co-Tylenol 7.5%

Cosanyl DM 6%

Cotussis 20%

Creamcote #1-#4 10%

Daycare 10%

DayQuil 10–25%

Demazin 8.5%

Dimetapp 2.3%

Dimetane Decongestant
  2.3%–3.5%

Dr. Drakes 2.3%

Dristan Cough 12%

Dristan Ultra 25%

Endotussin NN 4%

Ephedrine Syrup 3%

Formula 44 Cough 10%

Formula 44 D 20%

Furosemide Sol 11.6%

GG Cen 10%

GG Tussin 3.5%

Halls 22%

Head and Chest 5%

Kaochlor 5%

Kaon Elixir 5%

Kay Ceil 4%

Marax Syrup 5%

Mercodol with Decaprin 5%

Metoclopramide Sol .01 %

Naldecon 5%

Naldecon DX 5%

Night Relief 25%

NN Cough Syrup 5%

Nortussin 3.5%

NovafedA 5%

Novahistine Cough 3.5%

Novahistine Cough and Cold
  5%

Novahistine Elixir 5%

Novahistine DH 5%

Novahistine DM 5%

Novahistine DMX 10%

Novahistine Expectorant 7.5%

Nyquil 10%

Nyquil Cough 25%

Pediquil 5%

Periactin Syrup 5%

Petussin 8.5%

Phenergan Expectorant
Plain 7%

Phenergan Expectorant with
  Codeine 7%

Phenergan Expectorant VC
  Plain 7%

Phenergan Expectorant PC
  with Codeine 7%

Phenergan Fortis 7%

Pinex 3%

Potassium Chloride Sol 10%

Prednisolone Oral Sol 1.8%

Prednisone Sol 5%

Promethazine Syrup 7%

Promethazine with Codeine
  7%

Promethazine DM with
  Codeine 7%

Quelidrine 2%

Quibron Elixir 15%

Quiet Night 25%

Robitussin 3.5%

Robitussin AC 3.5%

Robitussin CF 1.4%

Robitussin DAC 1.4%

Robitussin DM 1.4%

Robitussin PE 1.4%

Romilar III 20%

Romilar CF 20%

Rondec DM Syrup and Drops 0.6%

Roniacol Elixir 8.6%

SK AP AP Elixir 8%

Sudafed Cough Syrup 2.4%

Tedral 15%

Temaril Syrup 5.7%

Tempra Syrup and Drops 10%

Terpin Hydrate 42%

Terpin Hydrate with Codeine 2%

TheoElixir 20%

Thera-Flu 10%

Tolu-Sed 10%

Tonecol 7%

Triamininc Expectorant 5%

TrindDM 5%

Tylenol Liquid and Drops 7%

Tylenol Extra Strength Liquid or Drops 8.5%

Vicks Cough 5%

Viromed 16%

Wal-Act 5%

Wal-Phed 0.01 %

IRON AND VITAMIN SUPPLEMENTS

Ce-Vi Drops 5%

Feosol Elixir 5%

Fer-in-Sol Drops 0.2%

Fer-in-Sol Syrup 5%

Fumeral 5%

Ganatrix 15%

Geralix Liquid 15%

Geraplex FS 15%

Geraplex Liquid 15%

Geritol 12%

Geritonic 20%

Gerizyme 18%

Gevrabon 18%

Iberet Liquid 15%

Mol Form Liquid 4.8%

Niferex 10%

SSS Tonic 12%

Zymalixir 1.5%

Zymasyrup 2%

MOUTHWASHES

Asring-O-Sol 65%

Cepacol 14%

Chlorhexidine Wash 11.6%

Colgate-100 15%

Dr. Tichener's 70%

Flourigard 6%

Isodine 35%

Listerine 26%

Listermint 12%

Mouth Wash and Gargle 14%

Odara 48%

Oral Pentacresol 30%

Scope 18.5%

Note: Some mouthwash percentages can vary from 15% to 25%

TOOTHACHE RELIEF

Anbesol 70%

Anbesol Gel 70%

Betadine Mouthwash 8.8%

Blister Clear 37%

DeWitt Cold Sore 90%

Dalidyne 61%

Dents Toothache Drops 60%

Double Action Kit 60%

Gum-Zor 22%

Jiffy 56.5%

Numzit 10%

Pfeiffer Cold Sore 85%

Rid-A-Pain Dental Drops 20%

Rid-A-Pain Gel 7.5%

Teething Lotion 4.5%

Toothache Drops 20%

HAND SANITIZERS

Purell 65% ethyl alcohol

Products Available in Alcohol-Free Formulation

ANTI-DIARRHEAL

Dia-Eza

Kaolin-Pectin

Kaopectate

Pepto-Bismol

Rheahan

TOOTHACHE/COLD SORE RELIEF

Benzodent

Chloraseptic

Canacirl

Carmex

Ora-Base

Ora-Base with Benzocaine

Ora-gel

Proxigel

S.T. 37

Tanic

COUGH AND COLD RELIEF

Actifed

Actifed-C

Adult Noctec

Alupent Syrup

Chloraseptic

Codimal Expectorant

Corricidin

CreonDM

Delsym

Dilantin

Drixoral

Efficol Cough

Hycodan Syrup

Hycomine Syrup

Ipsatol

Liquiprin (acetaminophen)

Loratadine Syrup

Mediquel Naldecon Syrup

Naldecon DX

Nydrazid

Omnituss

Orthoxreal

Ryna

Sudafed

Sudafed Plus

Triaminic DM

Triaminic Cough and Cold

Triaminicol

Tussionex

Vistaril Suspension

Wal-Minic DM

Wal-Minic Cough and Cold
  Relief

HAND SANITIZERS—CAN INCLUDE ISOPROPYL ALCOHOL, BENZALKONIUM CHLORIDE, POVIDONE-IODINE, OR TRICLOSON

Safe Hands

Safe4Hours

Gentlecare

GUIDELINES FOR A HYPOGLYCEMIC DIET

This information is adapted from the University of Wisconsin Hospitals and Clinics Authority "Health Facts for You," produced by the Department of Nursing and printed with their permission.

Hypoglycemia

WHAT IS IT?

Hypoglycemia is a medical term for low blood sugar (glucose). Glucose is the sugar that our bodies use for energy. In most people, a normal level of blood sugar is within a range of 70 to 99 mg/dL. Hypoglycemia can be a concern for people with diabetes, but it also affects people who do not have diabetes.

SYMPTOMS

Symptoms may occur within 2 to 4 hours after a meal. People have some or all these symptoms:

Hunger	Double or blurred vision
Sweating	Fast pulse rate
Shakiness	Headache
Weakness	Anxiety
Fatigue	Craving for sweets
Nausea/vomiting	Flushing
Numbness/coldness in arms or legs	Confusion
Mood swings	Irritability

Eating to Prevent Symptoms

Limit foods high in sugar and concentrated sweets. Eating these foods can cause a rapid increase in blood glucose. This may lead to excessive increase of insulin, which causes a rapid fall in blood glucose. Foods high in sugar include:

Cakes	Candy
Cookies	Gelatin, Jell-O
Pies	Nectars (agave)
Puddings and custards	Honey
Regular soda, lemonade, Kool-Aid, punch	Syrups (corn, pancake, maple)
Sugar, brown sugar	Fruit juice greater than 4 ounces
Ice cream, sherbet, frozen yogurt	Sweet tea and flavored coffee
Jelly and jams	

If you have something sweet, eat it with a meal. You may handle sweet foods better if eaten with a meal since the other foods at the meal reduce the effects of the sugar.

Limit or avoid caffeine. Caffeine causes an increase in adrenaline and can cause the same symptoms as low blood sugar.

Spread your intake of carbs throughout the day. Eating large amounts of rice, bread, cereal, or pasta at one time can cause your body to produce large amounts of insulin. This is much like simple sugars or sweets and can cause glucose levels to drop sharply.

Eat every 3 to 4 hours. Eating many small meals and snacks each day rather than 3 larger meals can help to regulate the amount of glucose in your bloodstream.

Aim for 2 to 4 servings of carbs at each meal (30 to 60 grams) and 1 to 2 servings (15 to 30 grams) at snack times. One carb serving has 15 grams of total carb.

Each of these foods contains about 15 grams of carbs:

1 regular slice of bread	1 small apple (tennis ball size)
½ English muffin, hot dog, or hamburger bun	½ cup fruit canned in its own juice
½ cup rice, pasta, cooked cereal	¾ cup high fiber cold cereal
1 small potato (about ½ cup)	1 cup plain, light, or Greek yogurt

Choose whole grains and increase high fiber foods. Whole grains take longer to break down. This helps to keep blood glucose levels more consistent. Whole grain breads and cereals, legumes/beans, vegetables, and whole fruits are high in fiber. These foods will help you eat at least 25 grams of fiber daily.

Include lean protein at each meal and snack. Our body breaks down protein more slowly than carbs. This mixture of carb and protein can give a long-lasting source of energy. Good sources of lean protein foods include skinless poultry, fish, low-fat cheese, eggs, peanut butter, and soy-based foods.

Enjoy foods high in healthy fats in small amounts throughout the day. Fats are also digested slowly and can help to balance the blood sugar. Choose healthy fats such as nuts, seeds, avocado, olives, and olive oil. Try to enjoy fats in small amounts because they are also high in calories and can lead to weight gain.

Keep some nonperishable foods on hand to prevent or treat low blood sugar symptoms. Granola bars with protein, or nuts and dried fruit mix are quick, healthy snacks. Keeping these foods on hand is a good choice instead of getting a high-calorie candy bar from the vending machine or store.

SAMPLE ONE-DAY MENU FOR A HYPOGLYCEMIC DIET

BREAKFAST

2 slices 100% whole wheat toast
   (2 carb servings)

1 egg or 2 Tbsp peanut butter
1 cup skim milk (1 carb serving)

AM SNACK

6 Triscuit crackers (1 carb serving)

2 Tbsp hummus

LUNCH

2 slices 100% whole wheat bread
   (2 carb servings)
2 oz lean turkey
¼ avocado, sliced

17 grapes (1 carb serving)
Raw carrot and celery sticks
1–2 Tbsp low fat salad dressing as
   dip

PM SNACK

1 cup Greek yogurt (1 carb serving)

EVENING MEAL

3 oz skinless chicken breast
½ large baked potato (2 carb
   servings)
2 Tbsp light sour cream
½ cup cooked broccoli

Small dinner salad with 1 Tbsp
   salad dressing
1 cup skim milk (1 carb serving)
1 cup strawberries (1 carb serving)

EVENING SNACK

3 cups light popcorn (1 carb serving)
2 Tbsp almonds

COMMONLY USED MEDICINES
(BOTH PRESCRIPTION AND OVER-THE-COUNTER)
THAT INTERACT WITH ALCOHOL

OLDER PEOPLE FACE GREATER RISK

Older people are at particularly high risk for harmful alcohol–medication interactions. Aging slows the body's ability to break down alcohol, so alcohol remains in a person's system longer. Older people also are more likely to take a medication that interacts with alcohol—in fact, they often need to take more than one of these medications.

TIMING IS IMPORTANT

Alcohol and medicines can interact harmfully even if they are not taken at the same time.

REMEMBER . . .

Mixing alcohol and medicines puts you at risk for dangerous reactions. Protect yourself by avoiding alcohol if you are taking a medication and don't know its effect. To learn more about a medicine and whether it will interact with alcohol, talk to your pharmacist or other healthcare provider.

Commonly Used Medicines (Both Prescription and Over-the-Counter) That Interact with Alcohol

SYMPTOMS/ DISORDERS	MEDICATION (BRAND NAME)	MEDICATION (GENERIC NAME)	SOME POSSIBLE REACTIONS WITH ALCOHOL
Allergies/ colds/flu	• Alavert® • Atarax® • Benadryl® • Clarinex® • Claritin®, Claritin-D® • Dimetapp® Cold & Allergy • Sudafed® Sinus & Allergy • Triaminic® Cold & Allergy • Tylenol® Allergy Sinus • Tylenol® Cold & Flu • Zyrtec®	Loratadine Hydroxyzine Diphenhydramine Desloratadine Loratadine Brompheniramine Chlorpheniramine Chlorpheniramine Chlorpheniramine Chlorpheniramine Cetirizine	Drowsiness, dizziness; increased risk for overdose
Angina (chest pain), coronary heart disease	• Isordil®	Isosorbide Nitroglycerin	Rapid heartbeat, sudden changes in blood pressure, dizziness, fainting
Anxiety and epilepsy	• Ativan® • BuSpar® • Klonopin® • Librium® • Paxil® • Valium® • Xanax® • Herbal preparations (Kava)	Lorazepam Buspirone Clonazepam Chlordiazepoxide Paroxetine Diazepam Alprazolam	Drowsiness, dizziness; increased risk for overdose; slowed or difficulty breathing; impaired motor control; unusual behavior; memory problems Liver damage, drowsiness
Arthritis	• Celebrex® • Naprosyn® • Voltaren®	Celecoxib Naproxen Diclofenac	Ulcers, stomach bleeding, liver damage

Source: National Institute on Alcohol Abuse and Alcoholism (NIAAA), https://www.niaaa.nih.gov/alcohols-effects-health/alcohol-use-disorder

SYMPTOMS/ DISORDERS	MEDICATION (BRAND NAME)	MEDICATION (GENERIC NAME)	SOME POSSIBLE REACTIONS WITH ALCOHOL
Attention and concentration (Attention deficit/ hyperactivity disorder)	• Adderall® • Concerta®, Ritalin® • Dexedrine® • Focalin® • Strattera® • Vyvanse®	Amphetamine/ dextroamphetamine Methylphenidate Dextroamphetamine Dexmethylphenidate Atomoxetine Lisdexamfetamine	Dizziness, drowsiness, impaired concentration (methylphenidate, dexmethylphenidate); possible increased risk for heart problems (amphetamine, dextroamphetamine, lisdexamfetamine); liver damage (atomoxetine)
Blood clots	• Coumadin®	Warfarin	Occasional drinking may lead to internal bleeding; heavier drinking also may cause bleeding or may have the opposite effect, resulting in possible blood clots, strokes, or heart attacks
Cough	• Delsym®, Robitussin Cough® • Robitussin A–C®	Dextromethorpan Guaifenesin + codeine	Drowsiness, dizziness; increased risk for overdose
Depression	• Abilify® • Anafranil® • Celexa® • Clozaril® • Cymbalta® • Desyrel® • Effexor® • Elavil® • Geodon® • Invega® • Lexapro® • Luvox® • Nardil®	Aripriprazone Clomipramine Citalopram Clozapine Duloxetine Trazodone Venlafaxine Amitriptyline Ziprasidone Paliperidone Escitalopram Fluvoxamine Phenelzine	Drowsiness, dizziness; increased risk for overdose; increased feelings of depression or hopelessness (all medications); impaired motor control (quetiapine, mirtazapine); increased alcohol effect (bupropion); liver damage (duloxetine)

SYMPTOMS/ DISORDERS	MEDICATION (BRAND NAME)	MEDICATION (GENERIC NAME)	SOME POSSIBLE REACTIONS WITH ALCOHOL
Depression	• Norpramin® • Parnate® • Paxil® • Pristiq® • Prozac® • Remeron® • Risperdal® • Seroquel® • Serzone® • Symbyax® • Wellbutrin® • Zoloft® • Zyprexa • Herbal preparations (St. John's Wort)	Desipramine Tranylcypromine Paroxetine Desevenlafaxine Fluoxetine Mirtazapine Risperidone Quetiapine Nefazodone Fluoxetine/Olanzapine Bupropion Sertraline Olanzapine	Monoamine oxidase inhibitors (MAOIs), such as tranylcypromine and phenelzine, when combined with alcohol, may result in serious heart-related side effects. Risk for dangerously high blood pressure is increased when MAOIs are mixed with tyramine, a byproduct found in beer and red wine
Diabetes	• Diabinese® • Glucotrol® • Glucophage® • Glynase®, DiaBeta®, Micronase® • Orinase® • Tolinase®	Chlorpropamide Glipizide Metformin Glyburide Tolbutamide Tolazamide	Abnormally low blood sugar levels, flushing reaction (nausea, vomiting, headache, rapid heartbeat, sudden changes in blood pressure); symptoms of nausea and weakness may occur (metformin)
Enlarged prostate	• Cardura® • Flomàx® • Hytrin® • Minipress®	Doxazosin Tamsulosin Terazosin Prazosin	Dizziness, lightheadedness, fainting
Heartburn, indigestion, sour stomach	• Axid® • Reglan® • Tagamet® • Zantac®	Nizatidine Metoclopramide Cimetidine Ranitidine	Rapid heartbeat; increased alcohol effect; sudden changes in blood pressure (metoclopramide)

SYMPTOMS/ DISORDERS	MEDICATION (BRAND NAME)	MEDICATION (GENERIC NAME)	SOME POSSIBLE REACTIONS WITH ALCOHOL
High blood pressure	• Accupril® • Calan® • Capozide® • Cardura® • Catapres® • Cozaar® • Hytrin® • Lopressor® HCT • Lotensin® • Minipress® • Norvasc® • Prinivil®, Zestril® • Vaseretic®	Quinapril Verapamil Hydrochlorothiazide Doxazosin Clonidine Losartan Terazosin Hydrochlorothiazide Benzapril Prazosin Amlodipine Lisinopril Enalapril	Dizziness, fainting, drowsiness; heart problems such as changes in the heart's regular heartbeat (arrhythmia)
High cholesterol	• Advicor® • Altocor® • Crestor® • Lipitor® • Mevacor® • Niaspan® • Pravachol® • Pravigard™ • Vytorin™ • Zocor®	Lovastatin + Niacin Lovastatin Rosuvastatin Atorvastatin Lovastatin Niacin Pravastatin Pravastatin + Aspirin Ezetimibe + Simvastatin Simvastatin	Liver damage (all medications); increased flushing and itching (niacin), increased stomach bleeding (pravastatin + aspirin)
Infections	• Acrodantin® • Flagyl® • Grisactin® • Nizoral® • Nydrazid® • Seromycin® • Tindamax® • Zithromax®	Nitrofurantoin Metronidazole Griseofulvin Ketoconazole Isoniazid Cycloserine Tinidazole Azithromycin	Fast heartbeat, sudden changes in blood pressure; stomach pain, upset stomach, vomiting, headache, or flushing or redness of the face; liver damage (isoniazid, ketoconazole)

SYMPTOMS/ DISORDERS	MEDICATION (BRAND NAME)	MEDICATION (GENERIC NAME)	SOME POSSIBLE REACTIONS WITH ALCOHOL
Mood stabilizers	• Depakene®, Depakote® • Eskalith®, Eskalith®CR, Lithobid	Valproic acid Lithium	Drowsiness, dizziness; tremors; increased risk for side effects, such as restlessness, impaired motor control; loss of appetite; stomach upset; irregular bowel movement; joint or muscle pain; depression; liver damage (valproic acid)
Muscle pain	• Flexeril® • Soma®	Cyclobenzaprine Carisoprodol	Drowsiness, dizziness; increased risk of seizures; increased risk for overdose; slowed or difficulty breathing; impaired motor control; unusual behavior; memory problems
Nausea, motion sickness	• Antivert® • Dramamine® • Phenergan®	Meclizine Dimenhydrinate Promethazine	Drowsiness, dizziness; increased risk for overdose
Pain (such as muscle ache, minor arthritis pain), fever, inflammation	• Advil® • Aleve® • Excedrin® • Motrin® • Tylenol®	Ibuprofen Naproxen Aspirin, Acetaminophen Ibuprofen Acetaminophen	Stomach upset, bleeding and ulcers; liver damage (acetaminophen); rapid heartbeat
Seizures	• Dilantin® • Horizant®, Neurontin® • Keppra® • Klonopin® • Lamictal® • Lyrica® • Tegretol® • Topamax® • Trileptal®	Phenytoin Gabapentin Levetiracetam Clonazepam Phenobarbital Lamotrigine Pregabalin Carbamazepine Topiramate Oxcarbazepine Barbiturates	Drowsiness, dizziness; increased risk of seizures (levetiracetam, phenytoin); unusual behavior and changes in mental health (such as thoughts of suicide) (topiramate)

SYMPTOMS/ DISORDERS	MEDICATION (BRAND NAME)	MEDICATION (GENERIC NAME)	SOME POSSIBLE REACTIONS WITH ALCOHOL
Severe pain from injury, postsurgical care, oral surgery, migraines	• Darvocet–N® • Demerol® • Fiorinal® with codeine • Percocet® • Vicodin®	Propoxyphene Merepidine Butalbital + codeine Oxycodone Hydrocodone	Drowsiness, dizziness; increased risk for overdose; slowed or difficulty breathing; impaired motor control; unusual behavior; memory problems
Sleep problems	• Ambien® • Lunesta™ • Prosom™ • Restoril® • Sominex® • Unisom® • Herbal preparations (chamomile, valerian, lavender)	Zolpidem Eszopiclone Estazolam Temazepam Diphenhydramine Doxylamine	Drowsiness, sleepiness, dizziness; slowed or difficulty breathing; impaired motor control; unusual behavior; memory problems

GUIDELINES FOR DIAGNOSING ALCOHOLISM

In this book we use the terms early, middle, *and* late stage *to emphasize the progressive nature of the disease of alcoholism. The presence of two or three symptoms in the list below might signify early-stage alcoholism. Four, five, or more symptoms ("moderate" to "severe" alcohol use disorder, AUD) indicate the progression of a serious, potentially life-threatening disease process. The National Institute on Alcohol Abuse and Alcoholism further breaks down the progression the following way:*

To be diagnosed with AUD, individuals must meet certain criteria outlined in the *Diagnostic and Statistical Manual of Mental Disorders* (*DSM*). Under *DSM-5*, the current version of the *DSM*, anyone meeting any two of the eleven criteria during the same twelve-month period receives a diagnosis of AUD. The severity of AUD—mild, moderate, or severe—is based on the number of criteria met.

To assess whether you or a loved one may have AUD, here are some questions to ask. In the past year, have you:

- Had times when you ended up drinking more or longer than you intended?
- More than once wanted to cut down or stop drinking, or tried to, but couldn't?
- Spent a lot of time drinking? Or being sick or getting over the aftereffects?
- Experienced craving—a strong need, or urge, to drink?

Source: National Institute on Alcohol Abuse and Alcoholism (NIAAA), NIH Publication No. 13 -5329, published 2003, revised 2014.

- Found that drinking—or being sick from drinking—often interfered with taking care of your home or family? Or caused job troubles? Or school problems?
- Continued to drink even though it was causing trouble with your family or friends?
- Given up or cut back on activities that were important or interesting to you, or gave you pleasure, in order to drink?
- More than once gotten into situations while or after drinking that increased your chances of getting hurt (such as driving, swimming, using machinery, walking in a dangerous area, or having unsafe sex)?
- Continued to drink even though it was making you feel depressed or anxious or adding to another health problem? Or after having had a memory blackout?
- Had to drink much more than you once did to get the effect you want? Or found that your usual number of drinks had much less effect than before?
- Found that when the effects of alcohol were wearing off, you had withdrawal symptoms, such as trouble sleeping, shakiness, irritability, anxiety, depression, restlessness, nausea, or sweating? Or sensed things that were not there?

If you have any of these symptoms, your drinking may already be a cause for concern. The more symptoms you have, the more urgent the need for change. A health professional can conduct a formal assessment of your symptoms to see if AUD is present.

However severe the problem may seem, most people with AUD can benefit from treatment. Unfortunately, less than 10 percent of them receive any treatment.

Ultimately, receiving treatment can improve an individual's chances of success in overcoming AUD. The *NIAAA Alcohol Treatment Navigator* can help you recognize and find high-quality treatment for alcohol-use disorder. If you drink excessively, seek medical help to plan a safe recovery, as sudden abstinence can be life threatening.

NOTES AND REFERENCES

CHAPTER 1: EVERY HUMAN SOUL

1. Marissa B. Esser, Adam Sherk, Yong Liu et al. (2020). "Deaths and Years of Potential Life Lost from Excessive Alcohol Use—United States, 2011–2015." *Morbidity and Mortality Weekly Report* 69: 1428–1433 (corrected and republished report).

2. The 51st Nobel Conference at Gustavus Adolphus College (October 6–7, 2015). "Addiction: Exploring the Science and Experience of an Equal Opportunity Condition." Available in archived videos on YouTube; see https://gustavus .edu/events/nobelconference/2015/. The conversation quoted here is from the 41-minute archived video "Eric Kandel, MD Presenting at Nobel Conference 51." See https://www.youtube.com/watch?v=Qb2V_g5FPwU&list=PLHuA oPzfQhGFS8jEE942HV07hvKfPotwJ&index=2.

3. Michael Beck, Sandra Dietrich, Herbert Matschinger, & Matthias Angermeyer (2003). "Alcoholism: Low Standing with the Public? Attitudes Towards Spending Financial Resources on Medical Care and Research on Alcoholism." *Alcohol and Alcoholism* 38(6): 602–605.

4. Survey conducted by researchers at Johns Hopkins Bloomberg School of Public Health: Colleen Barry, Emma Elizabeth McGinty, Bernice Pescosolido, & Howard Goldman (2014). "Stigma, Discrimination, Treatment Effectiveness, and Policy: Public Views About Drug Addiction and Mental Illness." *Psychiatric Services* 65(10): 1269–1272.

    "The more shame associated with drug addiction, the less likely we as a community will be in a position to change attitudes and get people the help they need," coauthor Beth McGinty concluded. "If you can educate the public that these are treatable conditions, we will see higher levels of support for policy changes that benefit people with mental illness and drug addiction." Dr. McGinty is quoted in the Johns Hopkins University newsletter *The Hub*: https://hub.jhu.edu/2014/10/01/drug-addiction-stigma/.

5. Statistics are gleaned from various sources including the National Institute on Alcohol Abuse and Alcoholism, the National Institute on Drug Abuse, the Substance Abuse and Mental Health Services Administration, and the Centers for Disease Control. For specific references see: Aaron White et al. (2020). "Using Death Certificates to Explore Changes in Alcohol-Related Mortality in the United States, 1999–2017." *Alcoholism: Clinical and Experimental Research* 44(1): 178–187.

Mark Gold (2020). "The Role of Alcohol, Drugs and Deaths of Despair in the U.S.'s Falling Life Expectancy." *Missouri Medicine* 117(2): 99–101.

Bridget Grant et al. (2017). "Prevalence of 12-Month Alcohol Use, High-Risk Drinking, and DSM-IV Alcohol Use Disorder in the United States, 2001–2002 to 2012–2013: Results from the National Epidemiologic Survey on Alcohol and Related Conditions." *JAMA Psychiatry* 74(9): 911–923.

Marc Schuckit (2017). "Remarkable Increases in Alcohol Use Disorders." *JAMA Psychiatry* 74(9): 869–870.

CHAPTER 2: ALCOHOL

1. Epigraph: Chauncey D. Leake, professor of medicine at Ohio State University, at a symposium called "Alcoholism," sponsored by the American Association for the Advancement of Science, 1957.

2. GBD 2016 Collaborators (2018). "Alcohol Use and Burden for 195 Countries and Territories, 1990–2016: A Systematic Analysis for the Global Burden of Disease Study 2016." *The Lancet* 392: 1015–1035. Conclusion (page 1026): "Alcohol use is a leading risk factor for disease burden worldwide, accounting for nearly 10% of global deaths among populations aged 15–49 years, and poses dire ramifications for future population health in the absence of policy action today. The widely held view of the health benefits of alcohol needs revising, particularly as improved methods and analyses continue to show how much alcohol use contributes to global death and disability. *Our results show that the safest level of drinking is none.* [italics added] This level is in conflict with most health guidelines, which espouse health benefits associated with consuming up to two drinks per day. Alcohol use contributes to health loss from many causes and exacts its toll across the lifespan, particularly among men. Policies that focus on reducing population-level consumption will be most effective in reducing the health loss from alcohol use."

3. Two classic reference texts on alcohol and alcoholism attest to alcohol's stimulating properties at low doses. In the conclusion to their comprehensive multivolume textbook, *Actions of Alcohol* (Amsterdam: Elsevier Publishing Co., 1970), authors Henrik Wallgren & Herbert Barry write: "Most studies of nerve conduction and transmission, EEG records, and behavioral performance indicate stimulant actions of low doses and depressant actions of high doses" (2:797).

   R. G. Grenell, "Effects of Alcohol on the Neuron," in *The Biology of Alcoholism,* eds. Benjamin Kissin & Henri Begleiter (New York: Plenum Press, 1972), summarizes: "Neuronal activity is stimulated by low concentrations and depressed by high concentrations of alcohol" (2:17).

4. The World Health Organization published its definitions in *Alcohol and Alcoholism—Report of an Expert Committee, Technical Report 94* (Geneva: WHO, 1955).

5. Berton Roueché, *The Neutral Spirit: A Portrait of Alcohol* (Boston: Little, Brown, 1960), 62.

6. Over 140 million people age eighteen and over in the United States drink alcohol. See Substance Abuse and Mental Health Services Administration, *Key Substance Use and Mental Health Indicators in the United States: Results from the 2018 National Survey On Drug Use and Health*, HHS Publication No. PEP19-5068, NSDUH Series H-54 (Rockville, MD: Center for Behavioral Health Statistics and Quality, Substance Abuse and Mental Health Services Administration, 2019), https://www.samhsa.gov/data/.

CHAPTER 3: WHAT MAKES AN ALCOHOLIC: PREDISPOSING FACTORS

1. For recent research on alcohol and hormones, see: Nadia Rachdaoui & Dipak K. Sarkar (2017). "Pathophysiology of the Effects of Alcohol Abuse on the Endocrine System." *Alcohol Research: Current Reviews* 38(2): 255–276.

   Vijay Ramchandani et al. (2018). "Stress Vulnerability and Alcohol Use and Consequences: From Human Laboratory Studies to Clinical Outcomes." *Alcohol* 72: 75–88.

2. Lieber summarized his research in an article titled "The Metabolism of Alcohol," in the March 1976 issue of *Scientific American*, 25–33. In this article, Lieber suggests that increased microsomal ethanol oxidizing activity (MEOS) in alcoholics is a possible factor in high acetaldehyde levels. Intensified MEOS activity would result in faster metabolism of alcohol to acetaldehyde. For a detailed review of Lieber's research on acetaldehyde levels in alcoholics and nonalcoholics, see Charles Lieber et al., "The Effect of Chronic Ethanol Consumption on Acetaldehyde Metabolism," in *The Role of Acetaldehyde in the Actions of Ethanol*, eds. Kai Lindros & C. J. Peter Eriksson (Helsinki: Finnish Foundation for Alcohol Studies, 1975), 23:83–104.

   For an update, see C. J. Peter Eriksson (2001). "The Role of Acetaldehyde in the Actions of Alcohol." *Alcoholism, Clinical and Experimental Research* 25(5 suppl.): 15S–32S.

3. Marc Schuckit & V. Rayses (1979). "Ethanol Ingestion: Differences in Blood Acetaldehyde Concentrations in Relatives of Alcoholics and Controls." *Science* 203(4375): 54–55.

4. Lieber speculated in "The Metabolism of Alcohol" that the high acetaldehyde level may be responsible for altering the mitochondria. He summarized: "The alcoholic may therefore be the victim of a vicious circle: a high acetaldehyde level impairs mitochondrial function in the liver, acetaldehyde metabolism is decreased, more acetaldehyde accumulates and causes further liver damage" (32).

5. Marc Schuckit (1980). "Alcoholism and Genetics: Possible Biological Mediators." *Biological Psychiatry* 15(3): 437–447.

6. The theory that acetaldehyde, rather than or in addition to alcohol itself, may be responsible for addiction gained popularity among researchers in the 1970s. Acetaldehyde's specific actions in the brain had not yet been pinpointed, but several researchers made intriguing proposals. See V. E. Davis & M. J. Walsh (1970). "Alcohol, Amines, Alkaloids: A Possible Biochemical Basis for Alcohol Addiction." *Science* 167: 1005–1007. See also G. Cohen & M. A. Collins (1970).

"Alkaloids from Catecholamines in Adrenal Tissue: Possible Role in Alcoholism." *Science* 167: 1749–1751.

7. Tammy Chung & Christopher Martin (2009). "Subjective Stimulant and Sedative Effects of Alcohol During Early Drinking Experiences Predict Alcohol Involvement in Treated Adolescents." *Journal of Studies on Alcohol and Drugs* 70(5): 660–667.

8. Marc Schuckit has been conducting research on the biological and genetic underpinnings of alcoholic drinking for more than four decades. His studies have consistently identified a genetic characteristic, which he calls "low level of response to alcohol" or LR, that increases the risk for alcohol-related problems; he continues his work to uncover related genes.

    Marc Schuckit (1984). "Low Level of Response to Alcohol as a Predictor of Future Alcoholism." *American Journal of Psychiatry* 151(2): 184–189.

    Marc Schuckit et al. (2016). "The Low Level of Response to Alcohol-Based Heavy Drinking Prevention Program: One-Year Follow-Up." *Journal of Studies on Alcohol and Drugs* 77(1): 25–37.

    Marc Schuckit (2018). "A Critical Review of Methods and Results in the Search for Genetic Contributors to Alcohol Sensitivity." *Alcoholism, Clinical and Experimental Research* 42(5): 822–835.

    See also Chung & Martin, "Subjective Stimulant and Sedative Effects of Alcohol During Early Drinking Experiences Predict Alcohol Involvement in Treated Adolescents."

9. R. D. Myers & W. L. Veale (1968). "Alcohol Preference in the Rat: Reduction Following Depletion of Brain Serotonin." *Science* 160(3835): 1469–1471.

10. Liisa Ahtee & Kalverno Eriksson (1972). "5-Hydroxytryptamine and 5-Hydroxyindoleacetic Acid Content in Brain of Rat Strains Selected for Their Alcohol Intake." *Physiology and Behavior* 8: 123–126.

11. R. D. Myers & C. L. Melchior (1977). "Alcohol Drinking: Abnormal Intake Caused by Tetrahydropapaveroline in Brain." *Science* 196(4289): 554–556.

12. Donald Goodwin, *Is Alcoholism Hereditary?* (New York: Oxford University Press, 1976); Donald Goodwin, *Alcoholism: The Facts* (New York: Oxford University Press, 2000).

13. Goodwin, *Is Alcoholism Hereditary?*, 77.

14. Benjamin Kissin & Henri Begleiter, eds., *The Biology of Alcoholism* (New York: Plenum Press, 1974), 3:10.

15. For recent FASD research, see: Johann Eberhart & Scott Parnell (2016). "The Genetics of Fetal Alcohol Spectrum Disorders." *Alcoholism, Clinical and Experimental Research* 40(6): 1154–1165.

    Sarah Mattson, Demma Bernes, & Laura Doyle (2019). "Fetal Alcohol Spectrum Disorders: A Review of the Neurobehavioral Deficits Associated with Prenatal Alcohol Exposure." *Alcoholism, Clinical and Experimental Research* 43(6): 1046–1062.

16. In 1980, Harvard Medical School received a $5.8 million gift from Joseph E. Seagram and Sons, Inc., U.S. subsidiary of the world's largest distiller and winemaker. The gift was to be used for research on the fundamental biological,

chemical, and genetic aspects of alcohol metabolism and alcoholism. Dr. Bert Vallee directed the research supported by the grant. From the *Harvard Gazette*, June 27, 1980.

17. D. Fenna, O. Schaefer, L. Mix, & J. A. Gilbert (1971). "Ethanol Metabolism in Various Racial Groups." *Canadian Medical Association Journal* 105(5): 472–75.

P. H. Wolff (1972). "Ethnic Differences in Alcohol Sensitivity." *Science* 175(4020): 449–450.

For recent research on ethnic and racial differences, see: Karen Chartier & Raul Caetano (2010). "Ethnicity and Health Disparities in Alcohol Research." *Alcohol Research & Health: The Journal of the National Institute on Alcohol Abuse and Alcoholism* 33(1–2): 152–160.

Erin Delker, Qiana Brown, & Deborah Hasin (2016). "Alcohol Consumption in Demographic Subpopulations: An Epidemiologic Overview." *Alcohol Research: Current Reviews* 38(1): 7–15.

18. Several research studies published more than four decades ago reported higher acetaldehyde levels in Asians than in whites. See M. A. Korsten, S. Matsuzaki, L Feinman, & C. S. Lieber (1975). "High Blood Acetaldehyde Levels after Ethanol Administration: Differences Between Alcoholic and Nonalcoholic Subjects." *New England Journal of Medicine* 292: 386–389.

J. A. Ewing, B. A. Rouse, & E. D. Pellezzari (1974). "Alcohol Sensitivity and Ethnic Background." *American Journal of Psychiatry* 131: 206–210.

T. E. Reed, H. Kalant, R. J. Gibbins, B. M. Kapur, & J. G. Rankin (1976). "Alcohol and Acetaldehyde Metabolism in Caucasians, Chinese and Amerinds." *Canadian Medical Association Journal* 115: 851–855.

More recent research confirms and expands earlier studies. See: Arthur Cederbaum (2012). "Alcohol Metabolism." *Clinics in Liver Disease* 16(4): 667–685.

Etienne Quertemont (2004). "Genetic Polymorphism in Ethanol Metabolism: Acetaldehyde Contribution to Alcohol Abuse and Alcoholism." *Molecular Psychiatry* 9(6): 570–581.

Etienne Quertemont & Vincent Didone (2006). "Role of Acetaldehyde in Mediating the Pharmacological and Behavioral Effects of Alcohol." *Alcohol Research & Health* 29(4): 258–265.

Howard Edenberg (2007). "The Genetics of Alcohol Metabolism: Role of Alcohol Dehydrogenase and Aldehyde Dehydrogenase Variants." *Alcohol Research & Health: The Journal of the National Institute on Alcohol Abuse and Alcoholism* 30(1): 5–13.

19. Ethnic group susceptibility to alcoholism, table from James R. Milam, *The Emergent Comprehensive Concept of Alcoholism* (Kirkland, WA: ACA Press, 1974).

CHAPTER 4: THE EARLY, ADAPTIVE STAGE OF ALCOHOLISM

1. George Koob, Michael Arends, & Michel Le Moal, *Drugs, Addiction, and the Brain* (Cambridge, MA: Academic Press, 2014).

George Koob & Jay Schulkin (2019). "Addiction and Stress: An Allostatic View." *Neuroscience and Biobehavioral Reviews* 106: 245–262.

George Koob & Nora Volkow (2016). "Neurobiology of Addiction: A Neu-rocircuitry Analysis." *Lancet Psychiatry* 3(8): 760–773.

George Koob & Michel Le Moal (2008). "Addiction and the Brain Antireward System." *Annual Review of Psychology* 59(1): 29–53.

2. Charles Lieber & Leonore DeCarli (1972). "The Role of the Hepatic Micro-somal Ethanol Oxidizing System (MEOS) for Ethanol Metabolism in Vivo." *Journal of Pharmacology and Experimental Therapeutics* 181: 279–287.

Charles Lieber (2004). "The Discovery of the Microsomal Ethanol Oxidiz-ing System and Its Physiologic and Pathologic Role." *Drug Metabolism Reviews* 36(3–4): 511–529.

3. J. H. Chin & D. B. Goldstein (1977). "Drug Tolerance in Biomembranes: A Spin Label Study of the Effects of Ethanol." *Science* 196(4290): 684–685.

J. H. Chin & D. B. Goldstein (1978). "Drug Tolerance and Biomembranes." *Biomedicine* 28(3): 141–143.

See also: D. B. Goldstein (1986). "Effect of Alcohol on Cellular Membranes." *Annals of Emergency Medicine* 15(9): 1013–1018.

For recent research on cell membranes, see: Saradamma Bulle et al. (2017). "Association Between Alcohol-Induced Erythrocyte Membrane Alterations and Hemolysis in Chronic Alcoholics." *Journal of Clinical Biochemistry and Nutrition* 60(1): 63–69.

Andrey Gurtovenko & Jamshed Anwar (2009). "Interaction of Ethanol with Biological Membranes: The Formation of Non-Bilayer Structures Within the Membrane Interior and Their Significance." *Journal of Physical Chemistry B* 113(7): 1983–1992.

4. Henrik Wallgren & Herbert Barry, *Actions of Alcohol* (Amsterdam: Elsevier Publishing Co., 1970), 2:496.

5. In an article titled "What Does It Mean When We Call Addiction a Brain Dis-order," *Scientific American*, March 23, 2018, Dr. Nora Volkow, director of the National Institute of Drug Abuse, offers a clear and concise explanation of "the neuroplasticity that underlies learning."

"Our reward and self-control circuits evolved precisely to enable us to dis-cover new, important, healthy rewards, remember them, and pursue them single-mindedly; drugs are sometimes said to 'hijack' those circuits . . .

"[Drugs] exert their effects on sensitive brain circuitry that has been fine-tuned over millions of years to reinforce behaviors that are essential for the individual's survival and the survival of the species. Because they facilitate the same learning processes as natural rewards, drugs easily trick that circuitry into thinking they are more important than natural rewards like food, sex, or parenting."

6. Numerous studies attest to alcohol's ability to improve the performance of alcoholics in a variety of mental and motor skills; see, for example, Wallgren & Barry, *Actions of Alcohol*, 479–618. In another early work, Jack Mendelson & Nancy Mello comment on the wide differences in functioning between alco-holics and nonalcoholics: "Most social drinkers will show significant signs of

intoxication at blood levels between 100 and 150 mg/100 ml and will be grossly intoxicated at levels above 200 mg/100 ml. Stupor and coma may occur at levels above 300 mg/100 ml. Alcohol addicts who have adequate liver function and who have developed a high degree of tolerance will not show such impairments. For example, alcohol addicts with blood ethanol levels between 200 and 300 mg/100 ml can perform quite accurately in tasks requiring psychomotor skills and good cognitive and memory function." Jack Mendelson & Nancy Mello, eds., *The Diagnosis and Treatment of Alcoholism* (New York: McGraw-Hill, 1979), 11.

7. Decades ago scientists recognized alcohol's "normalizing" effect on autonomic nervous system functions. For a general review, see Benjamin Kissin, Victor Schenker, & Anne Schenker (1959). "The Acute Effects of Ethyl Alcohol and Chlorpromazine on Certain Physiological Functions in Alcoholics." *Quarterly Journal of Studies on Alcohol* 20: 480–492.

CHAPTER 5: THE MIDDLE STAGE OF ALCOHOLISM

1. Howard Becker (1998). "Kindling in Alcohol Withdrawal." *Alcohol Health and Research World* 22(1): 25–33.

   George Breese, David Overstreet, & Darin Knapp (2005). "Conceptual Framework for the Etiology of Alcoholism: A 'Kindling'/Stress Hypothesis." *Psychopharmacology* 178(4): 367–380.

   George Breese, Rajita Sinha, & Markus Heilig (2011). "Chronic Alcohol Neuroadaptation and Stress Contribute to Susceptibility for Alcohol Craving and Relapse." *Pharmacology & Therapeutics* 129(2): 149–171.

2. For recent research on neurological adaptations and withdrawal, see, for example: Howard Becker & Patrick Mulholland (2014). "Neurochemical Mechanisms of Alcohol Withdrawal." *Handbook of Clinical Neurology* 125: 133–156.

   Ansel Hillmer et al. (2015). "How Imaging Glutamate, γ-Aminobutyric Acid, and Dopamine Can Inform the Clinical Treatment of Alcohol Dependence and Withdrawal." *Alcoholism, Clinical and Experimental Research* 39(12): 2268–2282.

3. Marty Mann, *Marty Mann Answers Your Questions About Drinking and Alcoholism* (New York: Holt, Rinehart and Winston, 1981), 52.

4. Benjamin Karpman, *The Hangover: A Critical Study in the Psycho-dynamics of Alcoholism* (Springfield, IL: Charles C. Thomas, 1957), quoted in Berton Roueché, *The Neutral Spirit: A Portrait of Alcohol* (Boston: Little, Brown, 1960), 129–130.

5. Marc Schuckit (2014). "Recognition and Management of Withdrawal Delirium (Delirium Tremens)." *New England Journal of Medicine* 372(22): 2109–2113.

6. On delirium tremens mortality, see: Abdul Rahman & Manju Paul, *Delirium Tremens* (Treasure Island, FL: StatPearls Publishing, 2020).

7. Markus Heilig, Mark Egli, John Crabbe, & Howard Becker (2010). "Acute Withdrawal, Protracted Abstinence and Negative Affect in Alcoholism: Are They Linked?" *Addiction Biology* 15(2): 169–184.

8. Charles Lieber (2003). "Relationships Between Nutrition, Alcohol Use, and Liver Disease." *Alcohol Research & Health* 27(3): 220–231.

9. Byung Joo Ham & Ihn-Geun Choi (2005). "Psychiatric Implications of Nutritional Deficiencies in Alcoholism." *Psychiatry Investigation* 2(2): 44–59.

10. Benjamin Kissin (1979). "Biological Investigations in Alcohol Research." *Journal of Studies on Alcohol* 8(supp.): 146–181; section quoted on pages 172–173.

11. Kissin, "Biological Investiations in Alcohol Research," 171.

   For recent research on the prefrontal cortex, see: Rita Goldstein & Nora Volkow (2011). "Dysfunction of the Prefrontal Cortex in Addiction: Neuroimaging Findings and Clinical Implications." *Nature Reviews, Neuroscience* 12(11): 652–669.

   Olivier George & George Koob (2010). "Individual Differences In Prefrontal Cortex Function and the Transition from Drug Use to Drug Dependence." *Neuroscience and Biobehavioral Reviews* 35(2): 232–247.

12. Marlene Oscar-Berman & Ksenija Marinkovic (2003). "Alcoholism and the Brain: An Overview." *Alcohol Research & Health: The Journal of the National Institute on Alcohol Abuse and Alcoholism* 27(2): 125–133.

13. Benjamin Kissin, Milton Gross, & Irving Schutz, "Correlation of Urinary Biogenic Amines with Sleep Stages in Chronic Alcoholization and Withdrawal," in *Alcohol Intoxication and Withdrawal: Experimental Studies,* Milton Gross, ed. (New York: Plenum Press, 1973), 281–289.

14. One research team reported sleep disturbances in alcoholics abstinent for as long as four years. See Althea Wagman & Richard Allen (1975). "Effects of Alcohol Ingestion and Abstinence on Slow Wave Sleep of Alcoholics." *Advances in Experimental Medicine and Biology* 59: 453–466.

   For recent research on sleep disturbances, see: Bhanu Prakash Kolla et al. (2015). "The Association Between Sleep Disturbances and Alcohol Relapse: A 12-Month Observational Cohort Study." *American Journal on Addictions* 24(4): 362–367.

   Gustavo Angarita, Nazli Emadi, Sarah Hodges, & Peter Morgan (2016). "Sleep Abnormalities Associated with Alcohol, Cannabis, Cocaine, and Opiate Use: A Comprehensive Review." *Addiction Science & Clinical Practice* 11(1): 9.

15. Clinical experience from Alcenas Hospital, Kirkland, WA, one of the few treatment centers in the country that stressed comprehensive nutritional therapy during and after treatment.

16. E. M. Jellinek, *The Disease Concept of Alcoholism* (New Haven, CT: Hillhouse Press, 1960), 139.

CHAPTER 6: THE LATE, DETERIORATIVE STAGE OF ALCOHOLISM

1. Aaron White, I-Jen Castle, Ralph Hingson, & Patricia Powell (2020). "Using Death Certificates to Explore Changes in Alcohol-Related Mortality in the United States, 1999–2017." *Alcoholism: Clinical and Experimental Research* 44(1): 178–187.

Recent CDC report: Marissa B. Esser et al. (2020) "Deaths and Years of Potential Life Lost From Excessive Alcohol Use—United States, 2011–2015." *Morbidity and Mortality Weekly Report* 69: 1428–1433.

2. Catherine Frakes Vozzo, Nicole Welch, Carlos Romero-Marrero, & Kyrsten D. Fairbanks (2018). "Alcoholic Liver Disease." Cleveland Clinic Center for Continuing Education. http://www.clevelandclinicmeded.com/medicalpubs/diseasemanagement/hepatology/alcoholic-liver-disease.

3. Lawrence Feinman & Charles Lieber commented on the relationship between fatty liver, hepatitis, and cirrhosis in "Liver Disease in Alcoholism," in *The Biology of Alcoholism,* eds. Benjamin Kissin & Henri Begleiter (New York: Plenum Press, 1974), 3:321: "Fatty liver and alcoholic hepatitis usually precede cirrhosis by many years and often eventually co-exist with it. However, there is no conclusive evidence that these latter lesions are necessary for cirrhosis to develop."

   Recent references on alcohol-related liver disease: Suthat Liangpunsakul & Dan Crabb, "Natural History and Cofactors of Alcoholic Liver Disease," in *Zakim and Boyer's Hepatology: A Textbook of Liver Disease* (7th ed.) (New York: Elsevier, 2018), 345–350.

   Ramesh Kumar, Rajeev Nayan Priyadarshi, & Utpal Anand (2020). "Nonalcoholic Fatty Liver Disease: Growing Burden, Adverse Outcomes and Associations." *Journal of Clinical and Translational Hepatology* 8(1): 76–86.

4. Robert Mann, Reginald Smart, & Richard Govoni (2003). "The Epidemiology of Alcoholic Liver Disease." *Alcohol Research & Health: The Journal of the National Institute on Alcohol Abuse and Alcoholism* 27(3): 209–219.

5. James R. Hoon (1974). "Hair of the Dog: A Gastrocamera Study." *Journal of the American Medical Association* 229(2): 184–85.

6. S. Chari, S. Teyssen, & M. V. Singer (1993). "Alcohol and Gastric Acid Secretion in Humans." *Gut* 34(6): 843–847.

   See also: Faraz Bishehsari et al. (2017). "Alcohol and Gut-Derived Inflammation." *Alcohol Research: Current Reviews* 38(2): 163–171.

7. Lata Kaphalia & William J. Calhoun (2013). "Alcoholic Lung Injury: Metabolic, Biochemical and Immunological Aspects." *Toxicology Letters* 222(2): 171–179.

   See also: Evangelia Simou, John Britton, & Jo Leonardi-Bee (2018). "Alcohol and the Risk of Pneumonia: A Systematic Review and Meta-Analysis." *BMJ Open* 8(8): e022344.

   Giacomo Bellani et al. (2016). "Epidemiology, Patterns of Care, and Mortality for Patients with Acute Respiratory Distress Syndrome in Intensive Care Units in 50 Countries." *Journal of the American Medical Association* 315(8): 788–800.

   Ashish Mehta & David Guidot (2017). "Alcohol and the Lung." *Alcohol Research: Current Reviews* 38(2): 243–254.

8. Benjamin Kissin & Maureen Kaley, "Alcohol and Cancer," in *The Biology of Alcoholism,* eds. Benjamin Kissin & Henri Begleiter (New York: Plenum Press, 1974), 3:481.

9. The statistics in this section were gleaned from "Alcohol and Cancer Risk," a fact sheet published by the National Cancer Institute. The fact sheet is periodically

reviewed and updated and includes numerous current references, all of which can be accessed online. See https://www.cancer.gov/about-cancer/causes-prevention/risk/alcohol/alcohol-fact-sheet.

10. Dahn Clemens et al. (2016). "Alcoholic Pancreatitis: New Insights into the Pathogenesis and Treatment." *World Journal of Gastrointestinal Pathophysiology* 7(1), 48–58.

See also: Ali Aghdassi et al. (2015). "Genetic Susceptibility Factors for Alcohol-Induced Chronic Pancreatitis." *Pancreatology* 15(4 suppl.): S23–S31.

Anton Klochkov, Pujitha Kudaravalli, & Yan Sun, *Alcoholic Pancreatitis* (Treasure Island, FL: StatPearls Publishing; 2020).

11. Jyoti Prakash et al. (2011). "Tobacco-Alcohol Amblyopia: A Rare Complication of Prolonged Alcohol Abuse." *Industrial Psychiatry Journal* 20(1): 66–68.

12. Dipak Sarkar, Katherine Jung, & Joe Wang (2015). "Alcohol and the Immune System" (editorial). *Alcohol Research: Current Reviews* 37(2): 153–155.

Gyongyi Szabo & Banishree Saha (2015). "Alcohol's Effect on Host Defense." *Alcohol Research: Current Reviews* 37(2): 159–170.

13. Fulton Crews et al. (2015). "Neuroimmune Function and the Consequences of Alcohol Exposure." *Alcohol Research: Current Reviews* 37(2): 331–341, 344–351.

CHAPTER 7: THE ALCOHOLIC

1. It used to be thought that blackouts were distinctive to alcoholism and a symptom of the disease itself. Recent research by White and others comes to this conclusion: "Blackouts are much more common among social drinkers than previously assumed and should be viewed as a potential consequence of acute intoxication regardless of age or whether one is clinically dependent upon alcohol." Aaron White (2003). "What Happened? Alcohol, Memory Blackouts, and the Brain." *Alcohol Research & Health: The Journal of the National Institute on Alcohol Abuse and Alcoholism* 27(2): 186–196.

CHAPTER 8: GETTING THE ALCOHOLIC INTO TREATMENT

1. Epigraph: This statement was made by Thomas Fleming, M.D, medical director of Little Hill–Alina Lodge, New Jersey, in a panel discussion organized by the magazine *Patient Care* and reprinted in their February 28, 1979, issue.

2. Anne Opsal, Øistein Kristensen, & Thomas Clausen (2019). "Readiness to Change Among Involuntarily and Voluntarily Admitted Patients with Substance Use Disorders." *Substance Abuse Treatment, Prevention, and Policy* 14(1); 47.

A review of this research, published on Recovery Research Institute's "Recovery Answers" website (https://www.recoveryanswers.org/research-post/mandated-treatment-motivation-change/), concludes: "This study and others provide evidence that counteracts some concerns about the negative effects of involuntarily admission for substance use treatment, which document positive perceptions of treatment and as good or better outcomes among patients who are mandated or involuntarily admitted to treatment."

3. From an interview with Wilbur Mills in *Overview* (Overlook Hospital, Summit, NJ) 1(3), Fall 1980. https://www.nytimes.com/1978/12/04/archives/wilbur-mills-offers-sober-testimony-to-an-alcoholic-past-entering.html.

CHAPTER 9: A GUIDE TO TREATMENT

1. Thomas Trotter, *An Essay, Medical, Philosophical, and Chemical, on Drunkenness and Its Effects on the Human Body* (1804). For a modern analysis of the significance of Trotter's work, see Griffith Edwards (2012). "Thomas Trotter's 'Essay on Drunkenness' Appraised." *Addiction* (Abingdon, England) 107(9): 1562–1579.

2. *Twelve Steps and Twelve Traditions* (New York: A.A. World Services, 1952), 74. *Alcoholics Anonymous*, 3rd ed. (New York: A.A. World Services, 1976).

3. *Twelve Steps and Twelve Traditions.*

4. Henrik Wallgren & Herbert Barry, *Actions of Alcohol* (Amsterdam: Elsevier, 1970), 1:5.

5. Administrative discharge from treatment statistics are reported in the Substance Abuse and Mental Health Services Administration's Treatment Episode Data Set (TEDS) for the years 2002–2011. According to the TEDS data, 1,071,091 patients admitted to treatment between 2002 and 2011 were administratively discharged—or more than 126,000 in the last available reporting year. For a clear and succinct report on the TEDS data, see William White, "Kicking People Out of Addiction Treatment: An Update and Commentary," September 11, 2015, http://www.williamwhitepapers.com/blog/2015/09/kicking-people-out-of-addiction-treatment-an-update-and-commentary-izaak-williams-and-william-white.html. See also William White, Christy Scott, Michael Dennis, & Michael Boyle (2005). "It's Time to Stop Kicking People Out of Addiction Treatment." *Counselor Magazine* 6(2): 12–25.

6. Alcenas Hospital was cofounded by James Milam and Dorris Hutchison in Kirkland, Washington, in 1970. In April 1981 the hospital was purchased by Comprehensive Care Corporation.

7. William L. White, "Recovery Durability: The 5-Year Set Point," July 31, 2013, http://www.williamwhitepapers.com/blog/2013/07/recovery-durability-the-5-year-set-point.html.

8. John Kelly, Keith Humphreys, & Marica Ferri (2020). "Alcoholics Anonymous and Other 12-Step Programs for Alcohol Use Disorder." *Cochrane Database of Systematic Reviews*, issue 3, Art. No. CD012880.

9. Marc Schuckit, *Educating Yourself About Alcohol and Drugs: A People's Primer* (New York: Plenum Press, 1995).

10. *Chalktalk* is a 1972 film of a talk Father Joseph Martin gave to military personnel. A Roman Catholic priest and an alcoholic in long-term recovery, Father Martin was an inspiring and impassioned educator and national leader in the battle to end stigma and enlighten the public about the disease of alcoholism. Father Martin's *Chalktalk* films and videos are still highly recommended for use in education and treatment programs.

CHAPTER 10: DRUGS AND THE ALCOHOLIC

1. Epigraph: From Richard Hughes & Robert Brewin, *The Tranquilizing of America* (New York: Warner Books, 1979), 41.

2. Charles Lieber (1976). "The Metabolism of Alcohol." *Scientific American* 234(3): 25–33.

3. Benjamin Kissin & Henri Begleiter, *The Biology of Alcoholism* (New York: Plenum Press, 1972), vol. 3, p. 112.

4. Benjamin Kissin discussed the concept of reactivation of physical dependence in his article "Biological Investigations in Alcohol Research," *Journal of Studies on Alcohol* 8 (suppl.), November 1979, 170–171.

5. Betty Ford with Chris Chase, *The Times of My Life* (New York: Ballantine Books, 1979), 307.

6. Ford, *The Times of My Life*, 310–311.

7. Hughes & Brewin, *The Tranquilizing of America*, 77.

8. National Institute on Drug Abuse, "Misuse of Prescription Drugs Research Report," https://www.drugabuse.gov/publications/research-reports/misuse-prescription-drugs/what-scope-prescription-drug-misuse. See also: https://www.cdc.gov/drugoverdose/data/prescribing/overview.html.

9. Alcohol use and prescription drugs, University of Michigan/NIDA studies: Sean McCabe, James Cranford, & Carol Boyd (2006). "The Relationship Between Past-Year Drinking Behaviors and Nonmedical Use of Prescription Drugs: Prevalence of Co-Occurrence in a National Sample." *Drug and Alcohol Dependence* 84(3): 281–288.

10. *Patient Care*, February 28, 1979, 45.

11. NIAAA, "Harmful Interactions Mixing Alcohol with Medicines," https://www.niaaa.nih.gov/publications/brochures-and-fact-sheets/harmful-interactions-mixing-alcohol-with-medicines.

12. *Physicians Desk Reference* (Oradell, NJ: Economic Book Division, 1980), 591.

13. See, e.g., Joe Kwentus & Leslie Major (1979). "Disulfiram in the Treatment of Alcoholism: A Review." *Journal of Studies on Alcohol* 40(5): 428–446.
S. C. Liddon & R. Satran (1967). "Disulfiram (Antabuse) Psychosis." *American Journal of Psychiatry* 123: 1284–1289.
A. H. Nora, J. J. Nora, & J. Blu (1977). "Limb-Reduction Anomalies in Infants Born to Disulfiram-Treated Alcoholic Mothers." *Lancet* 2(8039): 664.
J. M. Rainey (1977). "Disulfiram Toxicity and Carbon Disulfide Poisoning." *American Journal of Psychiatry* 134(4): 371–378.

14. Natalya Maisel et al. (2013). "Meta-Analysis of Naltrexone and Acamprosate for Treating Alcohol Use Disorders: When Are These Medications Most Helpful?" *Addiction* 108(2): 275–293.

15. Susane Rösner et al. (2010). "Opioid Antagonists for Alcohol Dependence." *Cochrane Database of Systematic Reviews*, issue 12. Art. No.: CD001867.
Daniel Jonas et al. (2014). "Pharmacotherapy for Adults with Alcohol Use Disorders in Outpatient Settings: A Systematic Review and Meta-analysis." *Journal of the American Medical Association* 311(18):1889–1900.

Bradford Winslow & Mary Onysko (2016). "Medications for Alcohol Use Disorder." *American Family Physician* 93(6).

16. B. J. Mason & C. J. Heyser (2010). "Acamprosate: A Prototypic Neuromodulator in the Treatment of Alcohol Dependence." *CNS & Neurological Disorders: Drug Targets* 9(1): 23–32.

17. Maisel et al., "Meta-Analysis of Naltrexone and Acamprosate for Treating Alcohol Use Disorders."

See also: Bradford Winslow, Mary Onysko, & Melanie Hebert (2016). "Medications for Alcohol Use Disorder." *American Family Physician* 93(6): 457–465.

CHAPTER 11: BEYOND PREJUDICE AND MISCONCEPTION

1. Ira Cisin (1979). "Discussion." *Journal of Studies on Alcohol*, 8 (suppl.): 52.

2. David Armor, J. Michael Polich, & Harriet Stambul, *Alcoholism and Treatment* (New York: John Wiley & Sons, 1978). On page 99, the authors describe the "normal" drinking criteria: "The recovered alcoholic who is classified as a normal drinker must meet *all* of the following criteria:

   1. Daily comsumption of less than 3 ounces of ethanol.
   2. Typical quantities on drinking days less than 5 ounces.
   3. No tremors reported.
   4. No serious symptoms."

Serious symptoms were then classified as "frequent episodes of three or more of the following: blackouts, missing work, morning drinking, missing meals, and being drunk. 'Frequent' means three or more episodes of blackouts or missing work in the past month, or five or more episodes of the other symptoms."

3. https://www.newsweek.com/americas-heaviest-drinkers-consume-almost-60-all-alcohol-sold-1520284 citing Philip J. Cook, *Paying the Tab: The Costs and Benefits of Alcohol Control* (Princeton University Press, 2007).

4. Di Castelnuovo, A., Costanzo, S., Bagnardi, V., Donati, M., Iacoviello, L., de Gaetano, G. "Alcohol Dosing and Total Mortality in Men and Women." *Arch Intern Med* (2006), 166(22):2437–45.

   Rehm, J., Shield, K. Alcohol consumption. In: Stewart, B.W., Wild, C.B., eds. *World Cancer Report*, 2014. Lyon, France: International Agency for Research on Cancer, 2014.

   Hartz, Sarah et al. (2018). "Daily Drinking Is Associated with Increased Mortality." *Alcoholism: Clinical & Experimental Research*, 42(11) 2246–2255.

5. *Alcoholism Report*, October 17, 1972.

6. NIAAA's 2017–2021 Strategic Plan is available online at https://www.niaaa.nih.gov/strategic-plan and can be downloaded as a PDF: https://www.niaaa.nih.gov/sites/default/files/StrategicPlan_NIAAA_optimized_2017-2020.pdf.

7. Mel Schulstad quote: W. White (2011). "Reflections on the Birth of Modern Addiction Counseling: An Interview with Mel Schulstad," www.williamwhitepapers.com (Pioneer Series). "Our duties were ill-defined, we worked endless hours, and we were paid a pittance, but it was the beginning of what we started calling a new profession."

8. J. F. Kelly, B. G. Bergman, B. B. Hoeppner, C. L. Vilsaint, & W. L. White (2017). "Prevalence and Pathways of Recovery from Drug and Alcohol Problems in the United States Population: Implications for Practice, Research, and Policy." *Drug and Alcohol Dependence* 181(supp. C): 162–169.

9. *Alcoholism Report*, August 25, 1978.

10. Keith Humphreys is quoted on page 212 of the 2012 report "Addiction Medicine: Closing the Gap Between Science and Practice," published by the National Center on Addiction and Substance Abuse at Columbia University. The full report can be downloaded as a PDF from the Parternship to End Addiction website: https://drugfree.org/reports/addiction-medicine-closing-the-gap-between-science-and-practice/.

11. Eaton's comment: *Alcoholism Report*, September 24, 1973; Bourne: *Alcoholism Report*, December 23, 1977; Brock: *Alcoholism Report*, January 27, 1978; Ohlms: *Alcoholism Report*, July 27, 1979.

12. M. Hayman (1956). "Current Attitudes to Alcoholism of Psychiatrists in Southern California." *American Journal of Psychiatry* 112(7): 485–493.

13. Conversation with George Vaillant (2005). *Addiction* 100(3): 274–280. Dr. Vaillant added: "If you want to treat an illness that has no easy cure, first of all treat them with hope."

14. John Kelly, Keith Humphreys, & Marica Ferri (2020). "Alcoholics Anonymous and Other 12-Step Programs for Alcohol Use Disorder." *Cochrane Database of Systematic Reviews* 3(3):CD012880.

SUGGESTED READING LIST

REFERENCES

Actions of Alcohol, by Henrik Wallgren and Herbert Barry. New York: Elsevier, 1970.
  Volume 1: *Biochemical, Physiological, and Psychological Aspects*
  Volume 2: *Chronic and Clinical Aspects*
The ASAM Principles of Addiction Medicine, 6th ed., by Shannon Miller, David Fiellin, Richard Rosenthal, and Richard Saitz. Philadelphia: Lippincott Williams & Wilkins, 2018.
  Section 1: Basic Science and Core Concepts
  Section 2: Pharmacology
  Section 3: Diagnosis, Assessment, and Early Intervention
  Section 4: Overview of Addiction Treatment
  Section 5: Special Issues in Addiction
  Section 6: Management of Intoxication and Withdrawal
  Section 7: Pharmacological Interventions and Other Somatic Therapies
  Section 8: Psychologically Based Interventions
  Section 9: Mutual Help, Twelve Step, and Other Recovery Programs
  Section 10: Medical Disorders and Complications of Addiction
  Section 11: Co-Occurring Addiction and Psychiatric Disorders
  Section 12: Pain and Addiction
  Section 13: Children and Adolescents
  Section 14: Ethical, Legal, and Liability Issues in Addiction Practice
The Biology of Alcoholism, edited by Benjamin Kissin and Henri Begleiter. New York: Plenum Press.
  Volume 1: Biochemistry (1971)
  Volume 2: Physiology and Behavior (1972)
  Volume 3: Clinical Pathology (1974)
  Volume 4: Social Aspects of Alcoholism (1976)
  Volume 5: Treatment and Rehabilitation of the Chronic Alcoholic (1977)
Facing Addiction in America: The Surgeon General's Report on Alcohol, Drugs, and Health, 2016, U.S. Department of Health & Human Services (HHS), Office of the Surgeon General, Washington, DC, November 2016.
  https://addiction.surgeongeneral.gov/sites/default/files/surgeon-generals -report.pdf
  Chapter 1: Introduction and Overview of the Report

Chapter 2: The Neurobiology of Substance Use, Misuse, and Addiction
Chapter 3: Prevention Programs and Policies
Chapter 4: Early Intervention, Treatment, and Management of Substance Use Disorders
Chapter 5: Recovery: The Many Paths to Wellness
Chapter 6: Health Care Systems and Substance Use Disorders
Chapter 7: Vision for the Future: A Public Health Approach

GENERAL WORKS

Beyond Addiction: How Science and Kindness Help People Change, by Jeffrey Foote, Carrie Wilkens, Nicole Kosanke, and Stephanie Higgs. Scribner, 2014.

Educating Yourself About Alcohol and Drugs, by Marc Alan Schuckit. Da Capo Press, 1998.

The Disease Concept of Alcoholism, by E. M. Jellinek. Hillhouse Press, 1960.

ALCOHOLICS ANONYMOUS

Not-God: A History of Alcoholics Anonymous, by Ernest Kurtz. Hazelden, 1991.

A.A. literature is not available through bookstores but can be purchased through A.A. World Services, P.O. Box 459, Grand Central Station, New York, N.Y. 10163; email: Orders@aa.org; online store: https://onlineliterature.aa.org/. Several favorite titles include:

Alcoholics Anonymous ("The Big Book")
Came to Believe
Living Sober
Twelve Steps and Twelve Traditions

DRUGS

I'm Dancing as Fast as I Can, by Barbara Gordon. Harper and Row, 1979.

Nursing 2021 Drug Handbook, 41st ed. Lippincott, Williams & Wilkins, 2020.

When Painkillers Become Dangerous: What Everyone Needs to Know About OxyContin and Other Prescription Drugs, by Drew Pinsky, Marvin D. Seppala, Robert J. Meyers, John Gardin, and William White. Hazelden, 2009.

HISTORY

Slaying the Dragon: The History of Addiction Treatment and Recovery in America, 2nd ed., by William L. White. Chestnut Health Systems, 2014.

Recovery Rising: A Retrospective of Addiction Treatment and Recovery Advocacy, by William L. White. Create Space Independent Publishing Platform, 2017.

INTERVENTION

I'll Quit Tomorrow, rev ed., by Vernon E. Johnson. Harper One, 1990.

It Takes a Family: Creating Lasting Sobriety, Togetherness, and Happiness, by Debra Jay. Hazelden, 2021.

Love First: A Family's Guide to Intervention, rev ed., by Jeff Jay and Debra Jay. Hazelden, 2021.

Get Your Loved One Sober: Alternatives to Nagging, Pleading, and Threatening, by Robert J. Meyers and Brenda L. Wolfe. Hazelden, 2003.

NUTRITION

Eating Right to Live Sober, by Katherine Ketcham and L. Ann Mueller. Signet, 2019.

Seven Weeks to Sobriety: The Proven Program to Fight Alcoholism Through Nutrition, by Joan Mathews Larson. Ballantine Books, 1997.

The G.I. (Glycemic Index) Diet, by Rick Gallop. Workman, 2010.

The Glycemic Load Counter: A Pocket Guide to GL and GI Values for Over 800 Foods, by Dr. Mabel Blades. Ulysses Press, 2008.

PERSONAL ACCOUNTS

Angela's Ashes: A Memoir, by Frank McCourt. Scribner, 1998.

Beautiful Boy: A Father's Journey Through His Son's Addiction, by David Sheff. Mariner Books, 2009.

Bill W: The Absorbing and Deeply Moving Life Story of Bill Wilson, Co-founder of Alcoholics Anonymous, rev ed., by Robert Thomsen. Hazelden, 1999.

Broken: My Story of Addiction and Redemption, by William Cope Moyers with Katherine Ketcham. Penguin Books, 2007.

Drinking: A Love Story, by Caroline Knapp. Dial Press, 1997.

Terry: My Daughter's Life-and-Death Struggle with Alcoholism, by George McGovern. Plume, 1997.

The Courage to Change: Personal Conversation About Alcoholism with Dennis Wholey, by Dennis Wholey. Houghton Mifflin, 1984.

SPIRITUALITY

The Natural History of Alcoholism Revisited, by George E. Vaillant. Harvard University Press, 1995.

The Spirituality of Imperfection: Storytelling and the Search for Meaning, by Ernest Kurtz and Katherine Ketcham. Bantam Books, 1993.

WEBSITES AND ONLINE RESOURCES

American Society for Addiction Medicine (ASAM)
www.asam.org

Faces and Voices of Recovery
www.facesandvoicesofrecovery.org

Facing Addiction with the National Council on Alcoholism and Drug Dependence (NCADD)
www.ncadd.org

GetHelpGiveHelp
www.gethelpgivehelp.info

National Institute on Alcohol Abuse and Alcoholism (NIAAA)
www.niaaa.nih.gov

National Institute on Drug Abuse (NIDA)
www.nida.nih.gov

Partnership to End Addiction
  www.drugfree.org
Recovery Research Institute
  www.recoveryanswers.org
Shatterproof
  www.shatterproof.org
  www.treatmentatlas.org
Substance Abuse and Mental Health Services Administration (SAMHSA)
  www.samhsa.gov

BOOKS LISTED IN ORIGINAL EDITION THAT ARE NOW OUT OF PRINT

Marty Mann Answers Your Questions About Drinking and Alcoholism, rev ed., by Marty
  Mann. Holt, Rinehart & Winston, 1981.
  One of the first women members of Alcoholics Anonymous, and the founder
  of the National Council on Alcoholism, answers the most frequently asked
  questions about drinking and alcoholism.
The Neutral Spirit: A Portrait of Alcohol, by Berton Roueché. Little, Brown, 1960.
  A lively, illuminating review of alcohol and its use from ancient to modern
  humans.
Primer on Alcoholism, by Marty Mann. Rinehart, 1950.
  An overview for both the alcoholic and the nonalcoholic of how people drink,
  how to recognize alcoholics, and what to do about them. Revised and updated
  in 1958 as *New Primer on Alcoholism.*
The New Handbook of Prescription Drugs, rev ed., by Richard Burack and Fred J. Fox.
  Ballantine, 1975.
  This handy reference book provides basic information on drugs, generic and
  brand price comparisons, and an illuminating look at the drug industry's con-
  trol over the flow of information to the medical profession.
The Times of My Life, by Betty Ford with Chris Chase. Ballantine Books, 1979.
  Chapters 38 and 39 of this special edition of the former First Lady's biography
  tell of her addiction to alcohol and pills, her family's intervention, her recovery,
  and her commitment to live "this beautiful new life of mine to the fullest."
The Tranquilizing of America, by Richard Hughes and Robert Brewin. Warner Books,
  1979.
  A hard-hitting, informative, and highly readable look at prescription drugs.
Alcoholism: The Nutritional Approach, by Roger J. Williams. University of Texas
  Press, 1959.
  A pioneer in the field of alcoholism and nutrition presents his genetotrophic
  concept that alcoholism develops from a genetically determined nutritional
  disorder in this short, easy-to-read book.
Nutrigenetics, by R. O. Brennan with William C. Mulligan. M. Evans, 1975.
  This fascinating and easy-to-read book presents the theory that combined genetic
  (hereditary) and nutritional (food/nourishment) deficiencies may cause hypoglycemia. Also included are the caloric and nutritional values of common foods
  and menus and snack suggestions.

Nutrition Against Disease, by Roger J. Williams. Pitman, 1971.

A guide to the prevention or control of disease through improved nutrition.

Is Alcoholism Hereditary?, by Donald Goodwin. Oxford University Press, 1976.

The author is a journalist as well as a physician and researcher, and he writes with clarity about the role of heredity in determining alcoholism. The discussion about his adoption studies conducted in Denmark is particularly informative.

Off the Sauce, by Lewis Meyer. Collier Books, 1967.

An anecdotal account by a man who finally made it "off the sauce" with the help of A.A.

Prodigal Shepherd, by Ralph Pfau and Al Hirshberg. Popular Library, 1958.

A priest's account of his addiction to drink and the courage he ultimately found to help himself and others.

A Sensitive, Passionate Man, by Barbara Mahoney. David McKay, 1974.

The slow, agonizing destruction of a life and a family by alcoholism has never been more graphically described than in this true-to-life account.

The Disease Concept of Alcoholism, by E. M. Jellinek. Hillhouse Press, 1960.

The classic work by one of the great pioneers in alcoholism theory and treatment, which catapulted the theory that alcoholism is a disease into public awareness.

INDEX

ABOUT THE AUTHORS

A clinical psychologist, the late JAMES R. MILAM, PH.D., has been a pioneering authority in the field of addiction. Dr. Milam first developed his extraordinary insight into the physiological bases of alcoholism while conducting research studies in the psychopharmacology of alcoholism in 1966. In 1970, Dr. Milam first published "The Emergent Comprehensive Concept of Alcoholism" and embarked on a decades-long campaign of public and academic presentations, workshops, and lectures throughout the United States and abroad to raise awareness of the disease concept of alcoholism and the effective treatment of this disease. Dr. Milam was cofounder and president of Alcenas Hospital from 1970 to 1981 and, thereafter, founded other treatment programs including The Milam Recovery Program and The Lakeside-Milam Recovery Centers to help thousands of alcoholics achieve sobriety and lead fulfilling, rich lives.

KATHERINE KETCHAM has been writing nonfiction books for over forty years and has coauthored sixteen books, ten on the subject of addiction and recovery. She is also the author of *The Only Life I Could Save: A Memoir.* Her books have been published in seventeen foreign languages and have sold nearly two million copies (www.katherineketchambooks.com). In 1998, Katherine pioneered treatment and recovery efforts at the Walla Walla Juvenile Justice Center, leading educational groups and working individually with youth and family members. In 2002, she founded Trilogy Recovery Community, a grassroots nonprofit recovery community organization.